Date Due

The White Ethnic Movement and Ethnic Politics

Perry L. Weed

The Praeger Special Studies program—utilizing the most modern and efficient book production techniques and a selective worldwide distribution network—makes available to the academic, government, and business communities significant, timely research in U.S. and international economic, social, and political development.

The White Ethnic Movement and Ethnic Politics

PRAEGER SPECIAL STUDIES IN U.S. ECONOMIC, SOCIAL, AND POLITICAL ISSUES

Praeger Publishers   New York   Washington   London

PRAEGER PUBLISHERS
111 Fourth Avenue, New York, N.Y. 10003, U.S.A.
5, Cromwell Place, London S.W.7, England

Published in the United States of America in 1973
by Praeger Publishers, Inc.

© 1973 by Praeger Publishers, Inc.

Library of Congress Catalog Card Number: 72-88987

Printed in the United States of America

ACKNOWLEDGMENTS

I am indebted to the Center for Urban Affairs at Northwestern University and the National Institute of Mental Health for their assistance in providing the financial support to enable me to write this book. Louis H. Masotti, director of the Center, gave me many pieces of ethnic literature and invaluable encouragement. John McDermott of the Chicago Community Renewal Society encouraged me to attend the June 1971 conference on ethnicity which inspired the idea of this book and also shared with me his extensive experience in group relations. David Roth, Midwest Coordinator of the National Project on Ethnic America of the American Jewish Committee, Monsignor Geno Baroni, director of the National Center for Urban Ethnic Affairs, and the Reverend Andrew M. Greeley, director of the Center for the Study of American Pluralism, have generously given to me their valuable time and thoughts. On more than thirty occasions David Roth furnished me with articles, bibliographic citations, and the names of individuals to further my research. Myron Kuropas, former president of the Republican Nationalities Council of Illinois, allowed me to attend regular meetings of the Council, provided me with literature, and generously shared with me his thoughts on and experience with ethnic politics.

Without the editorial assistance of my wife, Dorothy Fisher Weed, this book would never have been written. Tobe Harris edited the greater part of the book with patience and great editorial skill. I am indebted to Nancy Evans, Linda Huegel, and Carol Widrig for typing drafts, revisions, and final manuscript, as well as for their patience, promptness, and high competence.

Leon Despres, A. Abbott Rosen, and David Roth read the book and offered me the benefit of their comments.

PREFACE

In June 1971 the National Center for Urban Ethnic Affairs, headed by Monsignor Geno Baroni, sponsored a conference in Washington, D.C., on the concerns of white ethnic Americans. The conference brought to my attention an important aspect of contemporary urban America about which I knew little beyond something of the ethnicity of Chicago and which had generated very little serious literature. The interest and enthusiasm that the conference aroused in me led to the writing of this book.

The book is an attempt to untangle the complexity of American ethnicity. My primary interest was the recent rediscovery and resurgence of interest in white ethnic Americans. At the same time, I have attempted to put this phenomenon into historical perspective. As a political scientist and attorney with ten years experience in the Chicago courts, I have concentrated on my particular interests in group action and ethnic politics. My commitment to this project was reaffirmed by the scarcity of literature to be found on ethnic politics at the national level.

It is clear that the persistence of ethnicity and its significance in American society have neither been adequately explored nor systematically researched. Intensive survey research and analysis by the Reverend Andrew M. Greeley at the Center for the Study of American Pluralism has established that, in many situations, ethnicity is an independent predictor variable as important as socio-economic class.

There is a need for further serious thought and scholarly investigation.

CONTENTS

LIST OF TABLES

The White Ethnic Movement and Ethnic Politics

1

THE COMPONENTS OF
THE WHITE ETHNIC
MOVEMENT

INTRODUCTION

Most first-, second-, and third-generation Americans of European ancestry are Catholics and residents of the older industrial cities
of the North. As white ethnics, they are developing a new sense of
self-awareness. They are reacting to the black and affluent student
revolutions of the 1960s and to the economic stagnation and the social
and cultural disruptions that have recently affected their lives. Moreover, they are becoming increasingly positive about their own ancestral
cultural traditions, confused toward American culture, and in many
ways negative toward Anglo-Protestant dominance. White ethnics are
becoming a distinct minority. They have recently been described as
alienated, forgotten, troubled, disillusioned, frustrated, and angry.
Their shared grievances, coupled with their recent immigrant experiences, have drawn them together, both into their separate nationality
groups and into the larger category of "white ethnics."

Most of the growing attention paid since the mid-1960s to the
"backlash," "white ethnics," "blue-collar" Americans, and the "lower-
middle class" has been too vague and simplistic to foster understanding. Was the backlash only against racial groups or against other
groups as well? Who was lashing back at whom? Is a white ethnic
a "hard hat" or a "blue-collar" worker, is he a Wallaceite, a racist—
is he a member of the "little people," the "silent majority," or
"middle America"? Are non-Roman Catholic Americans such as
Orthodox Greeks and German Protestants also to be considered white
ethnic? Are Irish and German Americans, who are more thoroughly
assimilated than Americans from Southern, Central, and Eastern
Europe, less likely or more likely to identify with their ancestral
heritage? Are racial minorities part of the "white ethnic" category?

NUMERICAL SIGNIFICANCE

A United States Census Bureau survey conducted in November 1969 showed that 75 million Americans identified themselves with one of the seven major ethnic groups in Table 1. The survey found that

TABLE 1

Population by Ethnic Origin

Group	Millions
German	20.0
English	19.1
Irish	13.3
Spanish	9.2
Italian	7.2
Polish	4.0
Russian (mostly Jews)	2.2

Source: U.S. Census, Current Population Reports, Series P-20, No. 221, "Characteristics of the Population by Ethnic Origin: November 1969."

11 million Americans were foreign-born and that one-third of them said they usually spoke the language of their homeland in the home. This was the first time the Census Bureau had collected information on questions that specifically required identification as to origin or descent. Until then, the Census Bureau had to infer ethnic origin from information as to place of birth, country of origin, mother tongue, surname, etc. A later survey, in March 1971, found that 60 percent of the population sample identified themselves as having a single ethnic origin. This survey is reported in Table 2.

Since the 1970 census data on ethnic groups will not be released until the spring of 1972, the 1960 figures are the latest now available.

The 1960 census lists more than 33 million Americans in the "foreign white stock" category, which is defined by the Census as either foreign-born or children of at least one foreign-born parent. Of this figure, more than 9 million were themselves foreign-born. Table 3 shows the 1960 figures for foreign white stock for the eleven largest groups.

TABLE 2

Figures and Percentages of Population Claiming
a Single Ethnic Origin

	Total (in thousands)	Percentage
Race		
White	177,626	87.6
Negro	22,810	11.2
Other	2,412	1.2
Ethnic Origin		
English, Scotch, Welsh	31,006	15.3
French	5,189	2.6
German	25,661	12.7
Irish	16,325	8.0
Italian	8,733	4.3
Polish	4,941	2.4
Russian	2,132	1.1
Spanish	8,956	4.4
Central and South American	501	.2
Cuban	626	.3
Mexican	5,023	2.5
Puerto Rican	1,450	.7
Other	1,356	.7

Source: U.S. Census, Current Population Reports, Series P-20, No. 224, "Selected Characteristics of Persons and Families of Mexican, Puerto Rican, and Other Spanish Origins: March 1971."

In 1960 foreign white stock made up 18.4 percent of America's total population of nearly 180 million. Italian foreign stock constituted 2.5 percent of the total, German 2.4 percent, and Canadian 1.8 percent. In its definition of foreign stock population, the census excludes third and subsequent generations, which means that the ethnic population exceeds the census figures. Since the Irish, Germans, and Scandinavians entered the United States in large numbers during the latter half

TABLE 3

Figures and Percentages of Foreign White Stock

	Total (in thousands)	Percent	1969 Estimates
Italian	4,540	13.7	4,531
German	4,313	13.0	4,118
Canadian	3,154	9.5	
Polish	2,778	8.4	2,777
Russian	2,287	6.9	2,164
English and Welsh	1,955	5.9	
Irish	1,771	5.4	1,487
Mexican	1,725	5.2	
Austrian	1,098	3.3	1,035
Swedish	1,046	3.2	976
Czechoslovakian	917	2.8	885

Source: "Foreign White Stock by Country of Origin, Statistical Abstract of the United States," 1969, Table 34; and Pierre de Vise, "A Demographic Survey of Chicago's Ethnic Groups," unpublished paper presented to the Chicago Consultation on Ethnicity, November 1969.

of the nineteenth century, they here appear to constitute a far smaller portion of the total foreign stock than they would have earlier, while the Italians, Poles, Russians, and Mexicans, whose peak immigration occurred later, now take on much larger proportions.

The Census Bureau also compiles data on the mother tongue of the foreign-born. According to the 1960 census, for nearly 2 million immigrants, the mother tongue was English; for 1.3 million, German; 1.2 million, Italian or Spanish; and for more than half a million, Polish or Yiddish. For a significant number of immigrants, the mother tongues were French, Russian, Swedish, Hungarian, or Greek. A Census Bureau survey in November 1969 established that Spanish is spoken by more Americans than any other language but English, and that it is spoken in the homes of about half the population of Spanish origin. A 1970 Board of Education study in Chicago disclosed that almost 9 percent of Chicago's public elementary school pupils—or 37,840 children—had learning difficulties because they lacked a basic knowledge of English. More than 31,000 of these children were Spanish-speaking (over 50 percent of them Puerto Rican), along with 1,323 children who spoke Greek, 1,107 Italian, and 1,034 Polish.

In emphasizing America's ethnic diversity, The History of Violence in America, prepared by the National Commission on the Causes and Prevention of Violence, noted that between 1820 and 1945 immigration to America occurred in the following proportions:

British Isles	33%
Germany	16
Austria-Hungary	13
Italy	12
Russia and Poland	10
Scandinavia	6

The last complete estimate of the national stock of all Americans was made in a federal study conducted in the 1920s when the national quota system for immigration became law. The study attempted to trace national roots back to the first settlers. A 1950 effort to update the earlier figures showed that nearly 35 percent of all Americans were of British decent, more than 14 percent German; 9 percent Irish; 4.6 percent Italian; 3.2 percent Polish; and 2.7 percent Russian.

If we define "ethnic" as "any individual who differs by religion, language, and culture from the white Protestant Anglo-Saxon settlers," the figure would exceed 65 percent of the total population. Aside from "whites," America has no majority group. The largest minority is the so-called "WASP-NN," that is, White Anglo-Saxon Protestant Native-born of Native Parents. These account for less than a third of the population, but though they are a minority, it is misleading to think of them as such.

When Oscar Handlin in the introduction to his book The Uprooted, writes, "Once I thought to write a history of the immigrants in America. Then I discovered that the immigrants were American history," he overemphasizes the influence of immigration between 1845 and 1924. John Higham, historian of American nativism, contends that the founders of a society must be excluded from the immigrant category because as original settlers they firmly established "the polity, the language, the pattern of work and settlement, and many of the mental habits to which the immigrants would have to adjust." In 1790 the English constituted approximately 60 percent of the white population of the United States. Thus while white America is a nation of immigrants, it is more practical to consider the original immigrant group as natives, since they early became dominant and effectively preempted the crucial levers of economic and political power.

RESIDENCY

According to the 1960 census, the largest concentration of European immigrants and their children is in the Northeast and

comprises 34 percent of its total population. The Northeastern states
with the largest concentrations of foreign stock were Connecticut
(Italian, Canadian, Polish), Massachusetts (Canadian, Italian, Irish),
New Jersey (Italian, German), New York (Italian, Russian), Pennsylvania
(Italian, Polish), and Rhode Island (Italian, Canadian, British). In the
Midwest, large foreign stock populations were found in Illinois (Ger-
man, Polish), Michigan (Polish, German), and Ohio (German, Italian).
Massachusetts had the highest percentage of foreign stock in relation
to the total state population—40 percent. Rhode Island was second
with 39.5 percent, New York third with 38.7 percent.

Most white ethnics reside in the older industrial cities of the
Northeast and Great Lakes regions, as is illustrated by the two largest
American cities. In 1960, New York had a total population of 7,781,984,
consisting of 19 percent white foreign-born, 28 percent native white
with at least one foreign-born parent, 8 percent first- and second-
generation Puerto Rican, and 14 percent black. The overwhelming
majority of other New Yorkers who were the grandchildren and great
grandchildren of immigrants still thought of themselves, on some
occasions and for some purposes, as Jews, Italians, Germans, and
Irish. Immigrants and their children thus comprised nearly one half
of the city's total population in 1960. The major white ethnic groups
are shown in Table 4.

In Chicago, according to the 1960 census, more than one person
out of three was an immigrant or child of an immigrant. In 1930 when
Chicago's population was nearly the same as in 1960, the foreign white
stock was 65 percent of the total population. Figures in Table 5
specify the major ethnic groups in Chicago in 1960 and 1969 and give
their percentage in relation to the Chicago Standard Metropolitan
Area (SMA).

According to the Census Bureau's Congressional District Data
Book (April 1964), of the 50 Congressional districts with the highest
percentage of foreign stock, 39 were in the East (21 in the New York
City area), 30 were urban, 9 suburban, 9 mixed, and only 2 rural. In
1960, of the ten cities over 500,000 population with the highest percentage of foreign stock, all except San Francisco and Los Angeles were
in the North, only Seattle was in the Northwest, and all had more than
30 percent foreign stock—excluding Puerto Ricans. New York was
the highest (48.6 percent), followed by Boston (45.5 percent), then San
Francisco (43.5 percent), Chicago (35.9 percent), and Buffalo (35.4
percent).

A recent Connecticut survey of religio-ethnic groups in Bridge-
port, Hartford, and New Haven central cities found the distribution
shown in Table 6.

TABLE 4

Foreign White Stock in New York City, 1960

	Percentage of Total City Population
Italian	11
Russian (mostly Jewish)	7
Polish (mostly Jewish)	5
German	4
Irish	4

Source: Nathan Glazer and Daniel P. Moynihan, Beyond the Melting Pot, 2nd ed. (Cambridge, Mass.: MIT University Press, 1970), Table 2, "New York Foreign White Stock in 1960."

RELIGION

In the Northeastern and Northcentral United States, which include more than 58 large cities, the Roman Catholic population is more than one-third of the total population of 90 million. The 50 Congressional districts with the highest percentage of immigrants and their children sent thirty-one Catholics and six Jews to the House of Representatives in 1964, which indicates the strong Catholic and Jewish affiliations of these largely Eastern constituencies (39 of the 50). In his book, The Population of the United States, Donald J. Bogue writes, "The outstanding fact . . . is that Roman Catholics comprise a disproportionately large share of the population in the most heavily industrialized areas" and "have an excess of the urban working-class persons."

THE BLUE-COLLAR DIMENSION

White ethnics constitute a disproportionately high percentage of the blue-collar labor force. Close to one-half of all male workers of Irish, Polish, and Italian origin are, according to a November 1969 survey by the Bureau of the Census, employed in blue-collar occupations. This survey found that for males, 44.8 percent of the Irish, 49.1 percent of the Poles, and 50.2 percent of the Italians were blue-collar workers. For females, the proportion of Italian and Polish women employed as blue-collar operatives (25.3 for Italians and 19.2 for Poles) was substantially higher than the 15.37 average for all

TABLE 5

Chicago Ethnic Groups, 1960 and 1969

| National Origin | Total Foreign Stock | | Percentage of SMA 1969 | |
	1960 Estimate	1969 Estimate	Foreign- Born	Second- Generation
Poland	258,657	218,865	85	64
Germany	161,567	114,203	38	49
Italy	134,963	109,354	63	50
Russia	96,626	66,612	69	52
Ireland	85,120	57,363	64	64
Czechoslovakia	50,003	33,395	55	31
United Kingdom	52,039	39,019	67	42
Sweden	51,537	27,635	67	28
Lithuania	47,634	42,558	74	65
Austria	41,664	30,998	70	47
All countries	1,277,341	1,032,762	71	50

Source: Pierre de Vise, "A Demographic Survey of Chicago's Ethnic Groups," unpublished paper presented to the Chicago Consultation on Ethnicity, November 1969.

ethnic groups. The same survey showed that in educational attainment the Irish, Poles, and Italians lagged behind Jews, English, and Germans.

The Bureau of Labor Statistics defines blue-collar occupations to include the following census occupational categories: craftsmen, foremen, and kindred workers; operatives and kindred workers; and laborers, except farm- and mineworkers. Some analysts also include service workers and private household workers. Operatives—that is, those employed in mechanical industries such as manufacturing and mills—are the largest blue-collar occupational group in the private economy. According to the report of Assistant Secretary of Labor Jerome M. Rosow, entitled The Problem of the Blue Collar Worker, "forty percent of American families—including 70 million family members—have incomes between $5,000 and $10,000 per year and might be termed 'lower middle income.'" Sar Levitan, editor of Blue-Collar Workers, published in late 1971, agrees that 70 million persons living in families headed by blue-collar workers have annual incomes concentrated between $5,000 and $10,000. While precise numbers are not known, white ethnics represent a large part of this group. The November 1969 survey of the Census Bureau found that the following family heads by ethnic origin had median family incomes below $10,000:

Irish	66.4
Italians	62.4
Poles	61.7

Of the 21 cities over 500,000 population in 1960 ranked by the percentage of families with incomes of $10,000 a year or more, all but two, ranked within the $11-21,000 range, were in the Northeast and Midwest. In 1971 the Bureau of Labor Statistics reported that the labor force in 1970 consisted of the following:

	Number (in millions)	Percentage of Total
Blue-collar	27.8	35.3
White-collar	38.5	48.3
Service		12.4
Farm		4.0

Analysis of the 1960 census reveals the heavy concentration of blue-collar workers in the industrial Northeast and Midwest states. New York City, Detroit, Chicago, Cleveland, Boston, Gary, Buffalo, and Pittsburgh all have disportionately high percentages of blue-collar workers. Of the 21 cities over 500,000 population, only New York City (ranked sixth), Washington (seventh), and Cincinnati (eleventh),

TABLE 6

Religio-Ethnic Groups in Three Connecticut Cities

	Percentage
Black Protestants	15.8
Italian Catholics	15.4
Northern European Protestants	14.5
Irish Catholics	10.3
Jews (all national origins)	7.5
Eastern European Catholics	5.8
French Canadian Catholics	5.2

Source: Harold J. Abramson of the University of Connecticut, table distributed at the American Political Science Association Annual Meeting in Chicago, September 1971.

TABLE 7

Distribution by Religio-Ethnic Group of Blue- and
White-Collar Workers in Three Connecticut Cities

Religio-Ethnic Group	Blue-Collar	White-Collar
Spanish-speaking Catholics	90	10
Black Protestants	87	13
Polish Catholics	77	23
French-Canadian Catholics	75	25
Eastern European Catholics	69	31
Italian Catholics	65	35
Irish Catholics	50	50
Northern European Catholics	38	62
Jews	26	74

Source: Harold J. Abramson of the University of Connecticut,
Table distributed at the American Political Science Association
Annual Meeting in Chicago, September 1971.

figured in the first eleven by percentage of employed persons in white-
collar occupations. The last ten were all in the Northeast and Midwest
with Detroit (32.1 percent), Milwaukee (31.5 percent), Buffalo (30.4
percent), and St. Louis (30.2 percent), with Cleveland (24.8 percent)
the lowest.

The previously cited survey of religio-ethnic groups in Bridge-
port, Hartford, and New Haven central cities also disclosed the
distribution by occupational category shown in Table 7.

Blue-collar workers are strategically located in America and
the prominent segment of this group are the white ethnics.

SUMMARY AND DEFINITION

White ethnics easily number more than 40 million Americans.
They live in the Northeast and Great Lakes regions, generally in the
larger cities rather than rural areas, are predominantly Catholic,
but with large numbers of Jews in New York City and other Northern
urban areas, and lastly are heavily represented, except for Jews, in
blue-collar occupations. Irish-Americans, German-Americans, and
Jews are less likely to be a part of this broadly defined group than
Americans of Eastern, Central and Southern European descent.

To the extent that a white American thinks and acts in terms of his European origins, to that extent he is a "white ethnic," that is, the child, grandchild, great grandchild, etc., of European immigrants, thus still regarding himself, on some occasions and for some purposes, as a German, an Irishman, an Italian, a Pole, or a Jew. Also, of course, as an American.

A final note: there are more poor whites in the Northern metropolitan areas than poor blacks, and a disportionately high number of them are first-, second-, and third-generation ethnic Americans of European descent.

2

**DEFINITIONS
BY THREE
MAJOR SPOKESMEN**

MONSIGNOR GENO BARONI

The three major ethnic spokesmen in the last four years have
been Monsignor Geno Baroni, head of the Center for Urban Ethnic
Affairs at the Catholic University of America; Irving Levine, Director
of the National Project on Ethnic America; and the Reverend Andrew
Greeley, head of the Center for the Study of American Pluralism.
Each of them defines "white ethnic" somewhat differently. Baroni
accepts the phrase as an "unobjectionable label" that in recent years
has come into common usage to describe ethnic Americans. He does
not claim to have originated the phrase and acknowledges that "it has
gained widespread acceptance" among public and private agencies concerned with the restoration of urban life. He uses it to encompass the
most prominent segment of the white working class—first-, second-,
and third-generation Americans of European ancestry who live in the
Northern metropolitan areas. Ethnic America thus defines his constituency. While he concedes that many children and grandchildren
of European immigrants have moved upward and can be found in
various socio-economic strata, many are nevertheless still blue-collar
workers—"the backbone of the labor force in most of our Northern industrial cities, mining towns, and manufacturing cities." They still
reside in older, multi-ethnic neighborhoods or have relocated in predominantly blue-collar suburbs. "When you look at the major cities,"
notes Baroni, "and see who's left that's white, you see the working
class—not the bankers, not the professionals, but the working class
and the blacks. In a city like Detroit, two out of three persons are
either black or Polish." He emphasizes that many of these communities
are largely Roman Catholic. Baroni recognizes existing social realities: ethnic groups in urban America are already organized around
the parish, neighborhood, and social and fraternal groups. Residential

patterns, the lack of intermarriage, and voting tendencies show the continued importance of religio-ethnic loyalties, though the more obvious marks of cultural distinctiveness have diminished. Besides the ethnic and Catholic dimension, Baroni relies heavily upon the economic injustices and discontents of the white ethnics. For him the phrase "blue-collar" denotes families who earn between $5,000 and $10,000 per year. He relies on this dimension in his usage of "white ethnic groups," for he appreciates that the majority of working-class Americans of recent ancestry lack interest in their ethnic heritage. They do, however, share many common social and economic problems with those white ethnics who are conscious of their European heritage.

In evaluating the urban dimension of the definition of "white ethnic," Baroni stresses that of all whites the white ethnics are in closest proximity to the black and Latin ghettos of the older industrial cities and therefore in direct competition in jobs, education, housing, recreation, transportation, and street life. In rallying enthusiasm among white ethnics, Baroni has only occasionally resorted to such gimmickry as identifying white ethnics and himself the derisive epithet "pigs" and then saying that "pigs" is an abbreviation for Polish, Italian, Greek, and Slovak. Finally, while he includes the Irish in his definition, he does so reluctantly for two reasons: the Irish are early arrivals, closer to the English, and have been assimilated to a greater extent than the Eastern, Central, and Southern European ethnics; and secondly, and probably more important, they have dominated the Roman Catholic hierarchy, the urban political machines, and the majority of the labor unions. The Irish have been perceived as barriers to the economic and political advancement of the later immigrants and their children. Baroni's concept of "white ethnic" is likely to become the most popular one. He wants the category to be as broad as possible in order to enlarge the group for which he speaks and so that it may exert more influence for social and economic progress.

IRVING M. LEVINE

Irving M. Levine, an urban affairs specialist with the American Jewish Committee (AJC), insists on the term "white ethnic" and has named his AJC program "The National Project on Ethnic America." His interest in the white ethnic working class originated in the late 1960s as a constructive response to the conclusions about white racism in the Kerner Report. His use of such phrases as "white ethnics" or "white ethnic groups" represents a deliberate, conscious effort to refocus public attention on the needs of the white working class and to affirm their legitimacy.

But black progress remains his first priority. Urban American society, he believes, must be "depolarized," and depolarization will only occur when blacks and white liberals recognize and deal with the underlying problems of the white working class. Levine does not want to romanticize white ethnics. He has an interest in ethnic heritages. He is convinced that ethnicity is a persistent influence in the institutional life of America, and that America's Northeastern and Great Lakes working class is predominantly ethnic. Levine's insistent use of the phrase "white ethnics" has met considerable resistance. Union leaders, community organizers, scholars, and foundation executives deny its importance or consider it derisive. At the majority of the more than fourteen conferences on the urban North which Levine arranged, he has emphasized working-class discontent. But he reports that as debate progresses at these conferences, ethnicity inevitably is recognized as a critical factor. For Levine, the phrase "white ethnic" basically encompasses the white working class and ethnically aroused whites who have responded to the appeals of Joseph Colombo and the Jewish Defense League. Levine also sees white ethnics as allies of both middle- and upper-class Jews, as well as working-class Jews. He believes that ethnic attachments can be used to achieve social progress.

REVEREND ANDREW M. GREELEY

The Reverend Andrew M. Greeley differs from the other two ethnic spokesmen in style and emphasis. While he included the phrase "white ethnic" in his 1971 book, Why Can't They Be Like Us? America's White Ethnic Groups, he seems reluctant to define the phrase, and when he does, he writes about groups, not individuals. The term "ethnic" expands and contracts to suit his purposes. He sets up intellectuals as an "ethnic group" and then sharply criticizes the group's characteristics. He is disturbed that "white ethnic groups have become a social problem," and that the generalities "blue-collar" and "hard-hat" have been loosely applied to cover white ethnics. White ethnics, according to Greeley, will not be "bought off by an increase in real income or by community services." He is quick to advise American elite groups that "there are considerable numbers of white ethnics who are not blue-collar workers, and even substantial numbers who are college graduates and professionals." Greeley, a Catholic intellectual and sociologist, applauds the ethnic diversity and cultural richness of American society. For him, white ethnic groups are a "positive contribution," an "opportunity," indeed, collectives grouped around primordial bonds offering not only desirable cultural richness and variety but also "basic pillars of support for

the urban social structure." His energies are not directed toward
arousing white ethnic groups to action but to exploring and evaluating
their contribution to American life.

WHITE ETHNICS—A NEW MINORITY

These various definitions serve to emphasize that white ethnics
have become a new minority. Though an important part of American
life for the past 100 years, they have been largely ignored. But black
self-assertion, followed by the backlash in the urban North, the Kerner
Report, and the 1968 Wallace vote, all served to promote self-awareness among white ethnics. They have become associated in people's
minds with white racism and reactionary politics. They have been
publicly criticized and politically courted. Rhetoric has been directed
toward them and they have been called "the little people," "hard hats,"
or "the forgotten Americans"—all euphemisms for white lower middle-
class Americans of various ethnic backgrounds who are troubled,
confused, and angered by the rapidity of the social change taking place
around them. A new minority has been created that sees its common
enemies in the blacks, student radicals, and the white liberal establishment. In addition to sharing a recent immigrant experience and
Roman Catholicism, the majority of them are blue-collar and office
workers suffering from the economic squeeze caused by inflation,
higher taxes, and static real income.

White ethnics, to a significant degree, share a distinct group
outlook. While differences of attitude and behavior between Poles
and Italians are many, their perceptions of crucial domestic and
foreign issues are often similar. Both have reacted to the black and
affluent student revolution with more alarm than did other Northern
whites. Their support for United States involvement in Vietnam was,
until mid-1971, also stronger.

The phrase "white ethnic" has not been readily accepted. The
Reader's Guide to Periodic Literature places articles about white
ethnic groups under the heading "minorities," not because it rejects
the new term, but because of the long standing practice to place
articles about European immigrants and their descendants under that
heading. The Guide does not yet use the category "white ethnic" and
very infrequently uses the heading "ethnicity." The New York Times
reported in 1971 that the Ford Foundation was providing numerous one-
year advanced study awards for scholars of minority groups to encourage research in their history and culture. The news report disturbed many white ethnics for it gave the false impression that awards
were also to be granted their groups. The awards, however, were
intended only for racial, not ethnic, minority groups.

3

**THE MAJOR
INSTITUTIONAL
FORCES**

INTRODUCTION

Manifestations of the white ethnic movement occur in the institutional reactions of established organizations and also in the grass roots activities of white ethnic communities. Institutional reactions come from intergroup relations agencies, churches, foundations, political parties and governments, the communications media, universities, intellectuals, and organized labor. The leaders of these institutions recognize the growing alienation, frustration, and anger of the white ethnic working class and for the most part believe that positive ameliorative actions are needed.

The indigenous aspect of the white ethnic movement was initially negative and reactionary, exemplified by violent white demonstrations, marches, and riots, by neighborhood protection groups and gun clubs, and by the attraction of such men as George Wallace and Joseph Colombo. A positive development occurred in the early 1970s as white ethnics began to assert themselves by forming organizations, making demands on decision-makers and generally showing an attitude more positive than defensive toward themselves and their heritage.

Mainstream American institutions have responded to the groundswell of discontent, frustration, and anger which arose spontaneously in the mid- and late 1960s. These institutions and white ethnics may begin to cooperate for the purpose of social and economic progress, but whether the energy which originally fired the white ethnic working-class resurgence will exhaust itself or whether these institutions can give constructive direction to that energy remains to be seen.

THE NATIONAL PROJECT ON ETHNIC AMERICA

In late 1967 and early 1968, the American Jewish Committee (AJC), one of the oldest intergroup relations agencies in the United States, with 65 years of experience, undertook to use its specialized understanding of pluralism and group life to help develop more positive approaches and responses to the needs of lower middle-class white ethnics. Baroni's National Center for Urban Ethnic Affairs concentrates on action, whether at the local or national level. Greeley's Center for the Study of American Pluralism stresses the long overdue need for the study of ethnicity. AJC's ethnic activities fall somewhere between these two approaches by emphasizing social reordering without basically threatening existing institutions and seeking action through persuasion, not "demands" and demonstrations. AJC is committed to protect the civil and religious rights of Jews and to improve group relations for all Americans. The agency explores new social dynamics and then analyzes the components. Irving M. Levine, director of AJC's urban affairs department and a social worker by training, refocused the attention of the Committee on ethnic America and attracted the interest of some mainstream institutions to the problems of the white ethnic working class. Of three names mentioned in 1971 as the dominant personalities in the white ethnic movement—Levine, Monsignor Gino Baroni and the Reverend Andrew Greeley—Levine has been almost unanimously acknowledged as prime initiator and the most influential spokesman for white ethnics since 1968. By late 1970 Baroni had become the dominant force at the grass roots level, while Levine continued his outstanding influence with the mainstream institutions. When asked who was the first to go beyond accusations of racism in examining and dealing with the alienation, frustration, and anger of working-class white ethnics, Greeley points to Levine. Levine is now director of the American Jewish Committee's National Project on Ethnic America. He is a New York Jew of Lithuanian and Polish descent and a veteran of the civil rights movement of the 1960s.

Levine does not see his agency's role as that of an advocate. His program is aimed at reducing tensions between white ethnics and blacks in America. Levine is convinced that blacks and other poor minorities have the greatest moral claim on American society. But, as he argues, "We have a black problem and we have a white reaction to it. You can't solve the one without solving the other. Civil rights gains have been stalemated in many parts of the North and Midwest because the groups who are resisting have been left out." The "black agenda," as Levine calls it, "demands America's first priority because those needs are most critical. But the lower middle-class whites are the second agenda and we're going to have to deal with both agendas at the same time to get the black priority adopted." "The task is to push whites off a strictly negative anti-black agenda," Levine adds. "We have to make them conscious of their own realities. A new breed of ethnic leaders has to be developed who are as visible as the demagogues trying to exploit ethnic fears." These new leaders, according to Levine, can serve as "bridge persons" in forging single-issue coalitions or possibly even organic links with blacks. He talks of invading the national consciousness with the unfulfilled needs and legitimate anxieties of the white ethnic working class. At first Levine encountered great skepticism from liberal leaders, and they still have deep apprehensions concerning his activities. Levine urges America's progressive institutions to work with white ethnics to improve their neighborhoods and communal institutions. Housing rehabilitation, better schools and medical care facilities, more parks and recreational areas, sensitive handling of urban renewal, as well as other community supports are needed in the old ethnic neighborhoods. Dismissing white ethnic resistance to integration of neighborhoods, schools, and jobs as racist and labeling white demonstrators and rioters as bigots is counterproductive. Levine believes that white liberals have badly mishandled the whole question of "law and order" and have, by ignoring legitimate fears of both whites and blacks, lost a potential bridge of understanding and opened opportunities for the extreme right. For him, the battle cry should not be law and order but public safety for all, escort services for the elderly and for single women, storefront police stations, improved relations with the police, and effective drug addiction programs.

"There was a time not too long ago when blacks wanted activists like myself to 'get out of the black bag and go civilize whitey,' " Levine says. "We took their advice. Now these same black colleagues are saying, 'You don't love us anymore,' but they simply can't have it both ways. Pluralism is as American as cherry pie. Whites, too, have the right to assert a strategy." AJC continues its minorities programs in civil rights, economic development, housing, and social welfare.

AJC was also motivated in its ethnic program by what its leaders perceived as growing black anti-Semitism, as manifested, for instance, in the fierce Ocean Hill-Brownsville struggle in the late 1960s. Levine also cites the 1967 school board election in Wayne Township, New Jersey. The vice president of the board of education issued a statement urging the defeat of two Jewish board candidates on the ground that "most Jewish people are liberals, especially when it comes to spending for education . . . we could lose what is left of Christ in our Christmas celebrations in our schools. . . ." One Jewish agency staff member put it, "We needed new allies." Some blacks were singling out the Jews as the ultimate white racists. Levine understandingly

perceives these struggles as involving legitimate group interest, i.e.,
he defends "the interest of non-Jews to maintain their own traditions
and of Jews asserting their prerogatives and their traditions of what
they believed to be the best education. We said right away that both
struggles were legitimate. Not everyone agreed." But Levine never
condoned the anti-Semitic rhetoric of some blacks and some white
liberals. He feared the exploitation of latent anti-Semitism. Some
Jewish leaders saw graver consequences. As one said, "I'm scared
to death that we will become increasingly regressive, like Hitler's
Germany, trying to recapture the past by persecuting minorities and
dissenters."

The Project's literature states that it is "a depolarization program" and is associated with AJC's Institute of Human Relations
located in New York City. The National Project on Ethnic America's
advisory board consists of 41 members, most of whom represent
established institutions. More than a third of them are from the academic community and are recognized authorities on ethnic problems.
There are two or three representatives each from the federal government, local government, organized labor, newspaper media, black and
youth organizations, foundations, AJC, social welfare organizations,
and churches. Only one represents a growing community organization,
only three or four could be characterized as activists, but almost all
would be regarded as liberal in their political views. Michael Harring-
ton, head of the League for Industrial Democracy, is probably the most
radical member. None of the members is a working-class white
ethnic.

According to AJC literature, the agency became "convinced that
a society which protects pluralism and combats polarization is in the
best interest of Jews and other minority groups." AJC's aim is to
break down the so-called racist and hard-hat groups and the silent
majority into groups which share common cultures or self-interests
in order to prevent the majority of lower middle-class white ethnics
from congealing into a negative monolithic force. Not to do so would
be to allow the gun-club and violent home protection psychologies to
prevail. The lack of community analysis and positive programs
dealing with the needs of working-class and foreign-stock white groups,
Levine points out, runs the risk that fear of black progress may end
with political allegiance to a broader form of organized ultraconserva-
tism.

The initial activities of the American Jewish Committee were
primarily exploratory, but in January 1971 a two-year grant of $262,536
was received from the Ford Foundation. This assured vitality for the
National Project on Ethnic America and offered the means to expand
its program. Between 1968 and 1971 the Project, underwritten by
AJC, the Stern Fund, and others, was in its pilot stage and still

experimental. The most outstanding event of this period was when the AJC, in June 1968, convened the first National Consultation on Ethnic America. The Consultation was held at Fordham, the well-known Catholic university in New York City, and its purpose was to refocus public attention dramatically on America's ethnic groups. It was attended by more than 150 community activists and concerned thinkers, including representatives of ethnic neighborhoods, religious organizations, universities, labor unions, and intergroup relations organizations. For two days, the conferees concentrated on the problems, attitudes, life styles, and future prospects of lower middle-class white ethnic America. They examined the underlying influences at work in the lower middle-class white community and sought to develop new and effective strategies for reducing intergroup polarization in American life. In their examination, they tried to discard the easy labels of racism and bigotry with which these groups are simplistically dismissed by so many people concerned with racial justice in America. The National Consultation and the Philadelphia Conference on the Problems of White Ethnic America, which followed a week later, recognized the reality of white fears and sought new directions and strategies to change the traditional rhetoric of guilt and self-righteousness and to reduce fear, alienation, and anger. A third major Consultation on Ethnicity was convened by the American Jewish Committee in Chicago in November 1969. The two-day conference brought together educators, ethnic and religious leaders, and community organizers from across the country to inquire into the attitudes and life styles of ethnic groups, particularly those in Chicago. Conferees at the Chicago Consultation have kept in touch with one another through the efforts of the Project's Midwest coordinator and were reconvened in November 1971 to discuss ethnic studies. Through these consultations, the pilot project sought to attract the attention and resources of mainstream leadership and organizations at all levels.

The National Project has continued its program of local, regional, and national consultations to bring together leaders of ethnic groups, educational and religious institutions, community-action agencies, mass media, and civic and business organizations to study the implications of the rediscovery of ethnic America for the life of the nation. The consultations, among other things, have dealt with young workers, working-class women, mental health, and education. From these consultations various programs may develop to help ethnic leaders deal with their own groups in relation to the larger society. Action models may be forthcoming, such as an ethnic coalition committed to reducing intergroup tensions; a labor-supported community-action program for white workers; ethnic and cultural identity programs in mainstream institutions; new forms of fraternal, service, and religiously sponsored activities; and projects to promote mass-media consciousness of ethnic America. Through more than fifteen of these

conferences on ethnicity and the problems of the working class, the
Project has stimulated interest, concern, and action in such cities
as Detroit, Gary, Newark, Boston, Providence, New Haven, St. Louis,
Kansas City, Buffalo, Rochester, and San Francisco. In 1971 the
National Project opened a Midwest office in Chicago and appointed
David Roth Midwest coordinator to work with city-wide and neighborhood leaders to implement the Project's agenda in Minneapolis-St.
Paul, Milwaukee, Detroit, St. Louis, and Kansas City as well as Chicago.
Consultations are planned for Milwaukee and Minneapolis. The majority
of conferences thus far have had a white working-class focus and have
brought together representatives of unions, churches, ethnic organizations, community action groups, academic disciplines, the mass media,
and social service and government agencies. Ethnicity is a sensitive
subject for many of these representatives, and thus the working-class
approach is the safer one. But Project staff members still believe
that ethnicity is critical to an understanding of urban problems and
explore its influence at consultations whenever possible. Conferees
have concentrated on new strategies, issues, and leaders in an effort
to encourage cooperation among groups which might otherwise find
themselves in conflict, and to make them aware of the problems and
possibility of cooperation.

The conferences, coupled with support from the Project, have
spurred local projects ranging from an ethnic studies curriculum in
public and parochial schools in Chicago to a statewide coalition for
new priorities in New Jersey. In Baltimore, the Project spent a year
helping to organize a community-action program in a predominantly
Polish neighborhood. Black and white opposition developed against a
proposed new expressway that threatened the homes of both groups.
They organized and stopped the construction. Black and white ethnics
worked in 1971 on other problems that involved their mutual interests.
In Philadelphia, Project personnel organized a program to train
neighborhood leaders in the Kensington section, an area composed of
blue-collar Italians, Irish, Polish, and blacks. Staff from the Project
worked through a settlement house called Lighthouse and thus enabled
it to increase its services and attention to the social and economic
problems and frustrations of the Kensington whites while continuing
its programs for blacks. The National Project assisted the Italian
community in the North ward of Newark with advice and seed money.
Its assistance helped to provide a moderate political alternative to
the reactionary appeal of Anthony Imperiale.

In 1971, the National Project on Ethnic America published its "new
action agenda" for the next two years. Its goals included working with
community leaders and organizations, alienated young white workers,
working-class women, communications media, and educational institutions. Other goals included setting up research centers on ethnic group

relations at urban universities and establishing an ethnic studies
community relations service, as well as evaluating designs for neighborhood government systems and generally examining with scholars
the subject of ethnicity in America. In March 1971, the Project
co-sponsored with the Maxwell School of Citizenship and Public Affairs
a conference on neighborhood government. At the conference, leading
scholars and community activists evaluated the issues raised by
neighborhood government and explored different ideas for reorganiza-
tion of local government. A major paper, Neighborhood Goverances:
Issues and Proposals written by Donna E. Shalala, a political scientist,
was presented. It summarized and classified the demands for local
control, analyzed institutional efforts in that direction, and offered
the arguments of those who favor centralized control. Levine initiated
this conference because, as he said, "We need to formulate solutions
which will make possible a truly pluralistic society, one where a variety
of economic and ethnic groups are free to act out their own life styles
without foreclosing access or opportunities for others. One such
possibility, both exciting and complicated, is the idea of formal neighborhood government." In June 1971, the Project inaugurated the Group
Life Report. It will continue to report periodically on what is happening to white ethnic working-class Americans, emphasizing their
life styles, needs, problems, and community responses and describing
institutional responses to their world.

Another June activity of the National Project was a New York
City conference on the community relations impact of ethnic studies.
It was attended by 75 educators, ethnic group leaders, foundation
executives, writers, and scholars and was an effort to clarify some
concepts and approaches relative to ethnic studies. "Black studies"
have taken on concrete meaning over the past five years. "Ethnic
studies" is still an uncertain, confused, and theoretical term. The
conference attempted to draw upon the collective experience and
insights of its participants and to try to determine their meaning, how
they should be taught, and how to combine the goals of enhanced
individual identity and enriched intergroup relations. Another impetus
for the conference was the immediate possibility of the federal government's providing sizable grants for ethnic studies programs. The
staff of the Project is increasingly concerned with the tensions which
are developing over implementation and control of these programs,
and thought it an appropriate time to begin discussions. Three important occurrences at the studies conference underlined the basic
problems. Community activists and indigenous leaders feared that
the elites from educational institutions, foundations, and government
would dominate ethnic studies programs, operate them primarily for
their own benefit and the benefit of affluent young students and not for
the youth and adults of ethnic neighborhoods. Moreover, they resented

the middle-class professionals telling them what to do and how to do it best. Secondly, during the discussions, a young girl asked an embarrassing question: "Has anyone bothered to ask young people whether they are interested in ethnic studies?" Her spontaneous judgment was that the young were much more interested in youth culture. The third occurrence has had far-reaching implications for the white ethnic movement. It was a confrontation between a black public school administrator and Michael Novak, the most notable intellectual of the white ethnic movement. The black was quick to speak and to tell the conferees that their efforts were detrimental to and weakening the black movement. Most participants who responded to him did so curtly, but many equivocated. Later in the discussion, Novak not only rebuked the black and the equivocators but went on to sharpen the issue. It became increasingly clear that AJC and other establishment institutions could be expected to redirect much of their resources toward the white ethnics.

The conference on the impact on community relations of ethnic studies programs is illustrative of the constructive role played by the American Jewish Committee. It perceived itself as an explorer and synthesizer, not as an advocate. Dialogue and intelligent planning were its primary goals. It convened the conference to formulate guidelines and acceptable models for these programs. "Properly developed and introduced, an ethnic studies program can be a positive community relations tool as well as a valuable educational one," wrote Irving Levine in his letter of invitation to the conference. "But without adequate thought, demands by group after group for 'our own' program . . . can create polarization which damages both the learning process and the community at large."

During 1971, the National Project moved in various directions. As a part of its interest in the white ethnic working class, it focused particular attention on ethnicity in the suburbs, the alienation of white working-class youth, problems of working-class women, mental health, economic satisfactions, training social workers, and national lobbying for laws to establish ethnic studies centers, greater social security benefits, and tax concessions. Levine cites numerous instances where ethnicity remains a vital factor in suburban life. The Project has undertaken a study in Connecticut and Chicago of white working-class youth. When Levine discusses mental health, he is little concerned with psychiatry and established institutions for treatment. He describes "closed people who are moving in tunnels, frightened of a world where no one seems to be in control—least of all, themselves." He calls on churches, educational institutions, unions, and ethnic organizations to counteract the inertia of the lower middle class and demand new public and private mental health programs. Levine and his staff work closely with the print and electronic

media and their press conferences, news releases, etc., have produced reports, articles, and television coverage. The Project has
been willing to give seed money to community organizations. Levine
is not an ethnic determinist; his interest is rather in ethnic differences,
their significance, and their constructive possibilities. Ethnic experience and its concrete manifestations command his attention and
the Project's resources, not research and the ideas and writings of
ethnic elites.

Baroni and Greeley have some reservations regarding Levine
and the activities of the Project. Baroni believes Levine's "depolariz-
ing" programs will dissipate the energies of the white working class
in its quest for basic social and economic change. "It's too much
like 'defusing the ghetto,' " he says. "It's negative. I prefer the idea
of building a progressive majority out of a silent one." Greeley
dislikes Levine's tendency "to make white ethnic groups a problem."
He emphasizes that they are no longer immigrant groups, are no
longer poor, depressed, downtrodden, or uneducated. Both Baroni
and Greeley are offended by the fact that it was the American Jewish
Committee that first paid attention to ethnic Americans and remains
a dominant influence on behalf of a largely Catholic group, most of
whom are Irish, Italians, and Poles. They argue that the organized
agencies within the ethnic groups should take over the promotion of
white ethnic assertion. A publication of Baroni's National Center
states, "The Center feels that its approach is a genuine "inside"
approach. . . . The Center does not approach work people as 'the
enemy' or as 'people to be de-polarized' or as 'the people.'" Levine,
as well as Greeley, warned in 1969 that white ethnic groups remain
deeply suspicious of "outsiders," particularly when the outsiders are
"experts" or "social engineers." David Roth, the Midwest coordinator
of the National Project, has encountered similar suspicion and hesita-
tion in his dealings with ethnic Americans in Milwaukee, Minneapolis-
St. Paul, and other Midwest cities.

The American Jewish Committee has a long and distinguished
tradition of coping with group conflict and problems in the cities.
The Committee's ethnic project was conceived as an urgently needed
effort to ease tensions between whites and blacks and has been executed
to that end. The Project may not survive if its outside funding is not
continued, but by then it may have induced ethnic organizations to
promote and direct constructively the new pluralism. Its work is
remarkable, for, as a few prominent Jewish leaders have noted,
American Jews and their organizations are retreating from involvement
in social progress because of Jewish resentment over the continuing
silence of the Christian religious establishment regarding Israel's
safety, anti-Jewish attitudes among some black extremists, and the
movement toward separatism by ethnic and racial groups.

THE NATIONAL CENTER FOR URBAN
ETHNIC AFFAIRS

The dominant force in the white ethnic movement has become the National Center for Urban Ethnic Affairs. Located in Washington, D.C., at the Catholic University of America, it is an affiliate of the United States Catholic Conference, the Washington-based agency that meets social and other obligations of the combined body of American bishops. In June 1971 at Catholic University, the National Center sponsored a week-long national conference entitled "New Directions For Urban America—Workshop on Ethnic and Working Class Priorities." The more than 150 participants at the conference were community leaders, social agency representatives, labor leaders, academicians, clergy, authorities on ethnic studies, teachers, community organizers, politicians, and professionals such as representatives of the communications media whose services directly affect ethnic communities. Conferees ranged in age from mid-twenties to mid-fifties. Notable speakers and their topics included Ralph Nader— "Issues and Priorities of Urban America"; Michael Novak—"The New American Dream"; Richard Scammon—"Ethnic Circumstance— America at the Polls"; Robert Schrank (Ford Foundation)—"The New Work Force"; and Carl Holman (National Urban Coalition)—"New Directions Beyond Polarization."

At a luncheon in the Senate Office Building, the conferees were addressed by Senator Edward Kennedy (D-Mass.), who called the workshop participants and their direction "the most powerful force for the future of our country"; Senator Jacob Javits (R-N.Y.); Senator Charles Percy (R-Ill.); Senator Richard Schweiker (R-Pa.); and Congressman Roman Pucinski (D-Ill.) Senator Schweiker and Congressman Pucinski are sponsors of the Ethnic Cultural Studies Bills in the Senate and House respectively. Workshop speakers included John Perkins, Assistant Director of the Committee on Political Education (COPE) of the AFL-CIO, who discussed "Political Action and Change from the Bottom Up," and Edward Chambers, the Assistant Director of Saul Alinsky's Industrial Areas Foundation Training Center in Chicago, who spoke on "New Directions for Community Organization in the 70's." Panel discussions included "New Dimensions of Ethnic and Cultural Awareness in Urban Life," "Ethnic Factors in the Urban Ferment," and "Ethnic Groups and Social Change."

Prominent ethnic leaders in attendance ranged from Casimir Lenard, the conservative Executive Director of the Polish American Congress, to militant Reverend James E. Groppi, Milwaukee civil rights activist who is presently organizing that city's Italian-Americans.

During an Italian-American caucus, Groppi remarked: "I came back to my Italian neighborhood and it was hardly better off than some of the Black areas."

The Conference's 133 registrants came from the industrial cities of the Northeast and Great Lakes regions. Conferees interacted freely, displaying their diversity of styles and viewpoints. Speakers provoked energetic, often heated, discussions. In introducing Ralph Nader (who is, incidentally, the son of Lebanese immigrants), Barbara Milkulski, a Baltimore community organizer, noted that ethnic Americans were searching for heroes to "lead us out of the desert." In a speech reminiscent of muck-raking populism, Nader touched the audience's frustrations: "America's technology has not been used to improve the lives of urban residents. Price-fixing is rampant all over the country. . . . Economic interests buy public officials when they are candidates. . . . As in days of old the tactics of the Establishment are to turn the masses against the downtrodden, to keep the poor and the working class proving their patriotism. . . . Companies that pollute the air will try to divide and rule by persuading the worker that the dirty smoke is really 'the smell of the payroll.'"

The purposes of the workshop were to call on the insights of this gathering of speakers and participants to identify the issues, priorities, and rhetoric of the new ethnic involvement, to develop new directions for urban America, and to begin to organize locally and even nationally with the Center as the focal point. Much of the week's discussion centered on the need to organize separately the power of black and working-class white neighborhoods. Then, should the self-interests of the two groups coincide, they would be able, through ad hoc coalitions, to work for specific social and economic goals, with the possible corollary of improved intergroup understanding. Many local issues were considered, but the majority of critical local issues were soon seen to be reflections of national policy ones. The most frequently discussed were tax reform, the quality and variety of educational opportunities, housing, the economic and health problems of the elderly, and the employment and social hardship of working-class youth. Discussions of priorities stressed the contribution to American society of the cultural and ethnic heritage of the working class, and the importance this heritage should have for American society. Cultural pluralism was praised, the concept of the melting pot disparaged. Comparative ethnic cultural studies were urged by most conferees. The need for more effective ways to participate in local and national government was recognized as a top priority. Workshop participants spoke of discrimination and defamation against ethnic Americans by the society at large, particularly the mass media.

During the conference the following special interest caucuses were formed: community organizations, ethnic studies and community colleges, pastoral concerns, Italians, Poles, Hungarians, Slovenians. The Community Organization Caucus concentrated on developing a funding proposal for a network of community organizers. Its report was presented to the conference.

A policy statement drafted at the end of the week-long conference was entitled: "Ethnic Populism: Redefining Urban America." The preamble of the statement declared, "We summon ethnic people across the country to rise up in a new urban populism." It continued: "We must begin to construct our agenda for action. This agenda is based on defining the problem from an economic and social perspective. . . . What can be done about the fundamental inequities of our society? How can our social policies benefit all sections of the population rather than increase the power of a few? These are the fundamental challenges of the seventies. Thus, the central issue becomes that of redistribution of rewards, goods, and services . . . the change in distribution must be toward the needs of a multi-racial pluralistic society." While the statement did not necessarily reflect the views of the majority of the participants, the tenor of the workshop revealed a new sense of social and economic militancy among white working-class ethnics. The majority of participants left the conference strengthened in their desire for change in American society. Ethnos, the newsletter of the National Center for Urban Ethnic Affairs, reported in its July 1971 issue: "The workshop was a success in that it provided for participants a new 'beginning' to reexamine America's identity, purpose and direction in relation to who we are—the urban ethnic working people, and in that context, to evolve a new perspective for renewing hope in the American dream."

The National Center for Urban Ethnic Affairs owes its existence and vitality to its dynamic director, Monsignor Geno Baroni, son of an Italian immigrant coal-miner from Western Pennsylvania. He and Irving Levine have been the dominant personalities in the white ethnic movement. Baroni inspires and urges, relies on instinct; Levine, a rationalist, is a social engineer. Baroni took an active part in the civil rights struggle of the 1960s, both in the South and as assistant pastor of an inner-city parish in Washington, D.C. In 1963 he helped coordinate the civil rights march on Washington. In 1965 he was named by Cardinal O'Boyle to head the United States Catholic Conference National Urban Task Force. The Task Force was created in response to the conclusions and recommendations of the Kerner Report on Civil Disorders. The Task Force initially saw itself in terms of "black and white" but soon shifted its emphasis to include proposals for work in three areas—with blacks, Spanish-speaking, and whites.

The Task Force, on November 11, 1969, made a report to the bishops' meeting in Washington. This report, referred to as the Triple Task Force Report, was presented by representatives of the black, brown, and white communities. The Triple Task Force recommended that "an annual collection for human development" be established, and the bishops passed a resolution setting up "a National Catholic Crusade Against Poverty" and pledged to raise $50 million over the following several years to carry on the crusade. The Catholic Conference's Task Force on Urban Problems committed itself to the development of an "urban mission policy." After the Campaign for Human Development was established, the Urban Task Force was phased out of existence in 1971. The bishops announced that the ethnic work would be carried on by a separate but affiliated program rather than by the Task Force.

In 1970 Baroni turned his attention to working-class white ethnics, convinced that inevitable group conflict could only be averted by dealing with the alienation of this group, most of whom are Catholic. He and Monsignor George Higgins wrote the September 1970 Labor Day Statement of the United States Catholic Conference, dedicated to white ethnic concerns. Monsignor Higgins of Chicago, head of the USCC's Social Action Program for many years and nationally prominent in labor circles, was one of the first supporters of Baroni's program. In November 1969, Baroni said that if we are to develop a new agenda for the 1970s:

> —We must go beyond the civil rights struggle of the 60's.
> —We must stop exploiting the fear of the ethnic, middle Americans.
> —We must bring together a new coalition to press for new goals and new priorities for all the poor and the near poor.
> —Including the Blacks—the Appalachians—the Indians— the Spanish-speaking—and the white urban ethnic groups.
> —Then we can develop a true cultural pluralism in this country and reduce the "inevitable group . . . conflict."

He speaks movingly of man's dignity as the "first and most important principle upon which we began to seek for solutions in our divided and bitter society." He calls for a moral response:

> While we admit that our nation has the material resources, the technology, the economic and industrial know-how and the wealth to provide a more human existence for every man, woman and child; something spiritual is lacking— the heart, the will, the desire on the part of affluent America to develop the goals and committments

> necessary to end the hardships of poverty and race in our
> midst. . . . This lack of national will—this lack of a
> national purpose or desire—this lack of a moral response
> to develop goals and committments to meet our sub-
> stantive problems of housing—education—health—unem-
> ployment—discrimination and so on—has created a crisis
> of belief on the part of the poor and youth—including
> many younger priests and nuns—in our democratic sys-
> tem of government and other institutions of society,
> including the Church.

He talks of replacing the despair following the assassinations of the
1960s with hope and a search for new leadership in the 1970s. By the
end of 1970 a major article in Newsweek (December 21, 1970) on
ethnic communities referred to Baroni as "chief strategist of the
nascent ethnic movement."

The National Center for Urban Ethnic Affairs did not formally
come into existence until 1971. It owes its existence to the efforts
of its founder, Monsignor Baroni, and to the Ford Foundation, which
provided the basic funding in 1971. Financial support and assistance
for the Center comes also from the National Urban Coalition, Catholic
University, the United States Catholic Conference, the Meyer Foundation, the National Credit Union Association, and the AFL-CIO COPE.
The Center's predecessor—the Urban Task Force—initially received
national attention by sponsoring an ethnic conference as had the American Jewish Committee's National Project on Ethnic America. Its
beginnings go back to this first national workshop on "Urban Ethnic
Community Development," held in June 1970 in Washington, D.C.
The United States Catholic Conference's Task Force on Urban Problems and the Catholic University of America sponsored the workshop,
and Baroni, as one of the directors of the former agency, developed
the five-day program after visiting numerous Northern cities and
finding that the white working-class "feel [s] neglected. They have
real needs and there are real myths about what's happened to them."
Prominent Catholic and Protestant clergymen, union spokesmen,
urbanists, local and national politicians, scholars, educators, and
community organizers made up the roster of speakers. The participants were primarily drawn from the industrial centers of the
Northeast and Midwest. They included parish priests, nuns, other
clergy, and laymen who represented the bishops in local urban task
forces, community organizers and neighborhood representatives,
spokesmen for white ethnic groups, students of urban and ethnic
phenomena, and representatives of the communications media. Reasons
for attending the workshop were various. According to the Reverend
James Sheehan, of Pontiac, Michigan, "People are having real problems

making it in our country. Some do have an ethnic vision of themselves."
The Reverend Daniel Bogus, of Polish extraction, pastor of a Catholic
church in an overwhelmingly black neighborhood in Detroit, attended
the workshop because, "I would do anything to bring about a better
understanding between races."

Senators Edmund Muskie and Charlès Percy, and Congressman
Roman Pucinski of Chicago, spoke to the conferees. Representatives
of the Economic Development Agency and the Office of Economic
Opportunity spoke of their agencies' interest in the problems of
working-class white Americans. Representatives of the workshop met
with John Gardner of the Urban Coalition and conferred with Senator
Edward Kennedy at his Capitol Hill office. The special purposes of
the workshop were:

1. To analyze ethnic factors in urban unrest.
2. To explore the use of federal and private programs
and resources in economics, cultural, and social development.
3. To share the practical experiences and insights of
community workers and professionals.
4. To confer with representatives of government agencies
to discuss the development of cultural, economic, and
social programs in urban areas.
5. To encourage clergy and lay participants to become
involved in their parishes and to identify, support and design programs for social, cultural, and economic development in their communities.

The conference generally served as a forum for white ethnic Americans
to air their grievances and develop a program for overcoming the
tensions between blacks and white ethnics. One development was the
formation of the Diocesan Urban Task Force. Twenty-five workshop
participants who specialize in diocesan urban affairs conferred,
prepared a report, and made plans for future action.

The workshop received impressive news coverage. The New
York Times published a lengthy lead article on the workshop's personalities and activities. The Washington Post carried several
articles. The Catholic press and Washington Star covered the conference activities. The workshop received national television coverage
when it was reported on NBC's Huntley-Brinkley show and the Today
Show. Several syndicated columnists commented on it. The New York
Times reported that the "voices of the white ethnic working-class rose
in anger. . . . The occasion was an unusual conference of priests,
politicians and community workers, one that some participants believe
may signal the beginning of a major social movement among 40 million

people of European descent in scores of older industrial cities in the
Northeast and Middle West. . . . They poured out their resentment
and discussed strategies for self-help, like community organization
and legislative activity."

In November 1970, the United States Catholic Conference Task
Force on Urban Problems published a 117-page report on urban
ethnic affairs edited by Monsignor Baroni and entitled All Men Are
Brothers. It covered activities of the Task Force from its inception
until November 1970 and highlighted the growing self-consciousness
of urban ethnic working people to their own alienation and their growing
awareness of the necessity of strong self-assertion. A short interim
report entitled New Directions For Urban America covers the period
from June 1, 1970, to June 1, 1971. It outlines the Center's short-
and long-term goals, details its community development projects,
including four underwritten by the Ford Foundation, and lists other
programs and activities in which the Center is involved. The community development project is referred to in the interim report as
the "Center's Ford Foundation Project."

The Center's staff, according to the interim report, has visited
and surveyed programs in over 20 cities but plans to concentrate on
five community projects so that prototype organizations and projects
can be developed. In addition, the Center has given technical assistance
and money for program development to numerous existing community
organizations. It has also given encouragement and other forms of
assistance to programs in Northeastern and Midwest cities, such as
the Center for Migration Studies in New York and the Ethnic Cultural
Heritage Project in Pittsburgh.

The continued vitality of the National Center for Urban Ethnic
Affairs is due in a large measure to the energy, inspiration, and
vision of Monsignor Baroni. He was among the first to acknowledge
the needs and strengths of working-class white ethnics and to recognize
them as a critical factor in the urban crisis. He focused national
attention upon these American workers in 1970 by initiating and preparing the annual Labor Day Statement of the United States Catholic
Conference. It declared " . . . we propose to deal specifically in this
annual Labor Day Statement with the pressing problems faced by one
of the most neglected segments in American society—the so-called
white ethnic working class. . . . The Church's strength, its clergy
and laity is now more vitally needed than ever before to assist largely
Catholic ethnic neighborhoods in our cities to develop social, economic
and cultural programs. . . . " Copies were widely distributed as a
handout in many parishes on Labor Day weekend. "Nobody has done
anything for the white working class since Social Security," Baroni
complains. "Today there is a budding national movement of white
workers wonderfully parallel to where the Blacks were a few years

ago. My hunch is this one is going to move even faster." Baroni goes on, "George Wallace doesn't speak for these people. He only voices their basic insecurity by being anti. But there are positive elements in that insecurity which can be marshalled against polarization in our society."

The Center for Urban Ethnic Affairs has a staff of nine persons of considerable experience with the urban ethnic working class. And the staff has joined with a larger group of community leaders and associate professional specialists. Through this combination of staff, associates, and persons of the newly evolving discipline known as community resources, the Center can provide consultation, research, workshop assistance, and technical program development to groups, organizations, dioceses, and cities in areas of research, program development, leadership training, community organization, credit unions, manpower development assistance, and economic development. In his use of the Center's funds and personnel, Baroni has not emphasized research and study except as they relate to practical activity. His goal is social and economic change. Staff member James Wright, a former steelworker and a graduate of Saul Alinsky's Chicago-based school for community organizers, personifies, to a great extent, the ambitions and directions of the Center. Neither theoretician nor philosopher but rather a successful practitioner, he was hired away from the Calumet Community Conference in 1971 where he had been a dominant force in organizing that group, the first regional multi-issue community organization in America.

The Center has focused its resources on four projects.

Community Development Project

This demonstration project, funded by the Ford Foundation, permits the Center to survey community development in major American cities, to extend limited technical assistance to groups and programs, and to select five cities for concentrated technical and financial assistance. The organizations and cities selected are:

1. The Calumet Community Congress (Gary). This federation of 150 organizations is in Northwestern Indiana.
2. The South East Community Organization (Baltimore).
3. The North Ward Cultural and Education Center (Newark).
4. The New York Project (a mutual effort of the Congress of Italian Americans Organization, the local Urban Coalition, the National Urban Coalition, and the Center for Urban Ethnic Affairs to develop a new social movement in New York City, initially in the Italian community.)

5. The Black-Polish Conference and the Conference of
Ethnic Communities (Detroit).

While the Center has concentrated its resources in this project
on the above-mentioned organizations, it has also given technical assistance to development efforts in Cleveland, Philadelphia, Toledo,
Providence, Boston, Chicago, Pittsburgh, and other cities.

Credit Union Project

Since many urban problems are rooted in economic needs, the
Center has developed a supplemental credit assistance project which
will enable it to develop a "new" credit union approach in the cities
which will facilitate the capitalization of minority groups. This project is funded by the National Credit Union Administration.

National Urban Coalition Project

The Center and the National Urban Coalition have developed
several joint programs in urban ethnic communities and have co-
sponsored consultations of community leaders and national institutions.
The Center is consultant to the National Urban Coalition concerning
ethnic and working-class matters and has assisted the National Urban
Coalition in its efforts to create more representative local coalition.

Metropolitan Washington Research Project

The Center is identifying the working class of metropolitan
Washington, geographically, economically, ethnically, culturally, and
socially. This project, funded by the Meyer Foundation, may serve
as a model for developing similar urban profiles which will include
the ethnic dimension.

The National Center has engaged in other activities.

Federal Government

On several occasions, Center staff and ethnic community leaders
have met with White House staff and federal agency heads to discuss
federal response to urban ethnic community needs. On August 17,
1970, President Nixon met with Monsignor Baroni and other staff

members of the United States Catholic Conference to discuss the
economic and social anxieties confronting American workers. Meetings
have also been held with Senators Kennedy, Muskie, Harris, and
McGovern. The emphasis has been on OEO, HEW, and HUD programs
for the white ethnic working class.

National Institute of Mental Health

The Center arranged a joint consultation with leading social
scientists, mental health directors, and local urban ethnic community
leaders to explore the possibilities of programs of research and
services for working-class communities.

The National Urban Coalition

The Center and the National Urban Coalition have developed
several joint programs to benefit urban ethnic communities and, on
several occasions, ethnic community leaders have held joint meetings
with National Urban Coalition staff members to examine program
possibilities.

The Catholic University

The Center has held its two annual national conferences at the
University. A proposal for a three- to five-year research program
in "Evolving Ethnic Differentiations in American Metropolitan Areas"
has been developed, as well as another proposal for an "Urban Ethnic
Community Training Program." If funded, a one-semester program
would bring together students and community leaders from around
the nation in a joint effort to develop research and organization skills.
Relationships with several departments have been formed to develop
seminars and other interdisciplinary programs.

The National Credit Union Administration

The Center's Credit Union Project was funded in 1971 and has
been assisted by the Credit Union National Association.

The Campaign for Human Development

The national Catholic fund-raising drive to assist in developing
programs in poverty areas is called the Campaign for Human Develop-

ment and was initiated in November 1970. The Center has assisted
several groups in developing and submitting proposals for funding to
the Campaign's staff.

The National Police Foundation

Several meetings were held to discuss the need for police training
programs and the Center is currently arranging a demonstration program for urban ethnic communities.

* * *

The Center's location has facilitated staff relationships and
interaction with other agencies based in Washington—Common Cause,
the AFL-CIO, the Center for Community Change, the National Science
Foundation, the Bi-Centennial Commission, and the Polish American
Congress. The Center's staff has consulted with labor leaders to
determine the feasibility of collaborating to develop programs for
working-class communities. To this end, meetings have been held
with officials of the AFL-CIO, American Labor Alliance, and United
States Steel Workers of America. Consultations have also been conducted with newspaper and television journalists and syndicated
columnists concerning the communications media's insensitivity to and
lack of concern for working-class and ethnic Americans. Center personnel have channeled information to the media to improve their coverage of white ethnics.

A prominent Catholic scholar who is familiar with Baroni's
activities, believes that he is unaware of their effect. A Democratic
Party ethnic strategist with more than ten years of active involvement
in ethnic politics has compared Baroni's activism to that of the Black
Panther Party. The Reverend Andrew Greeley is highly critical that
Baroni and other Catholic clergymen are "seeking their own self-
validation by crusading for white ethnic rights." All three of these
observers would probably have been equally unsympathetic toward
such leaders as Martin Luther King and David Dellinger. Many black
leaders are suspicious, indeed hostile, to Baroni's activities, believing
them ultimately a racist strategy. Others—Carl Holman, president
of the National Urban Coalition, and James Gibson, another leading
black urban planner—disagree. So does Mayor Richard Hatcher of
Gary. Most black professionals in Washington, D.C., are working
with Baroni in his programs.

Baroni himself points to white ethnic alienation. He feels strongly
that one's ethnic heritage is a source of self-respect, pride, and
identity. He says, "I think God wants us to be free and liberated, in a
sense, in knowing our identity so the image of God can grow within

people. . . . And I think a person who loses his self-respect has a harder time dealing with people from other groups, other cultures— students, blacks, Chicanos."

The National Center for Urban Ethnic Affairs has been recognized by many mainstream leaders as a legitimate spokesman for ethnic America. Senator Schweiker placed a statement in the Congressional Record on June 10, 1971, which noted the Center's resolution in support of the ethnic studies center bill. The resolution has been unanimously adopted at the Center's second annual conference and presented to interested Congressmen and Senators at a luncheon held in the Senate Caucus Room. Schweiker acknowledged the Center as the legitimate voice and lobby of ethnic America for ethnic studies. Baroni has been cautious regarding the extent of his constituency and authority. Some observers had believed that he would use the second national conference of ethnic leaders as an occasion to announce his leadership of a national movement, but he made no such announcement. He is avoiding this kind of publicity while he travels around the country developing contacts with community organizations. When the Northwest Community Organization in Chicago held its annual conference in 1971, Baroni appeared and made a speech. When a group of young New York City Italians announced the formation of "Young Italians of America" in the summer of 1971, he traveled to New York City and spoke to the group. Baroni's strategy is to build a coalition of these organizations. With the backing of indigenous organizations, the National Center can represent white ethnic interests at the national level. Baroni will speak for them in the halls of Congress, at the White House, in the offices of private foundations, and everywhere he believes their interests need to be spoken for.

THE CENTER FOR THE STUDY OF AMERICAN PLURALISM

In announcing its grant of $264,694 to the National Opinion Research Center for research on white ethnic groups, the Ford Foundation acknowledged the importance of the Reverend Andrew M. Greeley in the ethnic resurgence since, for purposes of the grant, he was named director of a newly established Center for the Study of Ethnic Pluralism. The word "American," which evokes little controversy, has been substituted for the word "Ethnic" in the name of the new study unit. The Center is basically underwritten by the Ford Foundation grant but has received some grants from other sources. Commencing its activities in early 1971, its staff members during the first year have engaged in secondary analysis of existing data, collecting literature on American ethnic groups, and undertaking the

planning and designing of research projects. The Reverend Greeley
says that initially the Center will be an ethnic "think tank." A newsletter of the National Opinion Research Center, April 1971, emphasized the diverse ethnic backgrounds of the Center's staff.

One of the activities of the Center in the spring of 1971 was a
series of lectures at the nearby University of Chicago campus. Given
by academicians, they included such topics as "The Italians in America
Today," "The Politics of Black-Ethnic Cooperation," and "Family
Structure in American Ethnic Groups." The Center also plans to publish scholarly articles and reports oriented to public policy issues and
to sponsor conferences and seminars on ethnic subjects. It would like
to serve as a repository for ethnic research and writings and eventually
publish a journal and newsletter. The major areas of investigation and
study will be the ethnic factor in family life, voting behavior, voluntary
associations, and race relations. Greeley's researchers will try to
isolate ethnicity as a distinct variable by controlling, as much as possible, the factors of class, region, and religion. To a lesser extent,
the Center staff will explore the influence of religion.

The Center for the Study of American Pluralism exists because
of the vision, energy, and creative drive of its director—the Reverend
Andrew M. Greeley. Greeley has devoted himself to the study of
ethnicity and the cultural aspects of Roman Catholicism. He has investigated the attitudes and behavior of priests, voters and politicians,
families, urban dwellers. He has conducted research on the significance
of ethnicity and religion in intermarriage and the family, education,
race relations, and social and political change. He has written and
published more on the subject of ethnicity than anyone else. In 1971
his Why Can't They Be Like Us? America's White Ethnic Groups
raised many more questions than it answered. Besides the publication of numerous other books and the books he is currently writing
on the Irish, and on ethnic groups as part of the New Deal coalition,
Greeley's articles in learned journals, popular magazines such as
the New Republic and the New York Times Magazine, and less conventional journals such as Dissent, have been so frequent that they
are hard to keep track of.   He has a syndicated column in the Catholic
press. He is a lecturer at the University of Chicago and speaks frequently on ethnicity at colleges and universities and at the conventions
of learned societies.

Greeley feels compelled to comment on nearly everything written
or said about ethnicity or related subjects. When liberal book re-
viewers heaped praise on Mike Royko's Boss: Richard J. Daley of
Chicago, Greeley had ample grounds to criticize book reviewing practices, but his strong defense of Daley's style of politics revealed his
own ethnocentrism. In the Catholic press, Greeley had denounced what
he called "the-white-ethnic-as-social-problem" approach of Monsignor

Baroni and the Urban Task Force of the United States Catholic Conference. When the magazine City, an organ of the Urban Coalition,
carried two articles on the resurgence of interest in ethnicity and
then asked readers to respond to questions proposed by its editors,
Greeley was disturbed by their efforts and responded to the questions
with "I'm afraid the harsh, bitter truth is that most of those who
teach on university faculties, write articles for national journals,
advise governmental leaders, staff foundations and national agencies,
and worry about what's happening to American society, simply do not
know anything about what goes on in Hamtramck or Queens or the northwest side of Chicago." He believes that intellectuals who read the
New York Times are equally naive about the subject of ethnic groups
and the lower middle class. While his Irishness and strong distaste
for liberal intellectuals may too frequently be revealed, he remains
the most articulate and creative thinker and writer on the renewed
interest in ethnicity.

THE FORD FOUNDATION AND OTHER INSTITUTIONS

In January 1971 the Ford Foundation announced grants totalling
nearly 1 million dollars for action programs and research into the
problems of America's white working class. Protecting its flank,
the Foundation's press release on the grants stated: "The Foundation
stressed at the same time that it was continuing its work to widen
opportunities for blacks and other racial minorities." Besides the
three groups discussed in this chapter, the Center for Policy Research
and the University of Michigan received $271,348 for research on white
ethnic workers through interviews and surveys in metropolitan areas.
In announcing the grants, McGeorge Bundy, president of the
Foundation, observed:

> In the last year, a great deal has been said and written
> about the "blue-collar American," "the ethnic white,"
> and "the lower middle-class" worker. He is said to be
> "alienated," "forgotten," "troubled," "disillusioned,"
> and "angry." The number involved is estimated at between
> 50 to 100 million men, women, and children. Generaliza-
> tions about very large groups are full of exceptions, but
> it is clear that great numbers of working-class Americans
> have not been at the center of recent social concerns.
> It is important to know more precisely the economic and
> social roots of their anxiety and to explore ways of miti-
> gating their discontent.
> The organizations receiving these grants are seeking
> to deal with some of the problems of white working-class

American communities through constructive action and
through research on which effective policies and programs
may be based. The grants also are intended to widen
our understanding of the continuing role of ethnicity in
American life. The Foundation's active concern with enlarging equal opportunity for racial minorities will continue undiminished. The condition and fate of each of
these large segments affect one another. An institution
like ours, working to advance the well-being of American
society as a whole, can and should pay attention to both
at the same time.

Reverend Greeley advances two reasons for the grants: "What's
sauce for the blacks is sauce for everyone else. Secondly, the world
of the foundation, the world of the government, has awakened to the
existence of places like the northwest side of Chicago." Basil Whiting
of the Ford Foundation is more delicate: "We were concerned about
polarization and conflict in the cities of the northeast and saw a need
to try to reduce them. In addition," he says, "there are problems
relating to this segment of the population, which, while they are by
no means as severe as those faced by the black and poor, are real.
Finally, we wanted to explore the possibility of joint or parallel action
and cooperation between blacks and whites in getting services they
both need." Whiting is more guarded regarding the ethnic aspect of
the grants. "The foundation," he says, "didn't look at this in terms
of ethnicity. We're not emphasizing ethnicity. What we talk about
here in the program is not 'ethnic' but the working class."
    Other institutions such as the National Urban Coalition in Wash-
ington are working on the problems of the white ethnic working class.
The Coalition has an executive assistant for ethnic affairs and sends
representatives to most of the conferences on ethnicity.

4

**PERSISTENCE
AND RESURGENCE
OF ETHNICITY**

INTRODUCTION

Ethnic attachments are only one variable among the many by which Americans define themselves. Poles, Italians, Swedes, and others residing and working within old ethnic enclaves constantly think and act the way their ancestors and neighbors would expect them to. The Reverend Andrew Greeley's work is much concerned with the preservation of cultural links through the unconscious transmission of role expectations. He does not limit cultural identification to inhabitants of ethnic neighborhoods but documents the links among acculturated ethnics who reside elsewhere. A WASP or assimilated ethnic seeks enrichment and variety when he visits an ethnic restaurant or place of entertainment. The social activist uses ethnic origins to personalize causes and polarize ethnics on certain issues. The ethnic business or professional man, the ethnic priest, politician, or community leader often builds his career within the confines of his group and thus for him ethnicity serves as a means of social mobility and economic betterment. Lawyers accept or reject jurors on the basis of their ethnic origins. With the expanding ethnic middle class, and in reaction to the recent emphasis on black studies, scholarly and artistic interest in the customs of white ethnic groups has greatly increased. Educators are establishing ethnic studies programs. Scholars are investigating the immigrant experience and the persistence of ethnicity. Student degree candidates are writing dissertations on different aspects of ethnicity. Ethnic book clubs and educational and cultural journals are beginning to appear. Visits to the country of one's ancestors have become popular. Ethnic first names are becoming increasingly popular, and fewer ethnics are now modifying or discarding their surnames. This preservation of cultural links is deliberate. It is highly self-conscious and is limited neither to the lower middle class nor to the inhabitant of the ethnic enclave.

The intensity of one's ethnic attachment frequently corresponds to the strength of perceived threats from the outside. The threats from other groups which strengthen internal attachments may be immediate and concrete: the Yankees in Boston surrounded by organized ethnic communities; the Poles, Italians, and Lithuanians on the south-west and northwest sides of Chicago pushed by contiguous black and Puerto Rican expansion; the Jews in the New York City school system losing their hard-earned seniority to the blacks as the promotion rules are changed to accelerate black advancement. On the other hand, the threats may be more generalized. The Zionist movement after World War II and the Arab-Israeli War of 1967 dramatically affected American Jews because these events involved the creation and survival of a Jewish homeland; the brutal political repression of Czechoslovakians, Poles, and Hungarians deeply moved and activated many Americans who trace their roots to those countries. Ethnic loyalties can be quickly and passionately aroused when a Lithuanian sailor, seeking asylum on an American ship as in 1970, is returned to his Russian oppressors. Obviously, those with relatives in the old country feel the threats more strongly. Since World War II the Republican Party has directed a good deal of its energy toward attracting the votes of Americans whose origins lie in countries dominated by the Soviet Union. The Party's commitment has been called the "captive nations" strategy and originated with the intense reaction of Baltic and Eastern Europeans to the Yalta and Potsdam agreements. But the ethnic attachment to the homeland can be aroused even among such more fully assimilated white ethnics as the Irish. In August 1971 Chicago's Mayor Richard J. Daley and the Irish-American president of a large Chicago-based corporation headed a drive to raise 1 million dollars in Chicago in ten days to aid refugees from the civil strife in Northern Ireland. Daley also spoke of organiz-ing to exert pressure on Great Britain to withdraw its troops from Northern Ireland, and of the obligation to repay the Irish for the grand legacy given to Americans of Irish descent. A Daley-sponsored resolution put his newly formed committee, the Irish Relief Fund or the Friends of Ireland, on record as condemning "the bigotry of the government of Northern Ireland, which has resulted in blatant dis-crimination in jobs, housing and voting for a sizable section of the people of Northern Ireland." Shortly thereafter Colonel Jack Reilly, an aide to Mayor Daley, traveled to Dublin with a "substantial sum of money" for relief efforts in Northern Ireland. Reilly said that the money was "a gesture from the city of Chicago to the distressed population of Northern Ireland." Weeks later a Chicago attorney announced that he would head a commission of lawyers to seek the release of hundreds of persons detained in Northern Ireland under emergency detention powers used by the British government. In

September 1971 a Northern Irish rebel spoke to a crowd of Irishmen on the southwest side of Chicago. In his rolling Irish brogue he emphasized the close historic ties between Ireland and the United States and pleaded for assistance: "Please, for God's sake, give us your dollars and your support and it will only take six months to finish the job." His audience was most sympathetic; they jumped to their feet and cheered at the mention of the outlawed Irish Republican Army and scowled at alleged British atrocities. Earlier, Irish-Americans in New York City had picketed the United Nations after disorders in Northern Ireland.

Ethnicity is very important to small, highly visible minorities such as American Indians and Orientals since these groups cluster together for protection and self-defense. Ethnic identification becomes additionally significant whenever one comes into contact with others of different cultures and feels disoriented because the dominant society may offer so few means by which one can identify himself.

Three important perspectives should be kept in mind. First, the ethnic factor has always been an important dimension of American life. For many years, ethnicity was taken seriously by politicians, union leaders, businessmen, church administrators, and real estate developers and spectators. This is shown by the balanced ticket, ethnic appointments to public office, the ethnic caucuses among unionists, the profits in ethnic foods, restaurants, and entertainment, the ethnic parish, and the nationality suburb. While the ideal of the "melting pot" has, to some extent, played down the ethnic factor, the emergence of black consciousness, black nationalism, black power, and black capitalism has alerted scholars, intellectuals, and journalists to a long-standing dynamic of American life. They now have begun to examine seriously the persistence of ethnicity.

The second perspective requires that one differentiate between traditional manifestations of ethnicity and new or different manifestations—a nearly impossible task for the two are interwoven. The research and writings of Nathan Glazer, Daniel Moynihan, Michael Parenti, and Andrew Greeley primarily call attention to the survival of the ethnic factor but also serve to stimulate new expressions of ethnicity, of positive rather than negative identification. The American Jewish Committee seems bent on harnessing ethnic attachments to achieve positive social policies. Joseph Colombo's successes seem to be a novel and different expression. While he has tapped resentments that have built up over the years similar to those of New York's Jews and Irish in earlier times, it is, nevertheless, intense ethnic pride, the urban disintegration, black aggressiveness, and economic immobility which distinguish the Italian-American experience in New York City in 1971 from those of other groups. Meir Kahane's Jewish Defense League is similarly a recent development.

The third perspective concerns the future of ethnic attachments. After the resurgence spends itself, will ethnicity continue to influence attitudes and behavior in American society? Parenti believes they will persist; Glazer thinks they will gradually fade from the American scene. Greeley emphasizes that because ethnic groups are a combination of European cultural background, American acculturation, and political, social, and economic common interest, they will survive. "Not merely do different origins produce cultural differences," he argues, "the different experiences in America reinforce the old differences and create new ones." Parenti's prognostications are limited, but he does not foresee intermarriage occurring at a rapid enough rate to bring about large-scale assimilation, and he believes that the offspring of mixed marriages will maintain ethnic identifications. The persistence of ethnic attachments convinces him that ethnic loyalties may increasingly take their place alongside regional, class, and other group attachments.

WHITE ETHNIC ASSERTION

The predominantly Catholic white ethnic assertion of the latter half of the 1960s and early 1970s largely accounts for the renewed interest in ethnicity. White ethnics have been moving from a traditionally defensive and protective stance to an offensive and assertive one. Their encounters with black progress have been one of the primary causes for their assertion, another being their emergence into the middle class. These encounters, of course, are also linked with their recent alienation from American institutions and way of life. They feel neglected and forgotten.

Blacks are making conspicuous gains. In the 1960s they won civil rights and antipoverty laws. They received special federal assistance for more and better schools, housing, and jobs. In the 1970s they appeared to be consolidating their gains and making further advances. A black was named to the board of General Motors. The Ford Foundation undertook a six-year, $100-million program to increase minority opportunities in higher education. The Third Annual Black and Minorities Business and Cultural Exposition, known as Black Expo, raised $450,000 from the 479,050 persons visiting the Chicago Amphitheater and brought together the majority of influential black politicians to discuss black strategy for the 1972 elections. In the autumn of 1971 the Democratic national chairman promised to give blacks at least 20 percent representation on all party and convention committees and staff including, to the extent possible, the credentials and platform committees at the national convention, to add ten blacks to the party's policy council, and to more than double the budget of the minority affairs division of the Democratic National Committee. In October 1971, in a speech in Chicago, Mayor Richard Hatcher of Gary noted that the number of black officials had risen from 400 in 1967 to 1,860. He defined black politics as "defeating political arrangements where whites control and suppress blacks." He explained that "Black power and civil rights movements in the 1960s led to the organization of blacks, which in turn led to black power and solidarity, and an awesome demonstration of mass power in politics." The first black congresswoman announced in October 1971 that she would enter the presidential primaries in at least five states to try to win the Democratic Party's nomination for president.

In June 1971 the congressional black caucus, consisting of 13 black congressmen, held a political fund-raising dinner in Washington and for the first time in black politics raised $250,000. In March 1971 President Nixon and his aides were pressured into meeting with these legislators to discuss a list of 60 demands. Earlier they had embarrassed Nixon by boycotting his State of the Union Message. These racial assertions are unprecedented in American politics. Nixon felt obliged to reply to their specific demands and did so at some length. He accepted a few relatively marginal proposals but rejected most of them. This gave the black legislators the opportunity to stage a press conference in the Ways and Means Committee hearing room and to declare that his reply was "deeply disappointing." News-week was so impressed by their solidarity that it devoted the cover of its June 7, 1971, issue to a picture of the 13 black congressmen standing in front of the Capitol and featured an article on the new black politics. It noted that the caucus personified the "quickening black rush into the American political mainstream," and further emphasized that the political future of blacks lies in the central cities. Six cities, including Washington, Newark, and Gary, have black majorities. Eight others, including Baltimore, Detroit, and St. Louis, are more than 40 percent black, and one out of three Chicagoans is black. Blacks in increasing numbers are moving into the public agencies of many large cities and in a few instances are, in fact, taking over these agencies. The militancy of the black revolution in the 1960s and black political power and capitalism of the early 1970s have legitimized organization along racial-ethnic lines. Manhattan's black borough president has said that blacks in 1972 must "nationalize" the black vote if they are to have any influence in presidential politics. There is a National Conference of Black Elected Officials. The congressional black caucus held a convention of many of the nation's more than 1,850 black elected officials in the latter part of 1971 to consider a strategy to maximize their national influence in 1972. A few black political leaders have already advanced a "third-force" alternative. Blacks have their own anthem. In Chicago, Malcolm X

Junior College flies their green, black, and red flag alongside the American flag. Recent graduating ceremonies at the college included displays of the raised clenched fist, symbol of black resistance, and the use of the black handshake. To white ethnics, black nationalism is something very real.

It is in the white ethnic's response to this black emergence, coupled with assaults against him and America itself by affluent student activists, that he is not only reacting but asserting himself. Ethnic roots are a source of energy for the lower middle class. Ethnic identification has been recognized as a positive force and an acceptable framework for the social order of one's life. Norman Podhoretz, a prominent New York intellectual and the editor of Commentary, was quoted (Washington Post, April 11, 1971):

> The 70's are going to be a different period . . . just as the black assertion set the climate of the 60s, I think you'll find a comparable Catholic, white-ethnic assertion in the '70s. You have 40 million Catholics in the United States. They've never been organized as a political block around their resentments. Black assertion demystified political processes. But you can't stop there. You have an enormously potent force here, in this Catholic minority. . . .
> This Catholic assertion will set the agenda for the 1970s.

The late David Danzig, a scholar in intergroup relations at Columbia University, urged a program that would make ethnic groups behave more like a national coalition of minorities, forcing upon the American public a new awareness of their legitimate needs. There is no better representative of white ethnic assertion than Barbara Mikulski, Polish-American leader of the South East Community Organization in Baltimore. Looking to the future of the white ethnic movement, she wrote in the Jesuit magazine America (December 26, 1970):

> I want something positive. I want to see a national movement developed to help American ethnics, but not at the expense of any other minority groups.
> I have decided to be myself. I'm a woman, a Polish-American and a Catholic. . . . As I discover my own identity, I become more free and I want the same thing for all human beings. . . .
> When I graduated from college I had no heroes and a lot of people I have looked to since then are not around any more. I have come back to my origins. . . . I now see the Church as a vital force in saving the cities, which is the big challenge of our day. The framework is there. The

parish church and the parochial school can't solve all our
social problems, but they can play a big role in holding
together these neighborhoods and helping our ethnic communities. And if these ethnic communities don't make it,
the city won't make it.

The majority of ethnic Americans are recognizing that they have not
lost their foreign identity or ethnic consciousness in the American
melting pot. An enduring aspect of ethnic consciousness is its re-
silience. For many, ethnicity has meaning into and beyond the third
generation. A high level of nationality consciousness has always
been maintained by the churches, local newspapers, and political
organizations wherever there are large concentrations of ethnic
groups. Both immigrant neighborhoods and residential movement
demonstrate that ethnics prefer to live among those who share their
cultural heritage and immigrant experience. It was always erroneously
assumed that ethnic identity would diminish with acculturation. Rather,
it has persisted and, in some cases, been intensified. Ethnic activists
believe that heightened group identity will engender cooperation, inspire self-confidence and self-respect, and develop indigenous leadership. These qualities will then enable ethnic communities to influence
decisions involving their welfare. Ethnic power will thereby be a
recognized force in the political arena. Harper's Magazine of September 1971 carried the autobiographical article "White Ethnic" by Michael
Novak, at present the most articulate intellectual spokesman for white
ethnics and by his own admission in the subtitle ". . . a man disin-
herited by the authorized American fantasy." Novak writes, "I am
born into a history not Anglo-Saxon and not Jewish . . . and thus I
am privy to neither power nor status nor intellectual voice." The
magazine's cover depicts two wrestling arms—one in a blue workshirt,
with dirty fingernails, scars, and muscles, and the other, cleaner and
slighter, in a pinstripe suit, white cuffs, and gold cufflinks. The
picture bears the caption "The Ethnics v. The System."

Backlash

Initial expressions of ethnic unrest were indigenous or grass-
roots in origin and were not encouraged by the elites of mainstream
institutions. Increasingly, however, elites are recognizing the assertion of white ethnics and are attempting to give a constructive direction to the movement. In the late 1960s the assertion was in large
part reactive and racial. Blacks and Puerto Ricans were perceived
as the enemies. White ethnic reaction was generally local rather
than national. It occurred most intensely in the larger industrial

cities of the Northeast and Midwest, but even in this context there
were widely divergent stimuli to ethnic expression. Generalizations
are difficult because the urban context has wide variations. Italian-
Americans in New York City were moved by forces different from
those that provoked their counterparts in Newark. The interests and
fears of Polish-Americans in Gary were not the same as those of
Polish-Americans on the northwest side of Chicago. Indeed, the concerns of Polish-Americans on the northwest side of Chicago differed
from their counterparts on the southwest side. Since 1970, the
reactionary, negative, and destructive phase of ethnic self-awareness
seems to have given way to a more positive phase. White ethnics are
struggling to identify and redefine themselves in positive terms, to
organize and thereby appreciate their political potential, and to construct alliances. Appeals to racial fears and hatreds have become
somewhat less effective. It is too early, at the time of this writing,
to evaluate the new ethnic potential, but it is likely that the presidential
campaigns of 1972 will produce strong and explicit ethnic appeals.
And if leaders like Colombo, Mikulski, and Novak have their way, the
white ethnic will be highly visible in the 1970s. Most the assertions,
of course, will be at the local level and involve concrete issues.
While an effective national organization with broadly based support
is unlikely, a loose coalition on specific goals is a distinct possibility.

George Wallace in the North

One of the first signs of white ethnic discontent and alienation
was the attraction of George Wallace. He actively courted ethnics
as early as the 1964 presidential race in such cities as Gary. But
Wallace made his strongest and most systematic appeal in his bid
for the presidency in 1968. He received 13.53 percent of the popular
vote, and though the majority of his support came from the Old South,
he received over 4 million votes outside of that region. In Illinois
(8.5 percent), Indiana (11.4 percent), Michigan (10 percent), and Ohio
(11.8 percent) he captured more than 1.5 million votes. The Pennsylvania (8.1 percent) and New Jersey (9.1 percent) electorate gave him
nearly 650,000 votes. His vote in these industrial states would have
been greater if organized labor had not opposed him. The leaders
of the AFL-CIO perceived Wallace as a threat to their power. In his
book The Making of the President 1968, Theodore H. White asserts
that organized labor was "roused to the greatest political exertion of
its history," and he characterizes its effort as "unprecedented in
American history." Wallace appealed to the fears and prejudices of
residents of the industrial centers of the North. He claimed to be a
friend of the white workingman, spoke on the issues of race (busing,

housing, and so on), of law and order, and vigorously attacked their
common enemies. Those who wore beards and long hair, the liberals,
the bureaucrats, student and black activists, the intellectuals, the
universities, and the mass media fell under attack. Wallace was the
first national figure to recognize white ethnic grievances. The "little
people," as Wallace called them, listened, and many voted for him.
In September 1968 placards in the streets of Chicago demonstrated
the sources of the candidate's support: "Italian Power for Wallace,"
"Polish Want Wallace." In Gary, Cleveland, Flint, Baltimore, and
Newark, angry white workingmen waved Wallace banners and pasted
Wallace stickers on their lunch pails and the bumpers of their cars.
For the majority of Wallace voters from the North, their vote expressed their disillusionment and sense of neglect. Wallace had
moved into the vacuum left by government, universities, foundations,
and the church. The liberal revolution of the 1960s had not only
ignored the needs and fears of white ethnics, but had made white
ethnics the scapegoats for the injustices of the blacks. The scapegoats
reacted. Wallace exploited the anguish of communities contiguous to
and threatened by black ghettos. He sought to divide rather than
unify blacks and whites of the lower and lower middle classes. Newspapers and television news in September and October revealed his
appeals to fear and racism, and publicized the reactions that he had
aroused. Violence was not uncommon at his rallies, where dissent
was not tolerated. In his book on the 1968 campaign Theodore H.
White reports an incident that occurred at a Wallace rally in a predominantly ethnic suburb of Chicago:

> While Wallace spoke, violence sputtered on the fringe of
> his Cicero crowd. A youth carrying a McCarthy placard
> found himself assailed; the attackers kicked his ankles;
> a fat middle-aged blonde woman pushed through the crowd
> and screamed, "Shoot 'em, kill 'em!" The youth carried
> a sign saying, DON'T LET WALLACE MAKE THIS A
> POLICE STATE. The fat woman clawed his face, slapped
> it. The crowd, approving her, yelled, "You nigger-loving
> homosexual!" "Take a bath, you dope addict!" An
> apparently Jewish reporter was taking notes, and several
> yelled, "Hey, you Hebe, you Jew bastard—how you doing,
> Moishe, you writing backwards?"

Following Wallace's substantial electoral support in the urban
North, social reformers like Irving Levine of the American Jewish
Committee and some politicians realized that the white ethnic is
very much a part of the political equation necessary to solve the
urban crisis. The prospect emerged that the race riots of the 1970s

would be between people and people rather than people and property.
While the urban white backlash has involved the entire American class
spectrum, the volatility of backlash and its political implications are
most dangerous in the lower middle class. This group consists
largely of second- and third-generation Europeans—ethnic subgroups.
Trapped in the cities because they cannot afford to move to the suburbs, victims of class prejudice, many white ethnics welcomed
Wallace's rhetoric and directed their anger at the blacks. Vice-
President Agnew's appeals to the "silent majority" and his attacks on
liberal institutions before the November 1970 elections were a somewhat more subtle effort to exploit ethnic disaffection.

Italian-Americans and Joseph Colombo

The strongest indigenous expression of the white ethnic resurgence in recent years has been the activities of Italian-Americans in
New York City. Italians in that city, according to the 1960 census,
are the second largest ethnic group, next to the Jews. On June 29,
1970, a crowd of Italian-Americans, estimated by the police to
approximate 40,000 and by rally sponsors at 200,000, gathered in
Columbus Circle on the southwest corner of Central Park for a unity
demonstration. They had, on previous evenings, been picketing the
New York offices of the Federal Bureau of Investigation. Their
purpose in these demonstrations was to protest the FBI's use of the
term "Mafia" and its alleged harassment of some Italian-Americans
suspected of criminal activities. An ad hoc committee of the Italian-
American Civil Rights League sponsored the demonstration.

The huge crowd cheered leading political figures, among them
former City Comptroller Mario Procaccino, unsuccessful candidate
in the 1969 mayoralty election. The organizers of the demonstration,
however, were disappointed that more Italian-American leaders did
not appear. Congressman Mario Biaggi (D-N.Y.) was there and
asserted that out of 22 million Italian-Americans, only 5,000, or less
than 1 percent, are involved in organized crime. Mayor John V.
Lindsay did not attend but sent greetings through Deputy Mayor Richard
Aurelio, the highest ranking Italian-American in city government.
Aurelio, however, was booed at the end of his speech. Mayor Lindsay
is distrusted by New York Italians, who perceive him as a champion
of blacks and Puerto Ricans and indifferent to their own needs.
Nevertheless, Aurelio smiled through the jeers, and the League unbent
sufficiently in its attitude toward him and the mayor to offer them
both honorary memberships. Aurelio accepted.

Congressman Adam Clayton Powell (D-N.Y.), defeated in the
June 1970 Democratic congressional primary in Harlem, exhorted

the crowd: "Right on! Right on!" Joseph Colombo, Sr., identified by the Justice Department as a national commissioner of the Cosa Nostra and head of one of New York's five mob families, received enthusiastic applause and cheers. "This day belongs to you, to you the people," said Colombo. "You are organized now, you are one, and nobody can take you apart any more." When the New York Times subsequently called Colombo "the leader of one of the six Mafia families in the city," Italian-Americans picketed the newspaper.

Most piers in New York harbor were closed the day of the demonstration as longshoremen converged on the rally. Downtown Manhattan's Little Italy, other Italian-American sections, and many Italian enterprises throughout the city closed their doors because of the demonstration. At the rally the crowd waved miniature American flags and listened to speeches extolling Italian-American loyalty to the United States. Italy's tricolor and the American flag flew from the statue of Christopher Columbus. While the rally was peaceful, the subsequent march to FBI headquarters was marked by violent incidents. The midafternoon march snarled traffic and tempers became short. A plate-glass window was broken, a few arrests were made, and two policemen suffered stab wounds when scuffling broke out about a block from FBI headquarters.

In a statement issued in advance of the demonstration, a coordinator of the rally declared: "What we resent emphatically is this myth that anyone whose name ends in a vowel is Mafia or Cosa Nostra. If there are criminals, let them be tried by the courts, instead of by newspapers that create fantasies of this Cosa Nostra." An Italian-American priest at the rally was overheard saying, "I've waited 41 years to hear these things." The resentments of Italian-Americans surfaced in a dramatic way during those two months of 1970. The FBI had become one symbol of the rejection of Italian-American culture by the dominant American culture. Italian-Americans had been conditioned to be ashamed of their heritage.

In a ten-page article in New York Magazine (June 7, 1971), Nicholas Pileggi wrote of "the Italian-American revolution" and the restiveness of New York's Italians "after 75 years of benign residence in their own neighborhoods." He noted that Colombo, like Meir Kahane of the Jewish Defense League, had "stepped into a leadership vacuum that had long existed among New York's low-income white working classes" and that middle and upper classes and professionals had abandoned the old neighborhoods and left them without leadership in education, politics, labor, neighborhood business, mass media, and the church. In the secondary schools of the city, for example, Italian-American children account for almost 18 percent of the students, but of the system's 90 high school principals, only one is Italian, and less than 10 percent of the city's schoolteachers are of

Italian ancestry. The reform movement in New York City government destroyed the neighborhood clubs and greatly reduced access of 1.6 million Italian-Americans to political power. Colombo's success grew largely out of political neglect and frustrations. For many years Italian-Americans exerted little influence in the local Democratic Party and received few top appointments and nominations. Four Jews and one black were on the 1970 Democratic ticket for top offices. The Jewish gubernatorial candidate avoided the Italian neighborhoods during his campaign and publicly berated an Italian audience for making demands for ethnic recognition. John Lindsay discovered the electoral power of Italian-Americans in New York City when an Italian beat him in 1969 for the Republican Party mayoral nomination. In the general election, two Italians, though defeated, received 58 percent of the total vote. A former Italian-American commissioner from the Lindsay administration believes that without avenues for improvement and self-expression, "Italian-Americans could be seduced into what is already discernible as a neo-fascist, black-shirt, law-and-order puritanism." Pileggi acknowledges other political and some intellectual manifestations of the new Italian-American resurgence but hails Joseph Colombo, Sr., and the Italian-American Civil Rights League as primarily responsible for providing an outlet for the frustrations and resentments of New York's Italians.

Any consideration of the Italian-American Civil Rights League must begin with the distinction between auspices and essence. While it is most likely that Joseph Colombo, Sr., founder and dominant leader of the League, has Mafia ties, most of the League's membership and most of those who derive ethnic reinforcement from association with the League have nothing to do with crime or the Mafia. Colombo may have harnessed the deep resentments, alienation, and pride of Italian-Americans for his own purposes, but he served as a catalyst for them. The League represents an assertion of Italian-American pride and protest. Italian-Americans look to him as their protector, spokesman and leader.

Several years ago, the Italian-American Anti-Defamation League was organized to improve the image of Italian-Americans. It had chapters in a few cities on the East Coast but never received the national attention that has been focused on the Italian-American Civil Rights League. When it was revealed that several members of its board of directors had reputed Mafia connections, it lost credibility and never recovered from the bad publicity.

The Civil Rights League was organized on April 30, 1970, when Colombo's 24-year-old second son, Joseph, Jr., was arrested on a federal charge of conspiring to melt down United States silver coins into more valuable ingots. He had no previous criminal record. On the night of the arrest, Colombo and some of his friends picketed

FBI headquarters. They marched back and forth in front of the headquarters, shouting "Italian Power" and loudly cursing J. Edgar Hoover.
On at least one occasion, nearly 1,000 Italian-American demonstrators
marched from the headquarters of the League to Saint Patrick's
Cathedral. Nightly picketing lasted for one year, and resulted in no
overt use of force by the local police or FBI. On some occasions the
numbers of demonstrators swelled into the thousands. The picketing
was coupled with a massive letter-writing campaign to the Justice
Department. Finally League officials stopped picketing on June 8,
1971, apparently because of pressure from Mafia chieftains who could
no longer tolerate Colombo's insistence on high visibility, a marked
departure from their traditional secrecy. Colombo explained the
discontinuation by declaring that they had accomplished their purpose.

Less than two months after the beginning of the FBI demonstrations, Colombo organized Italian-American Unity Day in Columbus
Circle, the most impressive Italian-American celebration in years.
Ignoring the annual Columbus Day celebration sponsored by the
established Italian-American organizations, he declared June 29, 1970,
the first holiday for Italian-Americans. United States Attorney General
John Mitchell was sufficiently impressed by the League's demonstrations or, at least, concerned enough not to offend the Italian-American
vote before the November 1970 elections, to announce, a month after
Unity Day, that the Justice Department and FBI would cease to use
the terms "Mafia" and "Cosa Nostra" in their press releases. Mitchell
explained that to avoid giving "gratuitous offense," these terms would
be replaced by designations without ethnic connotations, such as
"organized crime" or "the syndicate." The governors of New York,
Connecticut, Alaska, Texas, and South Dakota issued similar directives.

By August the League had formally become a charitable organization. Colombo appointed one of his friends, a former union organizer,
as president, and his eldest son vice-president. No one, however,
disputed that he was the boss. In November 1970 the League staged
a fund-raising affair at Felt Forum which grossed $450,000. Frank
Sinatra and other Italian-American entertainers donated performances.
By the end of 1970, League spokesmen claimed a membership of
45,000. There were 25 chapters in the New York area, with new
chapters opening across the country. Most of the League's membership and demonstration participants came from blue-collar and lower-
middle-class families living in the old neighborhoods. Few Italian-
American politicians, professionals, and middle-class suburbanites
have become involved in the League's activities. These people avoid
the company of sanitation workers, longshoremen, truck drivers, cab
drivers, and construction workers. In pursuit of one aspect of the
American Dream, the Italian-American middle class has fled to
Throgs Neck, Canarsie, and other suburbs.

League headquarters were established in a five-room suite in
an office building on Madison Avenue. The League chose as its
emblem an outline map of the United States in green, white, and red
enamel with the letter "I" superimposed on it. The "I" is intended to
symbolize unity. A wide variety of honorary members include Governor
Nelson Rockefeller, Mayor Lindsay, and defense attorney William
Kunstler. In March 1971, at a $125-a-plate testimonial dinner in
Huntington, L.I., the League honored Colombo as Man of the Year
and hailed him for "restoring dignity, pride and recognition to every
Italian." He was called the "guiding light of Italian-American unity."
More than 1,400 people attended the dinner, and a sum of more than
$100,000 was raised for the League.

Colombo's eldest son, representing the League, wrote in January
1971 to the vice-president in charge of production for Paramount
Pictures, protesting the novel The Godfather as a "spurious and
slanderous account of the Italian-American" and asking that Paramount,
in its film adaptation of the best-selling book, "delete the words
'Mafia' and 'Cosa Nostra' and the characterization of Italians as
'gangsters' from this movie." The novel had, in fact, been well received
by members of the Mafia since it exaggerated and romanticized their
political power, wealth, and influence in the business world. Instead
of condemning the Mafia, the book humanized it. Paramount was
flooded with letters describing the project as anti-Italian and threatening demonstrations, boycotts, wildcat strikes, and work stoppages.
The producer of the movie agreed to stop using the two terms and to
delete all offensive references from the script. This League victory
merited a front-page article and an editorial in the New York Times.
The producer was joined in his toning-down action by the producers
of the television series "The FBI." The Ford Motor Company assured
the League that in the television series it sponsored, the FBI agents
would not allude to ethnic roots. Many newspapers and magazines
stopped using the terms "Mafia" and "Cosa Nostra." In a campaign
conducted against corporations using Italian stereotypes in their
advertising, the League threatened to boycott their products. A popular
television commercial that featured the words "Mamma mia, datsa
soma spicy meatball" was discontinued by Alka-Seltzer. A canned
tomato sauce ad in which an Italian-American intoned "Datsa nice"
was discontinued.

One of the League's most recent undertakings is to build a $3.5-
million hospital and home for the aged in Brooklyn and to set up a
children's summer camp on the Jersey shore.

Colombo emerged as a public figure. He was a master of media
manipulation and propaganda. In little more than a year he rose from
obscurity to a notoriety which merited the cover of Time (July 12,
1971). The New York Times and other newspapers devoted considerable

coverage to him and the League, and numerous magazine articles
analyzed his activities and background. He appeared on television
news and interview programs. Despite his poor command of English
grammar and a strong Brooklyn accent, Colombo comes across as
self-confident and skillful. With straightforward responses, he con-
veys emotional conviction and sensitivity. His rhetoric is reminiscent
of the black activists:

> We feel we're being discriminated against. . . . And we
> say it's time that the Italian-Americans woke up and
> demanded what rightfully is theirs. If you're given a pre-
> sent you say "please" and "thank you." But anything that's
> coming to you you don't have to say "please." You can
> demand. And we know that every president who's elected
> he gives to all ethnic groups a piece of the pie, but where
> are we?
>   I say there is a conspiracy against all Italian-
> Americans. I feel that Mr. Nixon is behind it. . . . Mitchell,
> I believe, has a vendetta against Italian-Americans.

In May 1971 Colombo held a joint news conference with Rabbi
Meir Kahane to announce that his League and the Jewish Defense
League had joined forces to fight what he and Kahane called harass-
ment by the federal government. The alliance, according to Nicholas
Pileggi's New York Magazine article, was a logical development.
Colombo and Kahane had been sharing picket lines, membership, and
the same attorney for months. In May 1970, Jews and Italians from
the two Leagues had picketed a tool-makers association in Providence,
R.I., for sending a trade mission to Russia. Their followers had
signed each other up during lunch breaks in the garment factories.
They shared neighborhood stores and shops. They drove for the same
cab companies, paid off loans to the First National City Bank, and bet
with the same neighborhood Italian or Jewish bookmakers.
        Some steps toward alliance with N.E.G.R.O., headed by Gordon
Lynch, were also taken. One magazine wrote of the three leaders
constituting the "triumvirate of a budding national movement."
        But Colombo's career went into an eclipse when he was shot at
the second annual Unity Day Celebration on June 28, 1971. The shooting, less than an hour before the rally was scheduled to begin, took
place 25 feet from the stage and near the Christopher Columbus
statue in Columbus Circle. He was shot three times in the head and
neck and lay in a coma near death for many months. His assailant
was a 24-year-old black, a drifter of questionable mental and emotional stability. He had had numerous arrests, and had been accused
of committing sadistic acts. He apparently had a black female

accomplice and possibly one other accomplice. The assassination attempt would seem to have been carefully planned. But, almost immediately after the assailant fired at Colombo, he was cut down by three bullets fired by an unidentified man, who then escaped. The successful killer appears to have been either Colombo's bodyguard or someone posing as a part of Colombo's retinue.

Four theories have been advanced as motives for the attempted killing. Two involve blacks, two rival Italian-Americans. A black group calling itself the Black Revolutionary Attack Team called the Associated Press one hour after the shooting to take credit for it and vowed further attacks on exploiters of the black community. Law enforcement officers have not been able to substantiate this claim, though the rhetoric of black militants has focused increasingly on the Mafia because of its narcotics traffic in black neighborhoods. Black mobsters may have been trying to gain control of Mafia narcotics and gambling operations in the ghettos. Another possible motive may have been revenge. Colombo reportedly had made bitter enemies as he progressed in the Mafia hierarchy. The most commonly advanced theory is that Colombo had become too noisy and public, perhaps too powerful and independent.

Some evidence supports this last explanation. The Internal Revenue Service had refused to grant the League a tax exemption and was looking into the disposition of its $1-2 million in funds. Earlier, when Colombo was picked up by FBI agents, he had been carelessly carrying the names of several Mafia figures who had contributed to the League's benefit night at Madison Square Garden. Some commentators speculated that other Mafia bosses were angry because Colombo was not sharing the money. Several reports suggest that Mafia leaders could no longer tolerate Colombo's activities and had threatened to eliminate him if he did not voluntarily reduce them. Before the Unity Day celebration, some storefront offices of the League had been closed, the picketing of the FBI had ended, and League officials, including Colombo, had been assaulted. Mafia enforcers had told Brooklyn merchants not to close for Unity Day, tossed League buttons into trash cans, burned League signs, and asserted that Colombo was exploiting poor Italians and using their dues for his own benefit. Italian longshoremen, reportedly responsive to the prompting of Mafia bosses, withheld their support from the second Unity Day celebration. Colombo was said to have been asked by a Mafia chieftain to ease up on Unity Day preparations. He had refused. By insisting on remaining in the limelight, he had shed the traditional cloak of secrecy. His very success as a public figure may almost have cost him his life.

Immediately after the shootings, pandemonium broke out in Columbus Circle. Shouts of "a colored guy did it" and cries of "They got Joe! Joe's dead!" were heard everywhere. At least three black men were attacked. A musician who had been hired to entertain was assaulted by five or six men. Another black with a shaved head was beaten by a half dozen or more demonstrators who mistakenly assumed he was carrying a weapon. While he was being pummeled, shouts of "Kill him! Kill him!" came from the onlookers. Policemen who attempted to rescue the man were assaulted by the crowd. When he was finally extricated, blood was pouring from his head. At least two policemen had been injured, one severely in the back. Several black reporters were ejected from a press enclosure directly in front of the speakers' platform but were permitted to return after other newsmen interceded on their behalf.

The second Unity Day rally was held despite the shooting, but it is most difficult to draw any conclusions about its success or failure. The police estimated the crowd at 15,000, but observers place the number closer to 30,000. It lasted three hours. Fred Ferretti, reporting for the New York Times, wrote that the crowd seemed preoccupied with reports about Colombo's condition and "responded listlessly to the politicians and entertainers" who appeared before them. Ferretti reported numerous speakers urged Italian-American unity and concerted social action. As an expression of their unity, rally-goers extended their arms over their heads and joined hands. Manifestations of ethnic pride and protest permeated the rally. Vendors sold ethnic paraphernalia: buttons declaring "We're No. 1" and "Kiss Me, I'm Italian," Italian flags and pennants reading "Italian Power." Columbus Circle was bedecked with plastic streamers in red, white and green, the colors of the old country. Two politicians took advantage of the shootings to appeal to racial fears. Congressman Mario Biaggi, conservative Democrat from the Bronx, departed from his prepared text and blamed Colombo's shooting on "the same type of revolutionary that executed those two police officers" in May 1971 outside a Harlem housing project. Anthony Imperiale, former city councilman of Newark and political boss of the predominately Italian North Ward of that city, urged the audience not to forget that "the blood of the Roman gladiators" flowed in their veins and that they had to "fight for your place under the sun." Mayor Lindsay was invited, but the city comptroller was the highest-ranking city official to attend the rally. He stated that as a Jew he sympathized with Italian-Americans in their fight against defamation and discrimination. The League's president closed the rally with these words: "Go home but never forget, be proud to be an Italian all the time."

The tragedy of Joe Colombo, Sr., and his League is that the resentments, anger, and feeling of alienation of lower middle-class Italian-Americans in New York and elsewhere have not found better

institutional expression. Since their arrival in this country, Italian-
Americans have suffered because of weak community organizations,
poor representation in the Roman Catholic Church, agencies of
government, and other mainstream institutions, and self-serving
politicians. That Colombo was able to tap basic sentiments so quickly,
and that the Mafia was apparently able to decelerate the movement
equally rapidly, says much about the failure of the larger society to
meet the needs of Italian-Americans. The Mafia still appears to be
the strongest institutional influence in New York's predominately
working-class Italian neighborhoods and in many Italian commercial
enterprises.

Most Americans do not understand what the Mafia is, either in
this country or in Italy. Heads of Mafia families in New York City
listen to the woes of their constituents, mediate between rival racke-
teers, assist deportable husbands, avenge dishonored fathers, and
give money to those in need. In many ways they resemble the old
ward heelers. But their only authority is by force and violence, and
they are the final judges. In his book From Caesar to the Mafia,
Luigi Barzini explains that the Mafia is a viable system governing
the life of Sicily and parts of southern Italy within the framework of
the lifeless institutions imposed on those regions from the north. He
makes the critical distinction between the Mafia engaged in the "subtle
art of promoting one's interests without killing anybody, [which] should
be written with a lower-case m," and the Mafia "with a capital M, the
fluid organization, the secret, far-reaching elite which governs
everything legal and illegal, visible and invisible." The former is
a social system, the latter a criminal syndicate. Colombo seems to
have succeeded not despite his Mafia ties, but because of them.
Mafia standing and power within the neighborhoods lent credibility
to the League. The success of demagogues like Imperiale and Wallace,
and the persistence of the Mafia as a major vehicle for social mobility, are reflections of the attitudes of the dominant WASP culture
which views Italian-Americans as inferiors and places a low value
on Italian culture and life style. Whether Italian-American assertion
will persist and whether it will express itself positively or negatively
is yet to be determined. But the resurgence of interest in ethnic
identity by Italian-Americans is not limited to Joseph Colombo's
activities.

In the last five years, Italian restlessness, discontent, and
pressure have been frequently expressed in local politics and public
decision-making. One of the first signs of discontent was a taxpayers'
revolt among small homeowners. In the spring of 1969 John Marchi
defeated incumbent Mayor John Lindsay for the Republican Party
mayoralty nomination. A sizable number of traditionally Democratic-

voting Italians registered as Republicans to vote in the primary.
Mario Procaccino captured the Democratic nomination and together
with Marchi won nearly three out of every five votes cast in the
mayoral election. Procaccino ran as a political conservative and
appealed to the so-called backlash vote. The 1969 election revealed
the polarized condition of New York City politics: Lindsay the liberal
versus Procaccino the conservative. The fight for a civilian review
board to consider complaints against policemen had defined the two
sides—West Side liberals and the minorities against white ethnics;
Manhattan versus the outer boroughs.

Long-entrenched machine politicians are losing their electoral
support as independent and reform-minded Italian-American challengers
bid for their political power. Arthur Goldberg, in his 1970 gubernatorial campaign, was decisively beaten largely because he had no
Italian-Americans as running mates and refused to court the Italian
vote. Nelson Rockefeller is not above aggressively practicing ethnic
politics. Lindsay has undertaken to cultivate better relations with
the Italian-Americans of New York City, and has tried to appoint more
Italian-Americans to his administration. Shortly after the Goldberg
defeat, the city stopped its condemnation proceedings against 69
Corona homes owned by Italian-Americans and agreed to relocate
the homes on nearby Parks Department land, ending four years of
bitter controversy. The Lindsay administration now takes the Congress of Italian-American Organizations (CIAO) seriously. The mayor
attended an annual dinner and dance in Brooklyn in the fifth year of
the social-action coalition's operation, and to his surprise was well
received by the 500 Italian-Americans at the affair. After two years
and numerous requests, city officials agreed to approve CIAO's day-
care centers and programs for school children during after-school
hours, as well as its programs for senior citizens. The centers
and programs were planned for predominantly low and lower middle-
class Italian neighborhoods.

A July 1971 newsletter, with a Brooklyn address, entitled
"Young Italians of America" announced the formation of an organization called Young Italians, because it had become "obvious that some-
how the young people do not get involved in the decision-making roles
in any of the established groups." During its short life, the Young
Italians complained to the mass media about "anti-Italian propaganda,"
reported to Italian-Americans about discrimination in the New York
State Division of Employment and about the use of the terms "Mafia"
and "Cosa Nostra" by the media and politicians, and sponsored an
Italian-American Conference in October 1971. Peter Mollo, the
executive director of the Young Italians, has appeared on radio and
television to protest the discrimination and adverse publicity that
followed the critical wounding of Joseph Colombo. Speaking on a

radio program about the White House Conference on Youth held in
April 1971 in Colorado, the executive director declared "the truth
was that Italian-Americans were systematically excluded from the
White House Conference as they are from all decision-making institutions of American life." He also spoke of serious community
problems during a television news program: "Italian-Americans in
New York City have the second highest drop-out rate in the public
school system and the third highest drug addiction rate." The director
also heads the Union Art School, which has been funded as an after-
school day-care center by New York City's Agency for Child Development. What this funding symbolizes, says the director, "is the ability
of all the ethnic groups in this neighborhood to succeed in getting
something we all want when we work together." The chairman of the
group recently declared in the local Brooklyn Heights Press (August
5, 1971): "We can learn from the successes of the other minority
groups in focusing attention to their problems, and apply that knowledge
in dealing with our own."

The Street Peoples Coalition is one of several organizations
that have been formed in New York City. Outside organizations such
as the National Urban Coalition, the American Jewish Committee,
and Monsignor Baroni's Center for Urban Ethnic Affairs have provided
financial and leadership support to programs in predominantly Italian-
American communities.

In the area of self-conscious cultural preservation, many things
are happening in New York City. The Center for Migration Studies
of New York, led by the Reverend Sylvan M. Tomasi, collects socio-
logical, demographic, historical, and legislative studies on the immigration of various ethnic groups. The Reverend Tomasi, who is a
Scalabrini priest with a Ph.D., has been particularly interested in
the immigration experience of Italian-Americans and has recently
co-edited a book entitled The Italian Experience in the United States.
According to his count, 160 articles and 40 books have been published
since 1966 on the subject of Italian-Americans, an unprecedented
number. An Italian-American Book Club recently began operating
in Yorktown Heights, New York. In Manhattan two successful actors
have been seeking worthwhile filmscripts about the experiences of
Italian-American immigrants. An organization located at Columbia
University's Casa Italiana and devoted exclusively to the study of
Italy's cultural life held its first discussion of Italian-Americans
since the Casa was founded in 1927.

Chicagoans of Italian descent seem to be at an earlier stage of
group assertion. Chicago, of course, has less than half as many
Italian-Americans as New York City. These have recently formed
an umbrella organization to advance socially and politically and to
combat discrimination and defamation. But so far it has done little,

has few members, and has not attracted much attention. The formation of Italian-American police and teachers associations to press for
more and better positions is evidence of other constructive developments. Some Italian-Americans in racially changing neighborhoods
and in competition for jobs have resorted to force and violence, but
these expressions have not been excessive or typical. The Civil
Rights League has had virtually no success in Chicago.

The League's experience in Newark, however, illustrates the
violent and radical aspect of its development. Mayor Gibson of Newark
has declared that whatever the future of American cities may be, it
will first become manifest in Newark. Less than three weeks after
Colombo was shot, the week-old offices of the Newark chapter of the
League were destroyed by arson. The storefront headquarters were
located in the city's predominately Italian North Ward. The president
of the Newark Chapter 35, Gus Ferrara, is a county correctional
officer, and the vice-president is head of one of the Newark locals of
the Patrolmen's Benevolent Association. The Chapter claims a
membership of over 5,000, 61 of whom signed up and paid $10 each
at a registration table set up in front of the burned-out headquarters.
When asked why he had undertaken to organize the League's chapter,
Ferrara said: "I got into it when my kid came home from school one
day and asked me if we had relatives in the Mafia."

Jews in the Urban North

The rapid growth of a self-conscious Jewish radical movement
in New York City and other northern industrial cities is similar in
many respects to the recent Italian-American and Roman Catholic
assertion. American Jews, living largely in the northern industrial
cities, were much involved in and affected by the black and affluent
student revolts of the 1960s. On the one hand, many Jewish teachers,
students, social workers, lawyers, and doctors actively participated
in these movements. But while upper and middle-class Jews not
directly involved in these movements continued to pay lip service to
the old liberal platitudes, they increasingly isolated themselves in
high-rise apartments and in suburbs, and in the late 1960s began to
blame the growing divisions within the country on radicals. Large
numbers of lower middle-class and working-class Jews in New York
City, Boston, and other urban centers of unrest reacted to black
advancement and rapid social change with fear and hostility. Many
of them voted for reactionaries like Mario Procaccino and became
part of the backlash. Some joined the Jewish Defense League. On
almost 100 campuses with substantial Jewish enrollments there have
sprung up Jewish radical groups of one kind or another. Among them

these groups publish some 35 newspapers. Some are radical Zionists; others accept Jewish dispersion and are somewhat critical of Zionism, while affirming the legitimacy of Israel; some concentrate on liberating Soviet Jewry; others attempt to radicalize traditional Jewish organization. The majority of these groups have renewed their loyalty to their Jewish roots and ideologically reconcile their devotion to the survival of the state of Israel with a dedication to universal liberation. These groups are displacing Hillel and other traditional campus Jewish organizations, which are rapidly expiring. Jewish radicals on American campuses find it difficult to rationalize certain social conditions in Israel as, for example, those that led to the 1971 violent street demonstrations in Tel Aviv and other Israeli cities by young Oriental Jews who call themselves Black Panthers. Most of them have emigrated from North Africa and the Middle East. They have threatened to visit United States cities with large Jewish populations to protest discrimination in housing, education, and employment by the present Israeli government.

The Jewish Defense League, in contrast to the student groups, is much more a part of the white ethnic movement. The League was founded in New York City by Rabbi Meir Kahane following the school crises in Ocean Hill and Harlem. Kahane firmly maintains that Jews need an aggressive organization to combat anti-Semitism. The formation and activities of his League are unique in the history of American Jewry. Most American Jewish leaders did nothing to protest Franklin D. Roosevelt's unwillingness to help the doomed Jews of Europe. There were few parades, demonstrations, or protest meetings. Kahane's group was first publicized after its members confronted blacks at Brooklyn College and elsewhere. Kahane's activities then shifted to the political captivity and religious persecution of Soviet Jews. Harassment of Russian visitors to the United States—diplomats, artists, and athletes—became a regular practice of the League. In March 1971 the League sponsored a sitdown near the Russian Embassy in Washington, D.C., to protest treatment of Jews in the Soviet Union. Police arrested 689 demonstrators. Three months later Rabbi Kahane and more than 37 of his followers protested at the Soviet Embassy again and at the State Department. The rabbi and other demonstrators were arrested outside the Embassy as they chanted, "The Soviet Union stinks." A dozen mice were released into a store in Providence, R.I., that sold Russian goods.

Kahane, like Colombo, has been successful at propaganda and mass media manipulation. He has aroused both Jews from the old neighborhoods and young Jews who feel that established institutions are no longer working for their benefit. He has challenged Jewish masculinity by constant reference to the image of the Jew as a passive victim of persecution. To prove Jewish manhood, the League

offers instructions in karate and the use of firearms and, for the more
enthusiastic, training camps. Kahane attacks middle-class Jews for
"selling out" in order to assimilate. When a major Jewish social
agency in New York City released files to the FBI, Kahane exploited
the scandal that ensued in the Jewish community. He justifiably
attacked Jewish community organizations in general for losing track
of their own poor, dropouts, addicts, and old people.

The League is based in New York City, publishes a newsletter,
and owes its existence and survival to the leadership of Rabbi Kahane.
Its motto is "Never Again." The common denominator in the various
chapters is a commitment "to protect Jewish lives and interests."
Kahane's organizational success is difficult to evaluate, for much of
the League's activity is cloaked in secrecy and many chapters are
evasive when asked about their membership. The New York City
chapter, the largest, has several thousand members. Philadelphia
claims a membership of 800. The Boston chapter has shrunk from
over 1,500 in the summer of 1970 to a few hundred, largely because
of disputes over the use of force and violence. The level of militancy
varies greatly. The New York City and Philadelphia chapters have
frequently resorted to disruption and violence and regard these as
acceptable tactics. The use and advocacy of violence has not been so
popular in such other cities as St. Louis and Chicago. The division
in the Boston chapter resulted in the formation of the independent and
moderate Jewish Survival Legion. The League's advocacy of violence
appears to be one of the major obstacles to its growth and acceptance
by the Jewish community. Jewish leaders and the Jewish middle
class are embarrassed by Meir Kahane's street-brawling. Criminal
charges of possession of dynamite may bring Kahane's career to a
halt. Jews have assimilated and succeeded in America. This gives
many observers reason to doubt that the League will increase in size
or influence.

To understand the Jewish Defense League, it is important to
appreciate the Ocean Hill-Brownsville conflict. In the academic
year 1968-69, teachers in New York City held three strikes, and
schools were closed for two months. A major cause of the strikes
was the conflict between the predominantly Jewish leaders of the
United Federation of Teachers and black militant educators—the
former defending the hard-earned rights of their members, such as
seniority, and the latter insisting on a decentralized school system
and more power and control over curriculum and teaching staff in
black schools. The union's leadership had won rights for their
heavily Jewish membership only through decades of strikes and
collective bargaining. Jewish religious and civic leaders found themselves confronted with racism in their communities to an extent that
was inconsistent with their own traditional liberal and progressive

stance. They had believed their people to be allies and not enemies
of the blacks. Black leaders found it easy to blame the Jews for
their lack of progress and made frequent appeals to the anti-Semitism
of their followers. The threat and actuality of black anti-Semitism
provoked Jews from the old neighborhoods who had daily contacts
with blacks. Many of them had "made it" into the middle class and
shared the same resentments, frustrations, and anger as Catholic
white ethnics. Black anti-Semitism strengthened their reaction
against black aggressiveness and progress.

Jews are a highly important ethnic group in America. They
have the strongest organizations of any minority. The horrifying
genocide carried out during World War II profoundly affected American
Jews and made most of them much more keenly conscious of their
heritage and cultural traditions. The state of Israel is now generally
accepted as a necessary political asylum for the remnants of European
Jewry. Israel has become the homeland, the embodiment of Jewish
tradition, and the bulwark of Jewish consciousness. Self-conscious
Jewish nationalism is very much alive in America. It found its
strongest recent expression during the Six-Day War in 1967. Politicians with substantial Jewish constituencies recognized this force.
Conservative Republican Congressman Philip M. Crane, representing
the north shore suburbs of Chicago where there is substantial Jewish
vote, spoke out forcefully against Russian anti-Semitism in Congress
on June 15, 1971. While Jews are one of the more acculturated
groups in America, they remain conscious of their origins and history.
As third- and fourth-generation Americans, they make greater efforts
to preserve their culture than any other major immigrant groups.
A new interest in their ethnic identity manifests itself in the desire
of an increasing number of Jews for religious and pre-school training
for their children. The established Jewish organizations have softened
their position on public aid to parochial schools. An increasing number
of Jewish organizations and newspapers have sprung up in high schools
and colleges. Jews are becoming increasingly conscious of their
level of tolerance for anti-Semitism. When a New York City radio
station broadcast black anti-Semitic poetry, many Jews responded
with alarm. When a Jewish social leader spoke to a Milwaukee white
ethnic audience, he was amazed at the degree of tacit anti-Semitism.
Conflicts with other ethnic groups have not been so dramatic as the
New York City school crisis, but in the suburbs of Pittsburgh and
Chicago conflicts have arisen between the parents of Jewish and
Italian schoolchildren. Jews want taxes spent for college preparatory
curricula while Italians favor technical and trade courses. Jewish
students are more interested in counterculture, black activism, and
student dissent than are their Italian-American counterparts.

A Closer Focus on Racial Backlash

The backlash is still very much with us. Had he not been crippled by a would-be assassin, George Wallace might well have run again for president in 1972 on a third-party ticket. His showing in the primaries indicates that he had considerable support. Frank Rizzo won the Democratic mayoral primary in Philadelphia in May 1971, and the election in November 1971, by appealing to the fears and prejudices of that city's electorate. His campaign was not unlike that waged by Mario Procaccino in New York in 1969. Michael Novak, in the September 1971 issue of Harper's Magazine, writes that the language of Spiro Agnew and George Wallace awakened "childhood memories in me of men arguing in the barbershop" and of his uncle "cursing the niggers in the mill, below, and the Yankees in the mill, above," and of everybody loving Uncle George because "he said what he thought." History reveals that much, perhaps most, of the backlash has earlier parallels in American history. Past American violence has been launched with a conservative bias. It has been unleashed against abolitionists, Catholics, radicals, workers and labor organizers, Negroes, Orientals, and other ethnic or racial or ideological minorities, and has been used ostensibly to protect the American, the Southerner, the white Protestant, or simply the established middle-class way of life and morals. Ethnic and religious violence in America's past, especially most of its mob and vigilante movements, has been retaliatory, committed by groups who felt threatened by the upward push of new immigrants or the blacks.

But by the late 1960s and early 1970s the Anglo-Protestant establishment seemed to be losing its dominant status. Many people regard the violence of the 1960s as dangerous because politically more purposeful than in the past and more intimately related to basic social issues. Old political alignments are weakening and new political groups are looking for allies and new arrangements. All of American society is involved in the inevitable conflict that accompanies the passing of an established pattern of social relationships and institutions. The consent of the subcultures that make up the United States—previously taken for granted and usually granted voluntarily—has diminished, and political unrest has increased. Racial and ethnic minorities have questioned and, in some instances, forced changes in the rules of the game. Demonstrations, vigilantism, and ghetto riots reflect deep and severe discontent. One half of the twelve successful or attempted assassinations that occurred in the United States during the 1960s were the result of minority conflict. The attack on Joseph Colombo at an Italian-American rally may be a preview to what is to come in the 1970s. New reactionary forces are courting white ethnics, while demagogues find opportunities to exploit legitimate fears and a sense of alienation. Racial conflict has converted many lower middle-class Americans to a status quo position on important public issues, a posture often not in keeping with their own best interests. In his New York Magazine article on the resurgence of Italian-Americans, Nicholas Pileggi cites the open enrollment controversy in New York City as an example to such misdirected appeals. During the discussions of the merits of open enrollment, no politician pointed out to white ethnic working-class voters the fact that Mayor Lindsay's open enrollment policy would benefit them more than it would the blacks and Puerto Ricans. Conservative spokesmen, Pileggi notes, alarmed the residents of New York City's Italian neighborhoods by their undisputed predictions that the admission of blacks and Puerto Ricans would lower academic standards. In Philadelphia, in the spring of 1969, a $90-million school bond issue was defeated by similar fears and resistance to increased taxes. With this first defeat of a school bond issue in the history of Philadelphia, the white ethnic communities lost as much as or more than the racial minorities.

Such negative or obstructionist power is not only racial but manifests itself in antimedia, anti-intellectual, and antigovernment expressions. Since 1968, Vice-President Agnew has been President Nixon's spokesman in blaming political unrest on permissive college administrators and the liberal-controlled mass media. George Wallace and Frank Rizzo attack intellectuals, black activists, and federal bureaucrats. Legislators pass bills to punish student activists by cutting appropriations for higher education. In Pontiac, Michigan, the Ku Klux Klan exploits white ethnic working-class opposition to busing school children, thus encouraging violence and heightening racial tensions. In addition to these reactions, many observers fear that the so-called positive and constructive revival of interest in ethnicity is also no more than a subtle form of backlash. One such observer is John Hope Franklin, former chairman of the history department of the University of Chicago and a black. He believes that the melting pot rationale is being abandoned because of the dominant majority's decision that certain groups cannot and should not be assimilated into the mainstream culture. Racial minorities and some ethnic minorities, he urges, are being indoctrinated in the belief that they will "be happier with their own kind" and can "console themselves by extolling the virtues of cultural pluralism." But Franklin also takes sharp issue with the Northern white rationale for blacks "huddling together in northern ghettos." The rationale goes like this: Blacks are a newly arrived group just as the Germans, Irish, and Jews were in the nineteenth century; they cluster together in order to advance themselves and preserve their culture, and they are happier together. But the post-immigration experience of the Europeans in America is far different from the post-migration experience of the black. For the black, the urban ghetto has become a dead end, while for most white ethnics, it has been only a temporary stage.

A close look at specific instances of backlash is necessary to demonstrate its existence and character. The phenomena of George Wallace, Joseph Colombo, and Meir Kahane are widely recognized, but little has been said or written about the vigilantism of the 1960s in Northern white urban and suburban neighborhoods. Residents of these neighborhoods felt threatened by the possibility of black rioters, looters, robbers, and rapists. In the New York City areas of Inwood, South Brooklyn, Corona, East Flatbush, and Bay Ridge, the ownership of guns increased, gun clubs were formed, self-defense leagues and home protection associations were formed. Men in bars spoke often of what they would do in the event of a race riot. Late in the summer of 1971, on Chicago's southwest side two 13-year-old white children were shot and killed and two black youths charged with the offense. Newspaper reports were cautious, but retaliatory shootings by white youths appear to have taken place. The killings may have been related to conflicts between black and white gangs. On one night during the wakes, 150 whites gathered at a neighborhood playground and with rocks and bottles attacked the police officers who tried to disperse them.

While vigilantism since the middle 1960s has not taken the law into its own hands, a few groups have come close to it. The North Ward Citizens' Committee of Newark is probably the best example. Before considering Newark, it is instructive to take a brief look at some other vigilante responses. In May 1964 the Maccabees, a neighborhood patrol group, was formed in the Crown Heights area of Brooklyn. Nightly radio-car patrols attempted to discover and report criminal actions, most of which were the result of teenage blacks coming into Crown Heights from adjacent areas. The 250 members of the Maccabees were predominantly Hasidic Jews. There was some reduction in crime. Then its rabbi leader was appointed assistant executive director of the New York City Youth Board, and the group subsequently became inactive.

In 1967 the People's Civic Association of the East New York, Brownsville, and Flatbush areas of Brooklyn organized a radio-equipped vigilante patrol of 350 members with five automobiles. It cooperated with the police in crime prevention and in reporting irregularities. Vigilante groups of tenants also formed to patrol large apartment buildings. Blacks also formed such groups to protect themselves against white violence, harassment, and crime in their own communities. Two such vigilante organizations were formed in Pittsburgh and Detroit. During the period of July through September 1968, white vigilantes were reported active in various areas of

Cleveland. They emerged in response to black turbulence in the
Hough section, a black ghetto area of the city. The New York Times
reported in September 1968 that the unsolved killings of two Cleveland
blacks in July of that year may have been the result of vigilante
action. But such killings were the exception, not the rule in the 1960s
and early 1970s. In the summer of 1968 an antiblack organization
calling itself Fight Back was organized in Warren, Michigan. It was
apparently similar in character to the North Ward Citizens' Committee in Newark. The National Action Group was also formed in
Warren in the summer of 1971 to fight the busing of school children.
While not a vigilante group, the National Action Group received the
support of the Ku Klux Klan and the National Socialist Liberation
Front. A federal indictment implicated two Klansmen in the dynamiting
of 10 Pontiac school buses. The group culminated its summer activities
by sponsoring a march when schools opened on September 6, 1971. The
march attracted a crowd estimated by police at 4,000 to 6,000 persons.
American flags were carried by many of the demonstrators. At a
rally after the march, demonstration leaders spoke of creating "freedom
schools" to circumvent court-ordered busing. Another rally sponsored
by the group five days before schools opened drew more than 5,000.
Pontiac is an industrial community. The majority of its white population are the children and grandchildren of European immigrants.
Some national observers view what happened during the Pontiac busing
enforcement as symptomatic of what will happen in similar situations
in other Northern school districts.

Newark: The Black Majority versus
the Italian Minority

"Wherever the cities are going," asserts Mayor Kenneth Gibson,
"Newark is going to get there first." Most observers agree with his
forecast. Newark experienced a major black riot in July 1967. After
World War II the white middle class began deserting the city for the
suburbs, and in the late 1950s the rate of desertion accelerated.
Between 1960 and 1967, the city lost a total of more than 70,000
white residents (in 1967 Newark's population was 400,000). Blacks,
Puerto Ricans, and Cubans took their places in dilapidated housing
areas with miserable living conditions. By 1967 the city had switched,
in a six-year period, from 65 percent white to 52 percent black and
nearly 10 percent Puerto Rican and Cuban. In 1962 seven-term
Congressman Hugh Addonizio had forged an Italian-black coalition
and overturned the long-time Irish control of City Hall to become
the first Italian-American mayor. Addonizio, who had been a liberal
in Congress, brought blacks into government and integrated the police

department before he lost office when he and some associates were
convicted of accepting kickbacks from contractors. By the time
Kenneth Gibson, a black, won the mayoralty in 1970, the black-Italian
coalition had broken up, largely over conflicts between the predominantly Italian police force and blacks who charged harassment and
brutality. The city had exhausted its bonding limit. Health and welfare costs, per capita, were 20 times as great as for some of the
surrounding communities. Taxable property was diminishing as
land, cleared for urban renewal, lay undeveloped year after year.
By 1967 property taxes had reached $661.70 on a $10,000 house—double
that of suburban communities. Three years later Newark's property
tax, nearly $10 for each $100 of assessed value, was one of the highest
for a large city in the United States. The ownership of real property
became too burdensome; owners were increasingly unwilling to
maintain the property, and few understood rehabilitation. In 1967, 74
percent of white and 87 percent of black families lived in rental housing. Civic leaders, formerly drawn heavily from the central business
district, moved to the suburbs and showed much less concern for the
city's welfare.

The educational system was near collapse with dropouts estimated
to be as high as 33 percent; unemployment, family breakups, and crime
were increasing. The United Community Corporation, the black-
dominated agency that administered the antipoverty program, came
into increasing conflict with the Italian-dominated city administration.
Italians have maintained a six-to-three majority on the City Council.
The decision to locate the state's new medical and dental college in
the black Central Ward pitted the black constituency against their
white councilman on almost every important issue. Black militants
regarded the proposed 150-acre site as an effort to dilute their
political power. Clashes occurred over the appointment of the
secretary of the Board of Education. Of the children in the school
system, 70 percent were black. Black militants proposed that the
position be filled by the city's budget director, a black with a master's
degree in accounting. The mayor appointed a white man with a degree
no higher than a high school diploma. These racial controversies
heightened tensions, and in July 1967 the Newark riot took the lives
of 23 persons, 21 of whom were black. By the late 1960s ultramilitants
seemed to have taken over, proclaiming wild dreams of separateness,
revolution, secession, and the establishment of an independent Africa
in America with Newark as its capital. Meanwhile unemployment
among young Italians in Newark was growing at the same time that
more black youths were finding employment. More blacks and fewer
Italians were going on to college.

Racial tensions since the 1967 riot have resulted in distinct
racial divisions, popularly called polarization. Since most of the

remaining inhabitants of Newark are black, Puerto Rican, and Italian-American, the whites have seized their common ethnic ancestry as a common bond around which to organize. The blacks have done likewise. Le Roi Jones, the black poet and playwright, who prefers to be known by his adopted African name Imamu Amiri Baraka, has used the rhetoric of black nationalism and separatism to rise to political power in the black Central Ward. Baraka has become a tribal chieftain. But he did not shun the system when Kenneth Gibson, a black man, ran for mayor in 1970. He supported Gibson's successful candidacy and has stayed in contact with him, for, as he says, they grew up together. He heads the Committee for a Unified Newark, a black cultural and political organization which has received considerable foundation, corporate, and governmental funding. Baraka has little patience with the predominantly white teachers union and reportedly was connected with a group of blacks who beat striking teachers in early February 1971. He asserts that the teachers, of whom the majority are white suburban residents, do not serve the best interests of Newark's black children.

The North Ward Citizens' Committee of Newark is the prototype of the white backlash group. It was formed during the summer of 1967 in response to real and anticipated threats from blacks, and though less active now as a vigilante group, it remains in existence as a political organization and provides headquarters for Anthony Imperiale. It was originally organized to conduct nightly radio patrols for the purpose of spotting and discouraging criminal activities and repelling, should the need arise, any incursion of rioters and looters from the adjacent Central Ward of Newark. Imperiale founded the organization following the racial confrontation in Newark brought on by the widespread black riots of June 1967. It was at first a traditional vigilante reaction—citizens banding together for self-protection under conditions of disorder and lawlessness. Imperiale says that the issue of the use of police dogs precipitated the formation of the Committee.

Imperiale is the son of an Italian immigrant. Most of the members of his Committee, and a large majority of the inhabitants of the North Ward, are of Italian ancestry. Besides his leadership of the North Ward Citizens Committee, Imperiale runs the North Ward Ambulance Squad, operates a service center in the ward and publishes a bimonthly newspaper, Newark Truth. He was elected a Newark councilman-at-large in November 1968, largely on the basis of popularity gained through his committee leadership. During the campaign he appealed to the resentments of Italian-Americans, who had come to believe that established institutions favored blacks and were hostile to their own grievances. He spoke frequently of restoring law and order to Newark and won an overwhelming victory as head of the ticket.

Imperiale's influence was declining in 1970 and early 1971, but in November 1971 he staged a political comeback by winning election to the New Jersey Assembly. Running as an independent for a seat from Newark's District 11B, he defeated the two major party candidates by 1,500 votes. He had been an unsuccessful candidate for the mayoralty in 1970 and lost subsequent bids for Democratic county committeeman and the Republican assembly nomination. After the mayoral victory of Kenneth E. Gibson in the June 1970 runoff, Imperiale declared "war" on Gibson's administration and in July of that year announced that he would form a coalition of "conservative" groups to counter the actions of what he called "radical organizations." He made his declaration at a meeting of several hundred of his North Ward Citizens Committee supporters. He explained that the "unusual" summer meeting had been called at the request of representatives of various allied groups who, he said, felt that an "emergency" existed in the city. He singled out the disturbance a few days before between police and the Young Lords, a militant group of Puerto Ricans, and accused the police of leniency and irresponsibility. "We are forming a state-by-state coalition," he declared. "We are calling in the Birchers and everybody else. So far we have received 101 favorable responses and we invite Wallace too." He went on to say that invitations to join the coalition have been sent to groups in all 50 states and he hoped to hold a National Convention of all groups in Newark by the end of 1970. He promised to bring busloads of conservatives into Newark during the next election to counter tactics at the last election by outsiders who came into the city and "kept the polls busy with hit-and-run agitation."

Imperiale's election in November 1971 as a New Jersey assemblyman from Newark was significant for two reasons. First, because of the 40-to-39 split between Democrats and Republicans in that body, he found that he held the balance of power, but both parties are reluctant to associate themselves with him or seek his support. A black Democratic assemblyman from Newark, referring to Imperiale, vowed not to vote with his party if it chose to deal with a "bigot." The Republican governor said that he would block an effort to get Imperiale's support: "I don't think the positions he has publicly expressed are compatible with the philosophy of the Republican party as I understand it and as I want to practice it." Imperiale replied, "I extend my hand in friendship but the governor should know I go over people not around them. . . . They're going to find out I don't push easily and I don't turn the other cheek. They don't have any right to say they don't want me." Secondly, in his campaign, Imperiale replied heavily on his old rhetoric, attacking black militants, anti-Communists, and "bums who rape, loot, and kill." He ran on the campaign slogan, "A Man Not Afraid."

An encouraging development in the North Ward has been the emergence of Stephen Adubato, a moderate, and the influence he exerts with the local Democratic organization. The organization offers a political alternative to Imperiale. Adubato works within the realities of shifting political power. Gibson replaced Addonizio in 1970. Mayor Gibson has no Italians on his staff, and there are no Italians in the city's two key antipoverty organizations, United Community Corporation and the Model Cities Program. The Board of Education, which is appointed by the Mayor, is now dominated by a six-man black and Puerto Rican majority. Adubato, an urban affairs specialist at Rutgers, thinks "the North Ward is restless because there is no delivery system for whites."

Following Imperiale's declaration of "war," Adubato spoke out against the former's irresponsible incitement and misguided activities. He criticized the failure of elected officials who live in the Ward to stand up to Imperiale. At a Columbus Day festival (termed the First Annual Columbus Festival) on October 11, 1970, Adubato launched what he called a project to focus attention on problems of urban white ethnics. Mayor Gibson and other elected officials attended as honored guests. Ethnic unity pervaded most of the speeches heard by the more than 1,000 persons who filled the halls of Thomm's Restaurant. Students of a local high school received the Vince Lombardi Award, named for the late football coach who exemplified a striving for teamwork and unity. In January 1971, when Adubato and the North Ward Young Democrats arranged a political forum entitled "Reform or Revolution—Answer to America's Problems" and invited Imperiale, Le Roi Jones, and others, the newspapers reported that Imperiale had circulated a letter among his supporters which read in part: "There will be a disruptive meeting of left-wingers in our ward Monday night at Thomm's." The rest of the letter urged his supporters to attend the meeting and voice opposition to such activities in the North Ward. Shortly before the start of the forum, a large number of Imperiale supporters congregated in front of the restaurant. Many young men carried signs protesting the appearance of Le Roi Jones. According to the owner of Thomm's restaurant, the tempers of the 400 people inside his place "were moving along too briskly for my taste." Imperiale and Adubato heatedly argued before the discussion began, and to avoid an outbreak of violence, the restaurant owner cancelled the discussion and no forum was held. Subsequently Adubato debated Le Roi Jones and Imperiale on the television show New Jersey Speaks. Jones agreed with him that Newark's business community was controlled by "white Anglo-Saxons who take the big share of the pie" while blacks and white ethnics such as Italians were receiving nothing. Harold R. Isaacs, a noted thinker on group conflict, found the exchange between Abubato and Jones alarming and perhaps a

harbinger of heightened group conflict. Isaacs saw an historical
parallel in the two men from Newark talking about separate white
and black agendas and the famous encounter between Marcus Garvey,
leader of a black separatist movement in the 1920s, and the head of
the Ku Klux Klan. The latter two had met, exchanged expressions of
mutual respect, and agreed on racist and separatist positions.

In June 1971 a slate of candidates loyal to Abubato won 72 out
of the 96 posts in the North Ward Democratic Party Committee and
elected him chairman. In that ward election, Imperiale was defeated
by a candidate backed by Adubato. During the same month Adubato
confronted Senator Edward Kennedy at an ethnic conference with the
inconsistency of his supporting black Congressman William Green
in the Democratic primary for the Philadelphia mayoralty while
Frank Rizzo, another candidate, took the same position on law and
order as his close political ally Mayor Delay. It was an embarrassing
moment and Kennedy was finally forced to reply that if his support of
Green was inconsistent, then he was inconsistent. Adubato has also
opened an office called the North Ward Educational and Cultural Center,
which is financed by Rutgers University and the National Center for
Urban Ethnic Affairs. The North Ward Center helps young Italians
to apply for college, finds them jobs, and advises them on how to
take advantage of the city's antipoverty programs.

Despite a 25-percent increase in the black population in the
last ten years, Newark's Italians, to a considerable extent, cannot
afford nor do they want to follow the Jews and Irish to the suburbs.
According to the 1970 census, blacks account for more than 55 percent
of the city's population and the Spanish-speaking make up nearly 10
percent of the total. The Italians, the only major white group to remain,
prefer city life among other Italians. In the face of racial conflict,
rising taxes, and urban decay, they show their strong attachment to
family and community. Community becomes the extended family. More
than 60 small social clubs remain active in the North Ward. On August
28, 1971, the New York Times ran a long article on the Italian community entitled "Newark's New Minority, the Italians, Demands Equity."
The article began by noting that the Italian minority, "spurred by
the growing power of Newark's black majority . . . has become increasingly conscious of its own identity and has begun demanding special
consideration as the city's new minority group." The leaders of the
largely lower middle-class Italian community want more antipoverty
programs, more city jobs, and Italian-American history in the class-
rooms. The New York Times article quotes Adubato: "Blacks have
got all these special programs to help them get to college, or to re-
habilitate their houses, or to help them find jobs. We white ethnics
don't get any of these things. All we want is equity." "A lot of people
confuse us with white Americans, which we're not," Adubato explained.

"We are the working-class people who haven't made it in America,
like the blacks, and we are still in the inner city competing with them."

Philadelphia: An Italian Runs Against the Blacks

Philadelphia has been described as an "undiscovered Newark."
It is the fourth largest American city, with a population of slightly
less than 2 million, and has been experiencing the same problems
as most other older industrial cities. Middle-class whites have been
fleeing to the suburbs while blacks and Latins migrate into the central
city. According to the 1960 census, Philadelphia ranked 15th of the
21 American cities with over 500,000 population in terms of families
with incomes of $10,000 or more each year. It ranked 14th in 1960
among these cities in persons employed in white-collar occupations.
The majority of Philadelphia whites who remain in the city do so because they can not afford to relocate in the suburbs. Blacks are on the
offensive; lower middle-class whites, mostly ethnics, who remain in
the city, believe they are threatened. Frank Rizzo, Imperiale's counterpart in Philadelphia, by seizing on the fears and racial animosities
of these whites, won the Democratic mayoral primary in May 1971 and
in November the general election. He presented himself as a law-and-
order candidate. He had been a policeman for 28 years and had become
police commissioner in 1967. Rizzo's victories in the primary and
general elections are part of a recent trend by which police officials
are winning the position of chief executive in many cities. So far they
have been elected as mayor in Los Angeles, Philadelphia, Detroit,
Minneapolis, and Waterburg. Former policeman Charles S. Stenvig
won a second term as mayor of Minneapolis. The former burglary
detective overwhelmed his black opponent, who was on leave as president of the Minneapolis Urban Coalition.
Meeting in June 1971, in the city of Philadelphia, where Rizzo
stripped the clothes off Black Panthers in the streets, members of
the all-black National Council of Police Societies publicly declared
themselves opposed to "indiscriminate" use of stop-and-frisk laws
and the use of preventive detention. The council voted to support
civilian review boards and promised to take "direct action" against
an officer "who abuses any citizen by the power of his office." The
council's action in Philadelphia placed it in clear opposition to the
law-and-order wing of the traditional police establishment.
But Frank Rizzo's emergence represents more than the exploitation of white racism. His electoral support reflects more than the
black-white cleavage. It also is the product of the long-standing
tensions between the native Protestant business and social elites
and the children and grandchildren of European immigrants, as well
as of the tensions among the various ethnic groups. In the general

election Rizzo, running as a Democrat, beat his bland Republican opponent—a Protestant aristocrat. In the primary, Rizzo defeated two blacks and a Jew. His three opponents were political liberals, he a conservative—another cleavage. The three liberals polled 483 more votes than the former police commissioner and brought out a record number of independent voters (127,000). It was no coincidence that some of Rizzo's heaviest support came from South Philadelphia's Italian-American neighborhoods. According to the 1960 census, the congressional district which encompasses South Philadelphia has over 50,000 first- and second-generation Italians—or 17 percent—ranking it fourth in the country, surpassed only by some districts in Brooklyn and the Bronx in numbers of Italian stock. More than 60 percent of residents in the same district are blue-collar workers. During his campaign, Rizzo frequently told the working-class Italian neighborhoods of Kensington and South Philadelphia that only in America could such a man as himself—with no high school or college degree and no personal fortune—became mayor of Philadelphia.

Before the turn of the century, Philadelphia was dominated by a Republican machine, the bosses of which were handmaidens to the Main Line business elite. The wealthy and socially prominent Main Liners gradually withdrew behind the scenes and took up a defensive posture in their exclusive suburbs. City politics were too "dirty," and they were preoccupied with preserving their wealth. These civic and business leaders were replaced as financial backers of the Republican machine by new, first-generation industrialists. The business elite's control gradually weakened to such an extent that the Republican ward bosses lost their unity and collected graft indiscriminately. The Democrats ended 68 years of GOP City Hall control in 1951 by slating blue-ribbon candidates from the old Main Line families who were willing to realign themselves with politics. The two Main Line reformers to be elected mayor in 1951 and 1955 perceived that the best interests of the city rested in the revitalization of the central business district and undertook to use the city's resources for that purpose. Thus they too were serving the interests of business, as the Republican bosses had done before them. Rizzo's election as mayor in November 1971 was to continue Democratic control of City Hall until 1975.

In the 1971 primary campaign Rizzo concentrated his efforts on white ethnics and wasted little campaign time speaking to black or moderately liberal audiences. He appealed to white owners of row-homes in working-class neighborhoods and to the inhabitants of the neat semisuburbs of the city's residential Northeast section. Many lower middle-class Jews voted for him. He polled considerable strength in the middle-class Irish and working-class Italian neighborhoods of Kensington and South Philadelphia. Rizzo himself was from South Philadelphia and was the candidate of the neighborhoods. He shared their background, values, and style of life. "My dad," Rizzo said, "set tough rules and you played the game by his rules or you didn't play. I remember as a young man there was no question as to who was right or wrong. There were no democratic formulas. Boom, you got knocked down. It was the system." The Democratic city chairman backed Rizzo. He represented a "father image" to the people from the old white neighborhoods. He would be an anchor in a sea of rapid social change.

Rizzo's primary campaign left no doubt where he stood on the major issue of the mayoralty race—law and order. He promised to keep the city safe and to act and talk in simple and direct terms. Blacks and Latins were to be contained—no riots, no marches, no demonstrations. He would tolerate no dissent by longhairs, militants, or student activists. In the primary race he promised 2,000 more policemen and tougher law enforcement. During Rizzo's four years as commissioner, the police force was expanded from 6,000 to 7,200 men and the budget increased from $60 to 92 million. He often spoke of his men as his "army." Rizzo symbolized security. On numerous occasions before the primary, he declared that he had to win big, to crush "them," to make sure characters from the left would not take over the town.

Rizzo's very candidacy grew out of racial conflict and his official police response to it. During his four years as police commissioner, he did not hesitate to call blacks "animals, barbarians, and savages." As early as November 17, 1967, he had demonstrated his toughness. On that date he personally directed the rout of several thousand black students from the school board's offices when two officers were blocked from arresting a student who had climbed onto the top of a car. Rizzo sent his men into action with clubs swinging. More than 40 persons, including innocent bystanders, were injured. Charges against those arrested at the scene were later dismissed. In August 1970, Philadelphians, spurred on by inflammatory reports in the local press, became anxious, not to say panicky, over a police killing followed the next night by the wounding of two police officers by gunshot. No evidence exists that these acts were related, but they occurred one week before the convening of the Revolutionary People's Congress, referred to by the local press as the Black Panther Convention. Rizzo heightened tensions by issuing statements and appearing on television denouncing "revolutionary" plots to assassinate policemen. He charged that the revolution was well-planned, well-organized, and centrally controlled: "These imbeciles who are doing the killing are instructed by the Black Panthers." Rizzo's statement encouraged confrontation politics. Whites and blacks looked upon one another with fear and suspicion. A black man with an "Afro" hair style was perceived as an enemy, a threat to one's security.

The day after the wounding of the two policemen, police staged a series of raids on Black Panther headquarters. Rizzo invited press and television representatives to ride with the police during the raids, and he made national headlines when his men herded the Black Panthers into the street, lined them up on the sidewalk, stripped them naked, and permitted the taking of news photographs. At press conferences during that week, Rizzo called the Panthers "revolutionaries" and "yellow dogs." He challenged them to send their best men against fewer of his best for a shootout anywhere and at any time. By the end of the week, people from the old white neighborhoods were urging Rizzo to run for mayor and affixing "Rizzo for Mayor" stickers to the bumpers of their cars. The urgings continued until February 2, when Rizzo announced his candidacy at a press conference in the police administration building.

During the primary campaign Rizzo spoke almost exclusively to the old white neighborhoods. "Pornography is so bad you can't take the family to the movies," he remarked. "We've got men riding in one-man patrol cars where you need a marine division." About black assertion, he declared: "All you have to do to get a job on the school board is to be a militant. Scream outside the administration building, and they'll hire you for $20,000." Rizzo had built a reputation. Once he appeared in a dinner jacket at a racial clash in South Philadelphia with a nightstick tucked into his cummerbund. He was the police commissioner who had warned civil rights demonstrators that "for every one of my men that gets hit with a brick, there are going to be some broken arms and legs."

Rizzo beat his Republican opponent, Thacher Longstreth, in the November general election. Longstreth, a former Princeton football player and an advertising executive, had been a city councilman and executive director of the Greater Philadelphia Chamber of Commerce. He sought to fuse a winning coalition of Democrats, blacks, Puerto Ricans, and most of the registered Republicans. He failed. The campaign was a bitter, name-calling battle that in general ignored the city's serious financial, housing, and education problems to concentrate on race and crime. Rizzo's "tough cop" image became the key issue. The contest was replete with overt appeals by both sides to racism and ethnic pride and fears. Longstreth referred to Rizzo as "the big bambino" and promised that "I won't need a bodyguard to walk the streets; I won't need to carry a blackjack in my pocket." Longstreth also said the Rizzo campaign motto, "firm but fair," means "firm with the blacks and fair with the whites." Rizzo's slogan— "Rizzo Means Business"—with pictures of the former police commissioner was posted almost everywhere. Rizzo claimed that his slogan was a pledge to keep small stores and industry in Philadelphia, but most voters were well aware of its other meaning. The Philadelphia Inquirer, one of the city's major newspapers, ran a cartoon

which pictured Rizzo as a bricklayer building walls between black
and white neighborhoods.

By winning his first political race with a nearly 50,000 plurality
in a heavy turnout, Rizzo replaced Mayor James H. J. Tate who was
ineligible by law for a third term. Rizzo, the choice of Mayor Tate,
is expected to a considerable extent to be under the control of the
local Democratic machine and the former mayor. Rizzo conducted a
cautious campaign. His speeches were generally before "safe"
audiences. At a streetcorner rally in his home district of Kensington,
Rizzo told a crowd of 1,300 cheering supporters that "my opponent
couldn't attract this many people if he walked on his hands. This
same man is the one who in 1969 said a family of four could live on
$4,000 a year. He's the guy who wants to give special taxing powers
to the schools." For the newspapers and television he depended
largely on news releases. His most important support came from
the regular Democratic organization, Mayor Tate, and the local
AFL-CIO federation. Rizzo's heaviest electoral pluralities came
from white ethnic communities, particularly the Irish and Italians.
For many of these supporters, "Rizzo Means Business" conveyed a
message of physical security and, to some extent, security against
being forced to take blacks into unions. News analysts wrote of
Rizzo's "earthiness for communicating to Philadelphia's ethnic minorities the message they wanted to hear—normalcy and safe streets."
Rizzo also won sizable support from the white middle class of northeast Philadelphia and cut deeply into the normally Republican white
middle-class wards. While Republican Longstreth drew more than
70 percent majorities in the city's predominantly black wards, this
fell short of the 80 to 85 percent majorities that the GOP nominee
had said he needed. Philadelphia has more than 270,000 black voters.
Almost all black leaders campaigned for Longstreth or against Rizzo.
Longstreth received pluralities among the Puerto Ricans, the liberals
(many of whom are Jewish), the WASPS who live in suburban-like
neighborhoods within the city limits, the young new voters, and the
young professionals and business people who live in the central city
and are resisting the flight to the suburbs. But he did not capture
sufficiently heavy pluralities in the predominantly Jewish wards.
Because blacks are moving into or nearer to their neighborhoods and
because their small businesses and shops are frequent victims of
crime, many Jewish voters were swayed by Rizzo's promises to
maintain the status quo. Rizzo's winning margin was not so spectacular
as had been predicted. A few weeks before the election predictions
ran as high as a 200,000-vote plurality, but Rizzo, running as the
regular Democrat, attracted less than 50,000 votes over his Republican
opponent in an overwhelming Democratic city. In 1960 Philadelphia,
with 68.1 percent, ranked behind only Boston, Detroit, and Cleveland

in the percentage of registered Democratic voters. A few days after
the election, Mayor-elect Rizzo announced his first appointment—his
younger brother, Joseph L. Rizzo, as fire commissioner. Joseph
Rizzo had been a member of the Philadelphia Fire Department since
June 1949 and was a battalion chief at the time of his appointment.
Rizzo passed over 17 higher-ranking civil service firemen to appoint
his brother. The appointee's salary jumped from $15,000 to $27,000
a year.

Rizzo is not Machiavellian. He believes that his tactics and
rhetoric are necessary and that they only reflect the divisions within
most of our northern industrial cities. Following his election as
mayor, Rizzo said, "I think the nation watched me for the reason that
we're getting back in the middle where we belong." He regarded the
election as a "law-and-order" referendum and his campaign as a
model for candidates to follow. "If they don't," he said, "they are not
going to win." Philadelphia, Newark, and New York are among the
oldest of our cities and are in advanced stages of social disintegration.
The inhabitants of these dying cities feel compelled to take sides, and
the Frank Rizzos and Anthony Imperiales and Joseph Colombos are
offering a simple choice.

Heightened Sensitivity to Ethnic Defamation

The Italian, Polish, and Mexican-Americans have mobilized to
eliminate what they perceive as defamation of their heritages. The
Italians formed the 30,000-strong Italian-American Anti-Defamation
League in the late 1960s, and Joseph Colombo's Italian-American
Civil Rights League galvanized support around its objection to the
use of the term "Mafia" by the government, the mass media, and the
motion picture industry. As Paramount Pictures undertook to film
The Godfather, the Grand Venerable of the Grand Council of the Grand
Lodge of New York State's Sons of Italy wrote a letter of protest to
the film company. It informed Paramount that the studio could expect
a boycott of the film, petitions of protest from all Sons of Italy lodges,
regional meetings to plan protests, a complaint filed with the State
Human Rights Division, and demands that no governmental authorities
give the production any cooperation.

The Italian-American Joint Civic Committee was organized in
Chicago in 1965 to fight defamation and discrimination. The Committee successfully lobbied for the inclusion of Section 20, entitled
"Individual Dignity," in the newly adopted Illinois Constitution.
Section 20, the first such clause placed in a state constitution, con-
demns communications that insult or incite hostility toward a person
because he belongs to a religious, racial, ethnic, regional, or national

group. Illinois State Representative Victor A. Arrigo, a delegate to
the Constitutional Convention, championed the provision while denouncing the "cancerous growth" of slurs that brand Italians as criminals.

The editor of a Polish weekly in Clifton, New Jersey, the Post-
Eagle, announced in 1970 the formation of an "I'm Proud to be Polish"
club and said he hoped to raise enough money to found a Polish Anti-
Defamation League. Less than a year later, Edward J. Piszek,
president of Mrs. Paul's Kitchens, Inc., of Philadelphia pledged
$500,000 for a national campaign to improve the image of Americans
of Polish descent. "Polish jokes should set up in a man a determination to prove they're not true," says Piszek. "In a positive way, it's
an answer to the jokes—instructively. You eliminate the opportunity
to originate the joke by proving it's not true." An unprecedented
campaign called "Project: Pole" began in Detroit in October 1971
and set as its goal "to place in proper perspective" the contributions
of Polish-Americans to American society. The first half-page
advertisement appeared in Detroit newspapers with the headline:
"The Polish astronomer Copernicus said in 1530 that the earth re-
volved around the sun. What was he trying to tell us?" Other pro-
Polish advertisements began to appear that month in newspapers
across the country, and particularly in Detroit, Chicago, Washington,
Philadelphia, Buffalo, and Hartford. At the same time 29 Polish newspapers commenced carrying "Project: Pole" ads. The Copernicus
advertisement was only the first of a series designed to educate
Polish and other Americans in Polish history. Famous Poles—Joseph
Conrad, Marie Curie, Frederic Chopin—were featured. One ad pro-
claimed: "Before there was a United States there was a Poland."
The ads include coupons with which one can order Poland, an art book
($6); "The Imagination of Poland," a 48-page colorful booklet that
details Polish achievements (50 cents); and a poster that "shows at a
glance the great men and women of Poland" ($1). "You have to go
through a daily newspaper with a magnifying glass to find anything
with a Polish theme," says Henry J. Dende, editor and publisher of
the Polish-American Journal, a national newspaper. "Because Polish-
Americans don't read much about themselves they relegate themselves
to second-class citizens." He observes, "The Polish joke is only
about three or four years old. But I think the opposition now stems
partly from the successful black revolution."

The Federal Communications Commission has repeatedly been
petitioned to censure television stations and networks that broadcast
Polish jokes, Mexican cartoon figures, and Mafia gangsters. An FCC
commissioner told the Communications and Power subcommittee of
the House of Representatives, which was investigating such complaints
in April 1971, that he would hate to have to enforce such a regulation.
He conceded that the number of complaints was increasing slightly,

but advised protesters to complain to the stations and networks, which, he felt, were better able to judge what viewers regarded as acceptable taste. The subcommittee heard strong complaints from the Mexican-American Anti-Defamation Committee and Nosotros, a Spanish-American civil rights group, about the Frito-Lay Company's "Frito Bandito" television commercials. The Committee called the advertisement "probably the most subtle and insidious of such racist commercials." Legal counsel for Nosotros has proposed a compromise: a "Frito Amigo" who gives away corn chips instead of stealing them. The cherry flavor of a children's powdered fruit drink mix was originally marketed as "Chinese Cherry," the label depicting a cartoon character with slanting eyes, buck teeth, and a pigtail. After several months the name was changed to "Choo-Choo Cherry" and the label character to an inoffensive railroad engineer.

The Urban Reporter notes that it has "many more advertisements that symbolically reaffirm the inferior status of Mexican-Americans by exaggerating Mexican racial and cultural characteristics and by reinforcing the myths that Mexicans are comical, lazy and thieving."

The hearings before the Communications and Power subcommittee were held to satisfy congressmen from predominantly ethnic districts. Representative Frank Annunzio (D-Ill.), the first witness, declared that the mass media continue to encourage the "scurrilous portrayal of ethnic Americans" and added that the "degrading guilty-by-association techniques have become intolerable." Annunzio and 60 other representatives have introduced resolutions calling for the establishment of ethnic antidefamation standards for the broadcasting and motion picture industries. The proposed resolutions would cover not only defamation, ridicule, and degradation of ethnic, racial, and religious groups but also the stereotyping of these groups. When the Italian-American Civil Rights League pressured Paramount Pictures to delete references to the "Mafia" or "Cosa Nostra" in the film The Godfather, Peter W. Rodino, Jr., a New Jersey Democrat who is an assistant majority whip of the House of Representatives, wrote Paramount on behalf of himself and "other members of Congress of Italo-American heritage," saying that the motion-picture and television industries had failed to establish or enforce standards to prevent productions "that defame, stereotype, ridicule, demean and degrade ethnic, racial and religious groups." At the June 1970 Italian-American Civil Rights League rally, Congressman Mario Biaggi (D-N.Y.) urged the mass media to "break away from the easy headline words and the continued indiscriminate use of 'Mafia' or 'Cosa Nostra' as synonyms for organized crime—an equation that carries with it the connotation that crime is the exclusive preserve of Italian-Americans."

Much of the recent effort to eliminate ethnic defamation can be attributed to politicians appealing to their ethnic constituents. Ethnic

politics in America never before emphasized defamation as strongly
as it does today. Congressmen who have proposed antidefamation
resolutions reflect the desires and demands of their constituents.
Most of them realize that government can do little to curb ethnic
derision and the cultural prejudice that spawns it. Their actions on
this issue indicate pressure from their districts which they cannot
ignore. One Catholic scholar of the ethnic movement believes that
the increase in defamation of Italians, Poles, and Mexican-Americans
is a displacement of the ridicule, debasement, and stereotypes formerly
reserved for blacks. The government, the universities, intellectuals,
television, and the film industry have become so highly conscious of
black sensitivity as to make black jokes less acceptable than Polish
ones.

GROUP CONFLICT IN AMERICA,
PAST AND PRESENT

   The history of conflict among ethnic, religious, and racial
groups in the United States should inspire caution among white ethnic
leaders in their advocacy of group assertion. Indeed, ethnic, religious,
and racial assertion throughout the world in the last thirty years has
resulted in unprecedented human slaughter. The 1960s rudely
awakened many Americans to an awareness of their heritage of violence. During this time, the National Commission on Civil Disorders
and the National Commission on the Causes and Prevention of Violence
issued at least four long reports systematically documenting group
conflict and violence in America. These reports—the most comprehensive studies of American violence—reveal its predominantly
ethnic, religious, and racial origins.
   American history is filled with ethnic, religious, and racial conflict, not class conflict. Intermittent group warfare has been the substitute for, or alternative to, class war. When white workers attacked
black scabs or imported Chinese laborers, when Irish workers
clashed with newer immigrants over jobs and promotions, the resulting violence, though viewed as class conflict, had a strong racial or
ethnic coloration. Ethnic groups moving into the industrial areas of
the United States provided a steady flow of cheap, unorganized labor
to replace the earlier groups as they became organized and demanded
a larger share of the profits of capitalism. What may have been
called an election riot originating in class conflict was often, in
actuality, an attempt to exclude some minority group from voting.
Class warfare in America has seldom occurred without the strong
influence of racial or ethnic antagonism and America's complex
hierarchy of status based upon religious, ethnic, and racial qualities.

Romantic frontier tales notwithstanding, most American domestic violence has been urban, not rural or frontier, a function primarily of the tensions between groups in large American cities. American historian Richard Hofstadter has concluded that it is ethnic, religious, and racial antagonisms that are the fundamental determinants of American violence. He observes that these predominantly urban tensions have been "exacerbated by other national circumstances: weak government, localism, and the diffusion of authority and power; extraordinarily rapid urban growth, large-scale migrations, and rapid social change; the inability or unwillingness of urban Americans to relinquish their gun culture; and finally, the development in the nineteenth century of a type of socially unchecked industrial baron, often an absentee, lording it over a distant and heterogeneous 'alien' working force with which he felt no ethnic, institutional, social or religious ties."

Historical Perspective

A brief survey of American history reveals numerous incidents of ethnic, religious, and racial violence. The period of the 1830s through the 1850s was marked by sustained urban rioting, particularly in the large cities of the Northeast. The riots arose from the rapid growth of the cities, the development of slums, Irish immigration, and the abolitionist movement. As early as the 1830s many Protestants had become aware of growing Catholic strength and had responded with nativism—the belief that America existed for "Americans" (native-born Anglo-Saxons and Protestants) and that foreigners were subversive. During this period, the most important ethnic antagonisms tended to be structured and polarized around the issues of Catholicism and Protestantism. The burning of the Ursuline Convent at Charlestown, Massachusetts, in 1834, marked the beginning of nativist mob action against Irish Catholics. The anti-Catholic Know-Nothing Party encouraged the use of violence for such purposes as keeping foreign-born voters from the polls. The bloody nativist riots of Philadelphia in 1844 grew out of Protestant resentment over the use of the Catholic Bible in addition to the Protestant Bible in public schools. When Protestants invaded the Irish Catholic suburbs of Kensington and Southward in Philadelphia, the Irish stood up to them, supported by armed Irish volunteers—the Hibernia Greens—but not before fire had destroyed many homes and churches. Both sides fired cannon, and 20 persons were killed and over 60 wounded. The American Protective Association (APA), organized in 1887, was the largest anti-Catholic movement outside the South and prospered until the turn of the century. A secret organization with rituals and customs similar to those of the Ku Klux Klan, APA drew its greatest strength from Protestants of low status in urban areas, especially in the West.

The Pentecost Riot in Hoboken in 1851 added another dimension to the assaults by nativists—attacks on liberal Germans by nativists joined by conservative Irish Catholic immigrants, who hated the liberalism and socialist ideals often espoused by the German Turn organizations. In this incident, a group of German workers and their families, including many Turners, were celebrating Pentecostal Sunday at a picnic when a mob of nativists and immigrants attacked. The Turners' counterattack led to a wild melee in which one person was killed and dozens were wounded. In St. Louis the 1854 election led to a riot arising from resistance to allowing German-Americans to vote; 10 men were killed and several wounded. The following year in Louisville, anti-German Know-Nothings captured the polls in the German section and, with the aid of police and sympathetic local officials, pulled immigrant Americans out of voting lines and beat them. Gun fighting erupted, and by evening 20 people had been killed and large numbers wounded.

Nativist riots were followed by riots between Irish and blacks, and indeed the greatest part of American violence has occurred between whites and blacks. In mid-July 1863, the New York City draft riots brought about the large-scale murder and lynching of as many as 1,200 blacks. These riots were more the result of inter-racial tensions than antiwar sentiment. Frequent large-scale episodes of racial violence marked the Reconstruction period in the South, as Southern whites who felt their supremacy challenged organized White Leagues, politico-military organizations, to counter and suppress any assertion by black freedmen. By 1877 radical Reconstruction had come to the same end as the brutally suppressed slave revolts, and the Southern caste system had become the prevailing social arrangement.

Immigrants carried their religious and ethnic animosities to the United States, where they often erupted in local political issues. In 1871 members of the Irish Hibernian Society harassed Orangemen parading in New York City, and during the resulting riots 39 were killed and 91 wounded, thus continuing the tradition of bloody clashes between Protestants and Catholics in Ireland on the anniversary of the defeat of James II by William of Nassau, Prince of Orange, on July 11, 1690. An underlying issue was control of the city government, increasingly dominated by the Irish.

On the West Coast in the late 1860s and 1870s, whites waged a campaign of violence to drive the Chinese out of California, where there were 50,000 by 1870. Whites objected to the crowding and smell of the Chinese districts, their prostitution and gambling, their alien customs and alleged monarchism. They also felt threatened by cheap Chinese labor that made unionization difficult. In Los Angeles, the Chinese district was known as "Nigger Alley," and in 1871 a fight there between rival Chinese groups precipitated a bloody anti-Chinese riot. When some intervening policemen were wounded, infuriated white mobs attacked the Chinese and a day-long slaughter left 18 Chinese dead by shooting and lynching. In 1882 Congress passed the Exclusion Act, barring Chinese immigration for ten years. The dislocation and confinement of Japanese-Americans in camps during World War II is another, more familiar, episode in American history of the treatment of an Oriental minority group.

After the 1870s and until the migration northward of Southern blacks during World War I, the country was relatively calm. There were, however, some notable exceptions; one being the anti-Italian riot in New Orleans in 1891. When 19 Italians reputedly associated with the Mafia were acquitted of the charge of murdering the New Orleans chief of police despite strong evidence of their guilt, a group of prominent civic leaders called a mass protest meeting which brought together more than 6,000 citizens. One civic leader of the rally led 50 men to the jail where they killed 11 of the Italians. There were other anti-Italian incidents. In New Orleans 3 Italians were lynched by similar mob action in 1896, and 5 more were murdered in that city in 1899. In New York City in 1902, when a Jewish funeral procession passed through an Irish district, Irish workmen began throwing nuts and bolts at the mourning Jews. When the largely Irish police force intervened, it was the Jews who suffered physical brutality at the hands of the police.

During the period of 1915 to 1919, when blacks began moving from an increasingly mechanized cotton economy to the jobs created in the North by the war effort, 22 major racial disturbances occurred. In all, whites took the initiative and blacks fought back. The worst of the post-World War I riots occurred in Chicago in 1919. Of subsequent race riots, two of the most notable were the Tulsa riot of 1921 and the Detroit riot of 1943. Harlem had a ghetto riot in 1935. however, it was a meager predecessor to the great ghettos riots which were to follow three decades later—Watts (1965), Newark (1967), and Detroit (1967).

Mexican-Americans in California and southern Texas have been repeatedly subjected to crowd violence. In 1943 in Los Angeles a mob of over 1,000 soldiers, sailors, and civilians broke into movie theaters, streetcars, and homes, dragged Mexicans into the street and stripped and beat them. The violence was called the Zoot-Suit Riot because the majority of those assaulted were youths wearing zoot-suits, the elaborate clothing worn by young Mexicans at that time. The Hearst papers had used the term "zoot-suit" for Mexican to such an extent that the two had become synonymous.

The massive immigration of Puerto Ricans to New York City, Philadelphia, and other northern cities during the 1950s precipitated many violent clashes with blacks in which killing and wounding has been common.

The urban vigilantism of the mid- and late 1960s is discussed later. It is too early to know whether it will end, persist, or take on a more sinister character. While this movement has employed force, very few have been killed or wounded as a result of its activities.

World Perspective

Ethnic and cultural conflicts since the end of World War II have resulted in an unprecedented amount of bloodshed and killing all over the world. The list is endless: Hindu versus Muslim, light-skinned Punjabis slaughtering dark-skinned East Bengalis, Sudanese Arabs killing Sudanese blacks, Watusi versus Bahutu, tribal civil wars in Nigeria and the Congo, Kurds killed by Iraqis, Indonesians and Malays killing Chinese in communal attacks, black Africans massacring Arabs in Zanzibar, Filipino Christians killing Filipino Muslims, increasing numbers of Irish Catholics and Protestants killing each other in Ulster, mutual killings of Turks and Greeks in Cyprus, Israelis and Arabs in continual conflict with the Arabs vowing to annihilate the state of Israel. In North America, Quebec separatists, Black Muslims, and Black Panthers have resorted to bloodshed, though on a much smaller scale.

According to a recent estimate by Robert D. Crane in "Postwar Ethnic Cultural Conflicts: Some Quantitative and Other Considerations" (ms. Hudson Institute, New York, March 1968), world-wide fatalities attributable to ethnic-cultural clashes for the period between 1945 and 1967 totaled nearly 7.5 million. Crane has documented 34 major incidents and hundreds of lesser ones. Wherever tribal, racial, ethnic, religious, or national groups compete for supremacy, tension and strain exist, and demonstrations, riots, and terrorism are commonplace. It is a strange irony that when man has seen the physical world as a totality from outer space, when science and technology have forced upon him an international perspective, when crises such as the starvation in Biafra are relayed instantaneously to the collective conscience of the world, and man's commonality is now global, that he seems ever more strongly driven to the separateness of the tribe.

American institutions dominated by Anglo-Protestants have set and enforced the rules of the game since the nation's beginnings, mediating America's pluralism and providing the power system—the larger coherence—to contain the nation's variety and frictions. But

America is rapidly becoming a nation in which no single style or ethnicity prevails. The power system embodied in the New Deal coalition has eroded. Roosevelt liberals, bereft of unified leadership, are fighting among themselves. Mediation by WASPS among competing interest groups is no longer possible under the old rules of the game because ethnic and racial minorities reject a position of subordination and inferiority. These groups have tested the limits of the authority they formerly accepted, forcing the dominant institutions to make explicit and justify their position. The WASP establishment can no longer merely pay lip service to minorities and to their pluralism of styles, beliefs, and cultures. However, if institutions dominated by Anglo-Protestants recognize the legitimacy of the contenders, they may continue to act as mediators. John Lindsay was reelected mayor of New York in 1969 because Jews, blacks, and Puerto Ricans trusted him more than they trusted the alternative candidates, both of whom were Italian-Americans. It is improbable that America will ever be integrated on ethnic and racial terms, or that the replacement of the dominant Anglo-Protestant culture with ethnic and racial pluralism can be anything but divisive as each group seeks what it conceives to be its just share of society's rewards.

America is not alone in undergoing a transformation of its political system. The weakening and collapse of power and social systems is a global phenomenon. Group assertion is occurring throughout Europe, Asia, and Africa, as dominated groups no longer accept their subordinate position, but rather seek a new identity, new terms of existence, a new society in which they belong and can find self-respect. Massive political shifts and realignments are the order of the day. Political theorist Harold R. Isaacs has recently generalized about "this fragmentation of man . . . one of the great pervasive facts of contemporary human affairs" as follows:

> It has come about as a result of the collapse or weakening
> of power systems—the larger coherences—that for periods
> of time managed to hold clusters of separate groups under
> the control of a single dominant group or coalition of groups.
> These systems created a certain coherence in which the
> differences and divisions were not so much submerged as
> held in their orbits by the gravity of the center. The force
> of this gravity was physical, economic, cultural, and—most
> heavily—psychological. The rules of the game were in-
> corporated into mystiques and mythologies of belief and
> behavior—all the assumptions of cultural and racial supe-
> riority/inferiority—which were internalized and accepted
> by all, rulers and ruled, victimizers and victims, and
> built into the system's institutions to keep it working. . . .

None of the proffered new coherences have sic worked.
Neither the feeble European capitalist-victor coalition
represented by the Versailles settlement and the League
of Nations, nor its broader-based successor, the United
Nations, could create a political system in which the power
struggle of the major powers—in effect reduced to two—
could be contained, much less the conflicts of the enor-
mously increased number of smaller nations, with all their
external and internal abrasions and collisions over national/
ethnic/racial/tribal/religious differences. Indeed the
Soviet and American power blocs that emerged after 1945
remained fragile and uneasy combinations precisely because
of the revised strength of old nationalisms and new drives
to self-assertion and self-esteem ("Group Identity and
Political Change: The Houses of Muumbi").

Isaacs then discusses the consequences of the end of empires. Since
1945, former empires have been divided into more than 70 new
nations. These newly-independent nations began their political lives
with regional, tribal, linguistic, racial, and religious divisions. In
most of them, according to Isaacs, such divisions have produced conflict: prolonged and bloody civil wars, military coups rooted in tribal
differences, and riots, collisions, and clashes.

The weakening and collapse of the old power systems have
affected Europe and North America too, but with far less bloodshed.
Minority cultural reassertion is on the increase in these areas of the
world. In Great Britain, the Welsh, Scots (who elected nationalist
members to Parliament), and Manx are restive, while the Irish
Catholics in Northern Ireland are increasingly willing to realize their
goal of separatism through violence. The Flemings and Walloons are
at odds over Louvain in Belgium. The Bretons are stirring in France,
the Basques and Catalans in Spain, the Jurassians in Switzerland. In
Eastern Europe cultural separatist movements largely directed
toward the Soviet Union remain alive. Separatist French-Canadians
persist in their drive to gain regional, linguistic, and political
autonomy for the province of Quebec and to sever its ties with Canada.
Black extremists in the United States advocate black separatism and
stronger ties with Africa.

The paradox of separatism is its lack of realism. In the face
of growing technological and economic interdependence, separatist
impulses seem doomed to failure, but their very existence at this
time in history bespeaks their tenacity and influence in a time of
shifting power systems and relationships.

CULTURAL PLURALISM AND ITS
IMPLICATIONS FOR AMERICA

The idea of cultural pluralism now contends with the melting pot ideal as the goal governing the relationship among the peoples of the United States. It is scarcely a new development in human history. The Roman Empire provides one of many historical examples of cultural pluralism. What has been astonishing about the American experience is the pervasive blindness to the fact that America is one of the most ethnically and culturally pluralistic nations in the world. The pursuit of the American Dream and its corollary, Americanization, made the persistent reality of America's cultural pluralism seem divisive. Immigrants and their children were destined to be socialized, integrated, and, indeed, Americanized, by being processed through the public shcools, taught and compelled to use the English language, and ultimately by intermarrying. The Americanizers won the ideological battle, and cultural diversity, though always present, was suppressed. Parochial schools have always been regarded as divisive. Ironically, public schools are now attacked for their committment to homogenization. Black educator Charles Hurst, formerly of New York City and now president of Malcolm X College in Chicago, built part of his reputation on his advocacy of a bilingual educational system incorporating both standard American English and the dialect of urban blacks. He has since reversed his position and now urges blacks to reject middle-class Anglo-Protestant language and style in order to assert their own identity, one which will command respect by being a vital original, not a poor copy of the WASP model.

Advocates of cultural pluralism recognize the United States as a nation of immigrant groups and encourage ethnic groups to retain the distinctive and creative aspects of their cultural heritages; they consider an ethnic group identity as no less compatible with American life and national loyalty than any regional, class, or other group attachment. Pluralistic substructures have and will continue to function as systems of self-definition, mediation, and interpretation within the larger society. Ethnics can thus behave politically as ethnics while remaining loyal to America. Cultural ties bear deeper meaning for individuals than that alternative too frequently offered by a highly complex and impersonal society, the rootless pluralism of mutually alienated groups.

The print and broadcasting media have contributed greatly to Americans' awareness of the diversity and fragmentation of their culture. When poor white ethnics see on their television screens blacks at the mayor's office making demands and receiving recognition and concessions, they begin to consider protesting their own condition. When the black is asked his name and his opinion on an issue, it seems as if he has acquired an identity, made a gap in the wall of the establishment. Television allows much rubbing-of-elbows among different groups.

The confrontation politics and national divisiveness of the late 1960s, it would seem, should have discouraged the advocates of cultural pluralism. Richard Nixon campaigned as the leader who would unite a divided nation, but the negative character of the activities of his vice-president in 1970 indicate that political expediency was more important to Nixon than national unity. Some social observers have argued that erosion of the WASPs' mediating function would create further disintegration—alienation and apathy alternating with outbursts of violence. They reason that if racial and ethnic minorities reject the ethic and style of the mainstream, the rules of the game, then they are less likely to accept each other. Whether correct or not, serious consideration of the role of government as well as public schools, the church, political organizations, and labor unions in integrating and Americanizing must be undertaken. In the past, these institutions were those best equipped to lessen the distrust, suspicion, and antagonism that arise from ethnic and racial and religious differences.

The direction and desirability of recent racial and ethnic assertion in the United States is still an unwritten chapter of American history. Andrew Greeley believes that ethnic loyalty is "a strong, positive force which might make available vitality and vigor for the preservation and enrichment of urban life for all members of the city." He has suggested that one possible use of the pluralism model is for the young who are seeking to create new clans, new tribes or communes. They may be able to "achieve the same goals by moving back into their grandparents' neighborhoods—an experience which would also have the happy advantage of revealing to them that intimate communities can be narrow, rigid, doctrinaire and, in many instances, quite intolerant of privacy, creativity and diversity."

After years of study of group relations and conflict, Harold R. Isaacs concludes:

> We are experiencing on a massively universal scale a convulsive ingathering of men in their numberless groupings of kinds—tribal, racial, ethnic, religious, national. It is a great clustering into separatenesses that will, people think, improve, assure or extend the group's power or place, or keep it safe or safer from the power, threat, and hostility of all groups similarly engaged.

He thinks it "at least barely possible" for us to survive the chaos of widespread group assertion if all groups in a given society abandon the "winner-take-all" philosophy and substitute an "all-win-a-little" philosophy. He approves the high value placed on group self-esteem

under a system of cultural pluralism. Group self-assertion promotes
the belief that, as Isaacs puts it, "all groups of men—indeed, all men—
are entitled to an adequate basis for self-esteem, that is to a respect
and therefore self-respecting status in both the social and the political
systems." Perhaps a spirit of change and an acceptance of diversity
will be salvaged from the unrest of the 1960s.

The United States of America, as a nation of immigrants, differs
from other immigrant societies such as Australia, Canada, South
Africa, and Latin America, in that the latter have drawn disproportionately from only a few favored ethnic stocks, while America is
populated by an unprecedented variety of immigrant stock. During
the period from 1820 to 1945 the United States received the following
ethnically diverse strains:

British Isles	33%
Germany	16
Austria-Hungary	13
Italy	12
Russia and Poland	10
Scandinavia	
Africa	
Spanish-surname	
Orient	
American Indian	

Moreover, within these categories are ethnically important divisions
such as the Irish Catholic and English Protestant, the Orthodox
Russian and Russian Jew, the Norwegian and the Swede. The founders
of the society, the original English settlers, established themselves
as the dominant group. They effectively took control of economic and
political power and became America's elite. The Anglo-Protestants
perpetuated the realities and myths of power that were necessary to
maintain their dominance. They established the rules of the game
and incorporated into them the mystiques and mythologies of cultural
and racial superiority and inferiority. They used legal force surrounded
by an air of legitimacy for such ends as economic exploitation; the
restriction of immigration by a national origin quota system that
clearly branded later immigrants as culturally undesirable; the confinement of the Indians largely to barren reservations; and the restriction of blacks to a degraded caste.

The Anglo-Protestant elite group has tenaciously resisted the
upward strivings of successive immigrant infusions. Subsequent
immigrant groups have had to compete fiercely with one another and
with the nativist establishment in their collective quest for the rewards of American society: economic security, economic advancement,

and status. Older, better established, more powerful ethnic and racial groups have had to grant or resist the demands for increased power and prestige of new and militant groups. The definition of Americanism was narrowed and rigidified by increasingly fine distinctions drawn between the characteristics of incoming ethnic groups and those of the resident WASPs. Being born an American did not automatically confer equal citizenship in the eyes of the larger society. Ethnic minorities have constantly had to affirm their Americanism and earn self-respect by striving to ascend the social and economic ladder. Horatio Alger became an article of faith in the mythology of Americanism.

These rivalries between the newcomers and the distrustful native Anglo-Protestant establishment, and between the economically competing and status-conscious ethnic minorities themselves, have created both friction and severe conflict. The Irish riots of New York City against black "scab" laborers or, in more recent times, the violent resistance by white ethnics to black migration into their previously all-white neighborhoods are examples of the violence that frequently flares from these rivalries. Differences in religion and social class render these conflicts all the more bitter and violent. Competition among ethnic and racial groups for resources which are scarce or presumed to be scarce, with the inevitable conflict that ensues, has been a basic social dynamic of the American experience.

The critical question is what level of conflict a society can tolerate and still remain civilized and in a state of ordered liberty. Lewis Coser and many other social scientists have concluded that group conflict has a positive and constructive aspect: when the patterns of relationships and the structures of society are no longer adequate to the social realities, group conflict forces a needed restructuring of the social order. The flexibility of the system determines the degree to which it responds to group pressure. The Spanish-speaking communities of America believe that their political power is incommensurate with their numbers, group consciousness, aspirations, and rights. If their demands are ignored or refused, their assertion will turn to frustration, anger, and probably ultimately violence. The recent Mexican-American riots in East Los Angeles illustrates some of the consequences of systematic rigidity.

On the whole, black assertion has succeeded in forcing important social changes and, by the early 1970s, in substituting a positive for a negative group consciousness. In September 1971, blacks held an economic, cultural, and political exposition in Chicago, known as Black Expo. It was the largest of the three annual expositions held in Chicago, and the largest of its kind in the world. The symbolic tying of a white and black ribbon marked its official commencement, and it inspired such pleasantries as "soul handshakes" between

political enemies like Mayor Richard J. Daley and the Reverend
Jesse L. Jackson. Advertisements in Chicago newspapers emphasized
that black "economic independence" depended on cooperation and involvement with whites. Hundreds of black businessmen and many of
the most prominent black politicians and entertainers participated.
At least 15 white companies had exhibit booths at Black Expo and
close to 200 white businessmen came to a pre-exposition business
breakfast. Whites were encouraged to attend the exposition, and many
did. It was estimated that in all nearly 500,000 people attended the
five-day affair.

But constructive and integrative assertion such as that represented by Black Expo is only one side of the coin: the prison riot in
September 1971 at Attica, New York, was racial assertion of another
kind. At least 42 men died in the brutal suppression of the rebellion.
Hatred between the black prisoners and the white guards representing
a predominantly white society outside the prison walls was probably
the single most important cause of the riot.

There are other incidents in which the rhetoric of destruction
preached by black extremists has become an ugly reality. Racial
violence in the American military is at an all-time high. The judicial
system also reflects the divisions within American society as black
defendants appeal to black jury members in strong racial terms, and
black jury members often refuse to convict blacks. If ordered liberty
is to survive, injustices and inequities in a society cannot be accepted
as excuses for criminal behavior under some vague notion of "political
crimes."

Incidents of terror and violence—stabbings, shootings, beatings,
and burnings—persist in the racially changing neighborhoods of large
northern cities and show no signs of decreasing as racial and ethnic
assertion becomes more militant and aggressive. In September 1971
two black youths shot and killed two 13-year-old white children in a
racially changing working-class neighborhood in Chicago. Approximately 150 white residents, angered over the killings, roamed the neighborhood and threatened violence to black residents.

Ethnic and racial group assertion and the resultant conflict take
many forms—passive resistance, demonstrations, acts of terrorism,
urban ghetto riots, and assassinations. We have already noted that of
the twelve successful or attempted assassinations that occurred in
the United States in the 1960s, six stemmed from minority group
tension. When Joseph Colombo, Sr., was seriously wounded in June
1971, his eldest son said, "It was a nut—the same kind of nut who
killed President Kennedy and Bobby Kennedy." An official of the
Italian-American Civil Rights League observed: "It seems like shooting civil rights leaders is 'in' in recent years." Whether such assassinations or assassination attempts are an endemic symptom of a new

American social malaise is still uncertain. The precedents are too
few. Moreover, the political unrest in America attributable to ethnic
and racial group assertion is part of a global pattern.

In 1971, America's discriminatory distribution of rights and
benefits to racial and ethnic minority groups was still pervasive and
there still existed a national intolerance against these groups' establishing their own satisfying ways of life. Interethnic conflict in America
has occurred and will continue to occur in politics, housing, religion,
education, unions, business, and crime. The raw material for such
conflict is present when two groups compete for a given amount of
resources. It most frequently arises when there are two large racial
or ethnic groups coexisting in the same geographical location, one
possessing more socio-economic and political power than the other.
In New York City the Italians are at odds with the Jews and blacks
for political power. The old all-white ethnic neighborhoods are under
increasing pressure from racial minorities seeking more and better
housing. The first black family to locate in an all-white neighborhood
in Chicago often suffers physical and verbal abuse: insults, rocks
thrown and shots fired through their windows, threatening phone calls,
and sometimes acts of arson. The same is true of other American
cities undergoing racial change.

In 1971, competition within the Roman Catholic hierarchy was
still bitter. Italians, Poles, and other nationalities have deeply
resented Irish dominance of the Catholic Church in America. Polish
Catholics formed their own national Church, but it was never able to
compete with the Irish-dominated Church. Many Italians still resent
the Irish for "Hibernizing" the Church and eliminating many Italian
Catholic customs.

The struggle between black school districts and the white,
largely Jewish teachers' union in New York City, the racial clashes
over education facilities between blacks on the one hand and Jews
and white ethnics on the other, the school busing controversies
throughout the North and the battle between the president of Chicago's
Malcolm X College and the predominantly white, heavily Jewish,
Cook County college teachers unions over control of the College—all
of these exemplify the conflicts in education. Competition for public
funds for education has a growing religious dimension as parochial
schools petition state and local governments for financial support.

The longstanding leadership of labor unions by the Irish, Germans,
and Jews is continually challenged by Italian, Slavic and, in a few instances, black insurgents. Whereas industrial unions, for the most
part, have been integrative and assimilative, the trade unions have been
much more rigid and exclusionist. Membership in such trade unions as
the ironworkers is passed from father to son, and members of racial
minorities are excluded by whatever means possible. During the ghetto

riots of the 1960s the shops and small businesses of white, primarily
Jewish owners were singled out as targets for looting and fire-bombing.
A study of the April 1968 riot in Chicago revealed that black-owned-
and-operated stores suffered relatively little destruction compared to
those of white owners. Moreover, small ethnic and racial entrepreneurs
such as construction contractors have always engaged in fierce competition with one another.

Domination of organized crime, once the realm of the Irish and
Jews has been taken over by the Italians, who are now challenged in
black communities by black criminal leaders and youth gangs. Studies
of youth gangs and their violent battles for territory have documented
their ethnic and racial character. Irish and Italian youth gangs are
still at war in Philadelphia. Irish, Puerto Rican, and black gangs—
the Young Lords, Latin Souls and Black P. Stone Nation—have almost
daily confrontations with rocks, bottles, knives, and guns in the Back
of the Yards area of the South Side of Chicago.

The United States military exhibits the same symptoms of racial
competition, friction, and violence. Between 1965 and 1970 hundreds
of servicemen were killed in outbursts of racial violence. The
Pentagon's civil rights chief issued a report in 1971 in which he related having found some black servicemen in the Far East so frustrated that they wept and suffered "verbal paralysis" in trying to tell
him their plight. "The frustrations of these men are so great and
their pent-up fury so high that many of them have exceeding difficulty
expressing themselves. . . . " His report noted that black and other
minority servicemen complained of discrimination in promotions and
job assignments. The report continued:

> We found that blacks and whites were moving farther and
> farther away from each other, resegregating through
> accelerated racial polarizations. This occurred on the
> base and also in the communities off the base. There were
> black bars and clubs and white bars and clubs.

Ethnic and racial conflict is not a well understood phenomenon.
There has been virtually no systematic and comprehensive analysis
of it. But many social scientists, as well as other scholars and
thinkers, now acknowledge the necessity for study and analysis of
group conflicts. The white urban backlash, wherein white ethnics
were perceived to be at odds with blacks, inspired much of the recent
interest. The term "white ethnic" is not particularly satisfactory
since the differences among the Irish, Italian, and Polish components
of the white ethnic group are often more significant than their simi-
larities. Individually these segments compete for what they believe
is their share of economic and political power and prestige. At a

five-day conference on white ethnics held at the Catholic University in June 1971, the tensions between the Irish and Italians erupted many times in overt, hostile exchanges, most of which were related to the "Hibernization" of the Catholic Church and to political rivalries.

Yet it is racial alliances which have been most significant in the social conflicts of the 1960s and early 1970s. The blacks in the ghettos of the urban North and rural South, the Mexican-Americans in southern Texas and southern California, the Puerto Ricans in New York, Chicago, and other cities, the Cubans in Florida, the Japanese in Hawaii, the Chinese in New York and California are not merely accepting their segregation but rather are maintaining it and drawing strength from it.

Ethnic and racial conflict is becoming more pronounced as groups gravitate toward poles which they perceive as expressing their identity. The primary elements of group identity—blood, faith, and land—become the centers around which people can rally or be brought to rally, whether to seek a change in their status or to defend whatever security they believe themselves to possess.

It is impossible either to delineate precisely the influence of race, ethnicity, religion, and geography or to assign each a quantitative significance. Yet the dedicated researcher learns that the analysis of any single conflict will reveal enough of its dynamics and of the interrelations of the groups involved to suggest practical solutions. Andrew Greeley makes a strong plea for further investigation of the ethnic factor in its broadest implications. He cites the results of two surveys which found an increase in anti-Catholic feeling among American Jews and found this increase most marked among college graduates and young Jews. Though he cautions that the findings are "highly tentative," he urges more study of Catholic-Jewish relations and recognition of the problems which flow from deteriorating relations, should such a study confirm that they are deteriorating. Greeley further cites findings about the racial attitudes of white ethnic groups and notes the differences among them, though he concedes that one need not rely upon statistics about attitudes to know that there is an acute problem in the relations between Irish Catholics and other Catholic groups, between the Poles and blacks in Chicago, and between the Jews and blacks in New York City. To mitigate ethnic and racial tensions, he proposes intergroup dialogue, cultural exchanges, the serious interest of competitive groups in each other's cultural institutions, and less demagogic political leaders.

Increases in ethnic and racial group conflict should always be viewed with alarm and met with institutional flexibility. But the American experience before the 1960s must also be remembered. Americans from very different backgrounds have coexisted for two hundred years in an atmosphere of relative peace and mutual respect.

The largest immigration in history occurred between the years 1860 and 1929, when 32.5 million people came to America. It was during this period, between the Civil War and the Depression, that America became an ethnically heterogeneous nation and suffered its highest level of ethnic group conflict. But the striking feature of the period is that the ethnic hostilities and prejudices did not result in more killings and greater destruction, given the magnitude of the adjustment which was made by so many diverse groups. Superficially when one thinks of ethnic relations, he recalls the attacks by the nativists upon the Irish, the Italians, and Roman Catholics in general; recollections of race relations may bring to mind the brutal suppression of the slave rebellions or the killings and terrorism committed by the Ku Klux Klan. Spectacular outbreaks of violence, many of which are episodic and ephemeral, have always received more popular attention than the evidence of harmonious intergroup relations. The latter constitutes, by far, the greater part of ethnic and racial group relations in the history of the United States.

Interethnic competition, friction, and conflict have not been nearly as disintegrative and destructive of the American fabric as one might expect, given the influx of over 40 million immigrants, the diversity and newness of American society, and the stakes involved. The traditions, values, and goals of family and group are frequently incompatible with one another and do not reinforce the style and substance of national government. The family buttresses old ties and former loyalties. Group differences place particular tensions on public institutions. The melting-pot rationale was primarily political, designed to define citizenship and promote political consensus. It did not encourage diverse group identities.

Nevertheless, the United States has functioned less as a nation of individuals than as one of groups, and its ethnic diversity and the protracted and diffuse nature of its infusion of immigrants have done more to strengthen the nation than to weaken it. Class conflict has been a relatively insignificant dynamic in America because the capitalists have had a succession of newcomers from which to draw their labor force. The working class was more often than not divided along ethnic and racial lines and seldom united against the upper or employer class. Large trade unions are still dominated by a single ethnic group. Industrial unions are still divided by ethnic conflicts.

The Constitutional prohibition against an established state religion was adopted because the Jeffersonians understood the destructive consequences of imposing a single set of cultural beliefs. A 1971 decision of the United States Supreme Court affirmed this prohibition when the Court ruled that the scheme of financial aid to parochial schools involved excessive entanglement of church and state.

American political ideology often rubs harshly against individuals or groups in their notions of how social and economic affairs ought to be structured. The federal government decrees, for example, that children will be bused to achieve racial balance and equality of educational opportunity, and that federal funds can only be used for projects where all citizens have an equal opportunity for housing and jobs. The implementation of the American people's constitutional guarantees is carried out despite the objections of many groups. The need for national community is said to override the parochial pull of separatism. The past success of America has been due to its commitment to constitutional government and to the rule of the laws men make rather than to the rule of men.

Government, along with public schools, political machines, labor unions, and business, has served to socialize and Americanize the diversity and variety of the peoples of the United States. These institutions have usually functioned to minimize the distrust, suspicion, and antagonism which arise from ethnic and religious differences.

The question for the 1970s is one of the extent to which America can tolerate intensified group assertion. The black revolution seems to have progressed to a constructive ideology. The rhetoric of destruction is still faintly heard, but black leaders who command constituencies are talking and acting within the established economic and political structures. It is too early to know where the growing white ethnic awareness will lead America. It seemed to have entered a constructive phase by the early 1970s. But if the black becomes stereotyped as the white ethnic's enemy, or if the white ethnic is stereotyped and ignored or ridiculed by the affluent white, the eventual victim could be the American democratic process. The white ethnic movement has rapidly become political. In only a few years the movement has begun to gain recognition and a few concessions. But confrontation and polarization must be kept to a minimum. This can only be accomplished if all contenders agree to the rules of the game. At the same time the mediating institutions—government, business, and labor unions—must not become arbitrary or inflexible to this end.

5

THE ROLE OF ETHNICITY IN THE COMMUNITY ORGANIZATION MOVEMENT

INTRODUCTION

The white residents of the older industrial cities of the North have increasingly organized themselves to exert pressure on public decision-makers. Reacting to their own lack of power and voice and to the success of black assertion, they have come together and formed interest groups and coalitions to press for change and reform. While the great majority of these residents are white ethnics, their individual group attachments may not be the dominant force uniting them. Whether racial considerations are at the roots of this movement is difficult to determine. In part, the movement is certainly a reaction to the winning of recognition, public offices, appointments, and benefits by blacks. Black mayors have been replacing their white ethnic predecessors. Blacks are making increasingly substantial inroads into the public school systems and now control many of the federal poverty and model cities programs. Traditionally, urban white ethnics acted through unions, political machines, and the liberal and urban wing of the national Democratic Party, but these institutions are now perceived by them as either ineffective or unresponsive to their needs. White ethnics seek new mediating and assertive agents.

The major new community organizations reflect their constituencies, their particularly local problems, and the organizational skills and goals of their organizers and leaders. The Calumet Community Congress (CCC) of Indiana is different from the Black-Polish Alliance of Detroit or the North Ward Educational and Cultural Center of Newark.

While economic and social class are more important in the former two organizations, ethnicity and race dominate Steve Adulato's organization in Newark's North Ward and its adversary, Tony

Imperiale's Citizens Committee. Only Italian-Americans like Adulato and Imperiale could have emerged as leaders in the North Ward.

CALUMET COMMUNITY CONGRESS

The Calumet Community Congress has become the largest and most successful community organization in America. As a federation of more than 150 local and diverse organizations in northwest Indiana, founded in December 1970, it is the first regional community organization in the nation and was almost immediately recognized by the national communications media as a potentially powerful workingman's organization. For its founding convention Senator Edward M. Kennedy sent a warm wire predicting that "perhaps in years to come the entire country will look to this Congress as proof that the democratic system can be made to respond to citizens united by common cause and concern." Four days after the formation of the CCC, the Washington Post carried an editorial praising the new organization: "both important and unusual because it unites the largely white ethnic working class into what can become a powerful force for rational social change."

As a workingman's advocate in northwest Indiana, the CCC has focused its energies against United States Steel, Inland Steel, North Indiana Public Service Company, Illinois Bell, Indiana Bell and General Telephone Company, and smaller corporations on a variety of environmental, consumer, and taxation issues. Through its efforts to reduce voter fraud in Gary and East Chicago, the CCC has raised the level of honesty in local elections.

CCC's structure permits it to deal with several issues, at the same time as its issues are those of its constituent groups. When one group has a particular local problem, the members of other groups can be mobilized to write letters, boycott, demonstrate, and so on.

No one has exerted greater influence on the development of the community organization movement than Saul D. Alinsky and the staff of his Chicago-based Industrial Areas Foundation Training Institute. Alinsky began organizing communities in the 1930s. His most notable success was the Back of the Yards Council in Chicago, which after his departure degenerated into a conservative white neighborhood protective agency. In the late 1950s Alinsky helped form TWO (The Woodlawn Organization) in a large black community on Chicago's South Side. Still a viable organization, it has become a model of effective community participation and organization, taking on Chicago's political machine, its most influential university, and its largest department store. Two graduates of Alinsky's Institute, James Wright and Michael Barnes, were the primary organizers of the Calumet Community

Congress. James Wright, of Irish and Mexican descent, had worked in the steel mills of Gary and been active in union politics and the development of black leadership in Gary in the late 1960s. He became the dominant organizer. Barnes, formerly a Catholic seminarian and grape boycott organizer on the West Coast, joined Wright during the early stages of organizing and remained after Wright moved to Washington, D.C., to lead the community organization division of Monsignor Baroni's Center for Urban Ethnic Affairs.

A close examination of the formation and activities of CCC requires a brief description of Gary, the largest city in northern Indiana and the second largest city in that state.

At the southern end of Lake Michigan, about 20 miles southeast of Chicago's Loop, Gary is the center of the world's second largest steel-producing area. It is a company town. In 1905 Judge Gary of the United States Steel Corporation chose the site as the location for a midwest steel center. To house its labor force, the Gary Land Company, a subsidiary of United States Steel, bought land near the major mill site, subdivided it, laid out the water, gas, and lighting systems, and built and sold homes. A 12-mile strip of lake frontage, including the ports of Gary and Buffington and the huge steel and related industrial complex is owned by United States Steel. In June of 1906 there were 344 people in the newly-created town; in 1960 over 178,000, of whom 39 percent were black. The 1970 census records a population, now over half black, of 175,000.

The white ethnic residential community of Glen Park, annexed in 1909, has recently tried to secede from the city. The census of 1910 showed that 56 percent of Gary's population was foreign-born, with Serbs, Poles, and Croats the most numerous. In 1960 the dominant nationalities among the foreign stock were the Poles, Yugoslavs, Czechs, Mexicans, and Puerto Ricans.

Industry has always dominated Gary. Of the workers residing there in 1960, 77 percent also worked there; another 9 percent worked in neighboring East Chicago. East Chicago, like Gary, is on Lake Michigan and in Lake County, Indiana, and resembles Gary in its socio-economic base and ethnic and racial composition. Gary is of relatively low socio-economic status. In 1960 only 23 percent of its employed males were engaged in white-collar occupations and the median family income was $6,004.

Lastly and most significantly, the steel corporations, as the dominant influence in Gary and northwest Indiana have taken little civic initiative and for decades have tolerated a corrupt political machine. Recently when the public schools were closed and unemployment ran well over 20 percent, they offered little assistance.

The blue-collar workers of northwest Indiana have been flagrantly neglected by their county political machine, the steel manufacturers, and their own union leadership. The union bosses ruled autocratically, concentrated only on mill issues, and ignored neighborhood problems such as clean air, clean water, and inequitable local property taxes. Many of the union bosses are allied with the local political bosses.

The potential alienation of these predominantly white ethnic workers caught the attention of the nation's communications media in 1964 when George Wallace won a substantial vote in Lake County in the Indiana presidential primary. Robert Kennedy offered them hope in 1968, and they gave him a majority of their votes in the 1968 presidential primary, but Humphrey did not inspire in them the same confidence Kennedy did. Wallace captured 16.4 percent of the votes cast in Lake County in the 1968 presidential race. Lake County Wallaceites, according to a study by Thomas F. Pettigrem of Harvard, typically were lower middle-class males with some high school education who highly identified with the working class and felt an acute sense of relative deprivation.

James Wright rejected the national media's image of Lake County's white ethnics as Wallaceites and racists. They were alienated because they were powerless, but they still favored economic reform and social justice. Following the 1968 election, Wright urged the Lake County Inner City Task Force, a coalition of churches working with blacks, to include the white working class in their leadership development and ghetto organizing plans. The clerics reluctantly agreed. At the Task Force's expense, Wright trained for a year at Alinsky's Industrial Areas Foundation Institute. The staff at the Institute teaches trainees the techniques to build, in its words, a "mass power organization." Alinsky graduates organize around what the people want for themselves and their community. They pick issues that are immediate, specific, and realizable. Organized action is always aimed, direct, calculated, and purposeful. Organizers remain within the experience of the people they are organizing. Wright returned to Lake County to work with Michael Barnes. They talked to people in bars, churches, on street corners, in mills, union halls, and shopping centers to identify problems. One of the first controversies Wright readily involved himself in was a labor dispute involving the issue of pollution by Du Pont Chemical in East Chicago. Herbicide wastes, hydrochloric acid, and sulphur dioxide were dumped into shallow holes, discharged into the Calumet River, or pumped into the air. Du Pont management refused to negotiate the union's demand for pollution abatement. Wright mobilized local leaders to enlist community support for the union from organizations such as the Izaak Walton League, the Indiana Save the Dunes Council, and public spirited citizens.

A local leader, a Slovak Catholic priest, was selected, according to Wright, because he was a Slovak, the same background as many of the unionists. Under the leadership of the Slovak priest more than 30 local groups formed the Citizens' League to Upgrade the Environment, joined with the small local of chemical workers, staged demonstrations, circulated literature on the extent of pollution by Du Pont, and badgered company officials. After only a few months Du Pont capitulated, agreeing to a nine-point pollution abatement program.

Other citizens' grievances arose and offered Wright and Barnes opportunities to organize more citizens. A school crisis developed in a Lake County township over the firing of 40 teachers who had been striking to gain recognition as a union. Community support was mobilized for the striking teachers, and citizen interest in the local public schools was aroused generally. Barnes organized homeowners from 17 suburban developments in one township to protest the flooding of their homes, which occurred every spring when a nearby river overflowed its banks and inundated the storm sewers. They pressured the developers into correcting the condition. A large laundromat was discharging pollutants into a small lake. A boycott was organized and the owners of the laundromat were forced to sign an abatement agreement.

Wright and Barnes generally operated behind the scenes. They found concrete problems and indigenous leaders. Most of the first half of 1970 was spent listening to residents of Lake County and developing local leadership and a county-wide network. Any local group greatly enhanced its strength and persuasiveness through such county-wide support. Soon the ad hoc supporting groups needed a permanent umbrella. Wright and Barnes had been supported as Task Force staff until the summer of 1970. Meetings were held to establish the skeleton of what was to be known as the Calumet Community Congress (the "Calumet" designation refers to a larger area than Lake County). Clergymen and church activists worked with Wright and Barnes and provided most of the money for the initial budget. In the fall of 1970 the Catholic Church was the primary source of CCC funding. Later national sources, such as the National Urban Coalition, provided some financial support. Before its founding convention, the Calumet Community Congress had already attracted opposition. John Krupa, Lake County Democratic Party boss, declared that at the root of the CCC "is the godless, atheistic force of communism." Krupa publicly denounced Bishop Andrew Grutka of Gary for endorsing the Congress.

Alinsky organizers have been trained to recognize that the "action is in the reaction." Krupa's repeated attacks gave them the opportunity to personalize and polarize. Krupa became the symbol of opposition to community self-help and people began to take sides—usually with the proposed regional organization. Wright recalls: "You could go anywhere those days—into the bars, the mills, the beauty parlors, the lodge halls, the gas stations, anywhere—and people were talking CCC and practically nothing else."

The strongest citizen participation and support came from the heavily industrialized areas of the county near the lake. The union leadership of the steel workers and other industrial workers in the area have not been enthusiastic about the formation of CCC. The emergence of community leaders outside of the mills threatens the existing union leaders. Moreover, some union officials do not want to jeopardize their friendly relations with management and with the regular county Democratic bosses. The Roman Catholic diocese of Gary, led by Bishop Grutka, provided crucial support and legitimization for the formation of CCC.

The Calumet Community Congress was officially created in December 1970 at a high school in Hammond. Located in Lake County, Hammond borders Gary, East Chicago, and Chicago, and the leading nationalities among the foreign stock in 1960 were Poles, Germans, Czechoslovakians, and Hungarians. Over 1,000 delegates, representing 143 organizations, attended the founding convention. A 62-year-old Scotsman, retired union organizer and picket captain at the 1937 Memorial Day massacre at the Republic Steel Plant in which 10 strikers were killed by the police, chaired the six-hour session. Selection of a Scotsman as chairman, rather than a member of a more recent immigrant group, precluded the arousal of ethnic sentiments. John Esposito, keynote speaker and a Ralph Nader associate, attacked United States Steel for poisoning the air and water in the Lake County region, refusing to abate the pollution, and failing to pay its fair share of local taxes. The delegates included unionists, Democrats, Republicans, clergymen, workers, students, housewives, and a few small business owners and professionals. An official of the 300-man chemical union, which had fought Du Pont on pollution, was elected president by the delegates. Other elected officers were representative of the diversity of the delegates. There were union officials, welfare workers, housewives, working students, clergymen, a cook, a roofer, a municipal employee, and a steel worker. Spanish-American delegates participated but there were only a few black delegates. The latter were generally suspicious. A parallel organization, the Black Alliance, held its founding congress on July 17, 1971, and, like CCC, traced its beginnings to the Lake County Project initiated in 1969 by the Inner City Task Force. The Black Alliance, also organized as a multi-issue structure, planned to develop its own organizational strength and, on certain issues, to ally itself with CCC.

Three days after its formal creation, the senate of CCC organized support for repeal of a variance which had exempted coke-ovens from the air pollution ordinance and which was scheduled to be voted upon by the Gary City Council the following week. United States Steel's coke ovens annually produced and discharged into the air 59,400 tons of air pollutants. This pollution was hazardous to the health of Gary's residents. Before CCC began its lobbying, it counted three councilmen planning to vote for United States Steel, two for repeal of the ordinance, and four undecided. Councilmen received a barrage of telephone calls and letters, newspapers were enlisted and applied pressure, numerous neighborhoods and groups met to voice their opposition to coke-oven pollution and packed the council hall on the night of the council vote. United States Steel lost 9 to 0.

CCC again tangled with United States Steel over the latter's share of state and local taxes. The giant corporation that built Gary has largely prescribed the practices of local taxation and benefitted from underassessments. CCC has also built strong cases of underassessment against Inland and Republic Steel. Inland Steel's Indiana Harbor Works in East Chicago, according to the CCC evaluation, should have been assessed at $20 million more than it was in 1971.

On the consumer front, CCC challenged the giant gas and electric utility, the Northwest Indiana Public Service Company (NIPSCO) and won some concessions. NIPSCO was, according to CCC, bilking customers out of their deposits, arbitrarily calculating rates and indiscriminately shutting off gas and electricity if bills were not paid promptly. CCC held community hearings throughout Lake County to gather grievances against NIPSCO and presented them at the utility's April stockholders' meeting.

While avoiding the endorsement of any political candidates, CCC also has projects on vote fraud (e.g., ghost voters) and political corruption.

Despite some early successes, the future of CCC is uncertain. It has been decentralized as area chapters have been set up throughout the Calumet region. Huge layoffs and serious unemployment in Lake County in 1971 did not enhance organizational growth and maintenance of CCC. James Wright foresees continued "union-busting tactics" to destroy CCC. The efforts to dismantle CCC have emanated largely from United States Steel, with lesser efforts from Democratic county boss Krupa. United States Steel has tried unsuccessfully to dissuade Bishop Grutka from substantially underwriting the Congress.

CCC has filled a vacuum. The traditional intermediate agencies that once served them, the political machine, the settlement houses, the churches and trade unions, have either ceased to function or substantively diminished in their mediating activities. CCC was not built on the basis of ethnic loyalties, but rather organized around issues germane to the mostly working-class residents of Lake County. Ethnic sensitivities were recognized and skillfully handled.

DETROIT'S BLACK-POLISH CONFERENCE — COOPERATION RATHER THAN CONFRONTATION

In Detroit two-thirds of the population is either black (44 percent) or Polish (20 percent), so the two groups necessarily live in close proximity. The city has had a poor record with its race relations. The 1943 race riot in Detroit, in which 34 persons died, was the bloodiest in the United States in the 1940s and 1950s. The black riot of 1967—in which 33 blacks and 10 whites were killed—was one of the worst of the 1960s. Detroit's experience was similar to that of other older Northern industrial cities. Middle-class whites were moving to the suburbs and being replaced by unskilled black migrants.

Against this background, blacks and Poles in Detroit are currently trying to work together. They perceive the city's problems as their own problems and realize that further conflict is counterproductive. The Black-Polish Conference was formed in 1968 to promote the general interest of the blacks and Poles of Greater Detroit and to dispel the myth that black and Polish people are incompatible. While it is still too early to draw conclusions about the success or failure of the Conference, it has survived, it has lessened tensions, it has served to strengthen the political influence of both groups, and it may well be a model for black-white cooperation.

The Black-Polish Conference evolved out of a seminar held on April 10, 1968, at Saints Cyril and Methodius Seminary, Orchard Lake, Michigan, sponsored by the Detroit Archdiocesan Priests' Conference for Polish Affairs. At that time, a resolution of black-Polish social equality was developed and endorsed by the priests at the Conference. The resolution expressed support for open housing and for equal opportunity in employment, education, and the use of public facilities. It moved black Congressman John Conyers, Jr., to invite the co-chairmen of the conference, the Reverends Daniel P. Bogus and Fabian B. Slominski, to Washington, D.C., for further discussion. Discussions between the three led to the idea of an alliance of blacks and Poles of Greater Detroit to advance mutual trust and work toward common goals. The Priests' Conference endorsed this concept. Initial meetings between civic-minded representatives of the two communities began in December 1968 and resulted in the establishment of the Black-Polish Conference. Leon Atchison, then administrative assistant to Congressman Conyers, recalls the first meeting:

> Well, the fur flew at that meeting. All the fears and animosity, the latent and overt hostility were very apparent. It was almost a shouting match. Anyone who was there would have thought it was the end for the Black-Polish Conference.
>
> But it was not the end. The meetings continued, and a healthy respect began to develop. People were candid. They got things out of their system, and the sincere people from both groups stayed. Since then, the conference has weathered some severe storms, and both it and the city of Detroit are the better for it.

Among leaders who actively support the alliance are Polish priests and black ministers, the president of the Polish-American Chamber of Commerce, the head of the local black businessmen's association, university professors and administrators, political figures such as Conyers and, though less enthusiastically, Polish Congressman Lucien Nedzi, civil rights workers, neighborhood organizers, journalists such as Krauewski of the Polish Daily News and Mitchell Lewandowski of the Hamtramck Citizen, leaders of the traditionally conservative Polish-American Congress, and Frank Ditto, head of a militant black organization called the East Side Voice for an Independent Detroit.

In 1971 the Black-Polish Conference had an executive committee comprised of the two co-chairmen, Father Bogus and Congressman Conyers, who alternate in chairing the organization's meetings. To avoid any appearance that the organization is political or church-dominated, both Conyers and Father Bogus have planned eventually to step down as chairmen. A steering committee, comprised of about 45 active members, meets on an average of once every two months. This group handles organizational business and decides what actions the Conference will undertake. Organized on a nonprofit basis, the conference has received some foundation grants to meet its operating budget. Its first major grant was for $50,000 from the Polish Priests' Conference and the New Detroit Corporation. The steering committee became the board of directors with the adoption of a constitution and bylaws. In 1971 three subcommittees were created by the steering committee:

1. Planning—its task is to develop programs and proposals for the board of directors.
2. Communications—headed by Stanley Krajewski, editor of the Polish Daily News, and Longworth Quinn, editor of the Michigan Chronicle. This committee has engineered an exchange of editorials between the two papers; its role is to promote communication between the two communities.
3. Education—its aims are to promote citywide black and Polish support for the ideals embodied in the Black-Polish Conference, through educational efforts in both communities.

Some clerical services and consultation aid is provided by the Archdiocese of Detroit, Human Relations Division. While the Conference has a permanent staff, it is small and relies heavily on volunteers.

In October 1969, the Conference sponsored a "get-together" dinner attended by blacks and Poles. Held at the Polish Century Club on Detroit's northeast side, the banquet brought together 300 black and Polish middle-class businessmen, clergy, and politicians, and was

primarily social. In a single sweep one speaker invoked the now leg-
endary names of two freedom fighters—General Casimir Pulaski of the
American Revolution and Rosa Parks of the Birmingham bus boycott.
The responses to questionnaires distributed at the dinner revealed
overwhelming approval of the concept of an alliance of blacks and Poles
for social, economic, and political advancement. Both groups have
subsequently held other affairs to promote fraternity, trust, and discussion of issues of mutual concern. The Conference tries to dispel old
stereotyping and friction by emphasizing commonalities.

The primary objectives of the Black-Polish Conference are outlined in the Conference's "Statement of Purpose." It reads:

> Two out of every three Detroiters is either Black or Pol-
> ish. Their predominance in the Detroit community should
> result in a great deal of interaction between the two groups.
> The Black and Polish communities often share the same
> neighborhoods, schools, and places of employment. This
> daily contact results in their sharing many of the same
> problems and goals.
>
> Our basic premise is that each community would be
> greatly aided in dealing with these common problems and
> goals if they worked more closely together. The Black-
> Polish Conference of Greater Detroit is, therefore, estab-
> lished for the following purposes:
>   * To promote increased knowledge of the history and
> culture of each community by the other through public meet-
> ings and cultural and educational programs;
>   * To develop and expand the channels of communica-
> tion between the two groups, particularly on matters of
> current community concern, not only between the leader-
> ship, but also between the individuals in each community;
> and
>   * To sponsor specific programs of mutual benefit to
> the Black and Polish communities.

To achieve these objectives the Conference has thus far undertaken numerous programs. A local action program has worked to unite
the civic, cultural, religious, recreational, and social organizations
of each group for concrete solutions to local problems such as personal
security in a neighborhood, garbage collection, and street lighting.
Conference staff encourage integrated meetings at which joint action
to improve local conditions has been undertaken. The staff offers
assistance whenever possible, including assistance to community
organizers, but it leaves the actual leadership to the indigenous leaders
of the cooperating clubs, associations, and churches. Using metropolitan Detroit churches as bases, the citywide Conference, according

to Jerry Ernst, its staff director, attempts to build parallel organizations of blacks and whites—each group mainly concerned with its own issues. When their issues and concerns coincide, they will seek each other's support.

The metropolitan affairs program aims to bring local groups together for a citywide cultural and social exchange. A dinner with a well-known guest as speaker and a reception in which food and entertainment have been furnished by each group exemplify these exchanges. Congressman Conyers goes to Pulaski Day dinners and Father Bogus attends meetings of the Booker T. Washington Businessmen's Association. Both deny that the Conference has been used to advance the political fortunes of the ambitious Conyers or any other black or Polish politician. "It's far too fragile a relationship for that," says Conyers. "We are still in the process of melting hostility."

The newspapers and television media have been encouraged to focus attention on the activities of the Conference. Some materials on black-Polish relations have been printed and distributed. One of these—the Conference newsletter, published periodically—keeps interested parties informed on the current activities of the Conference and provides editorial space for opinions.

Some effort has been made to establish a library and general cultural exchange center for blacks and Poles at the Conference's headquarters. A joint educational program is designed to sensitize each group to the traditions and cultures of the other, as well as to their shared interests. This program includes lectures, workshops, discussion groups, and seminars, and many of the sessions have been integrated.

The early work of the Conference was primarily organizational and crisis-solving. In the spring of 1969 the Republic of New Africa, a black nationalist group with the goal of establishing a separate black nation in the Southeast of the United States, held a convention in Detroit. Two Polish policemen patrolling near the convention were shot—one of them fatally. Police responded by arresting nearly everyone at the Republic of New Africa convention and nearly destroying the church where it was meeting. There were charges by blacks of police brutality, and bitterness began to grow. When a black judge released all the black prisoners against whom there was no substantive evidence—which included nearly everyone arrested—the Poles became increasingly angry and tense. Despite this crisis situation, the Black-Polish Conference met, and the heated exchanges at the meeting did serve to lessen tensions and promote some understanding. The Conference also helped to depolarize the 1969 mayoral election in which a Pole narrowly defeated a black.

While there have been several episodes like the nationalist convention and police killing, Father Bogus has stressed that progress will only come from seeking areas of agreement and common interest. "This, of course, requires some hard organizing and a realistic approach," he says. "You don't accomplish this goal through idealistic pronouncements about brotherhood or the value of good race relations." Among the areas of common interest so far have been elections to the at-large city council, representation on human relations commissions and on school and urban renewal boards, the location of urban renewal sites, garbage dumps, and new highway construction, the design of integrated public housing units, and the delivery and quality of city services. Father Bogus says, "We came together quite naturally around a political goal. We were both opposed to a move to elect Detroit councilmen on a citywide basis rather than a ward basis." Both groups promptly found a common interest on a question of practical politics— the election of Detroit's nine-member Common Council. Under the existing system of at-large elections in which all candidates run citywide, the blacks have two councilmen and the Poles one. If, however, each councilman ran in one district, both groups could increase, perhaps even double, their representation in favorably drawn districts. In Lansing, Polish and black state legislators from Detroit are jointly supporting a bill which would allow that change. They have the support of Conference members at home.

More than 90 local organizations co-sponsored the Second Annual Conference of Ethnic Communities of Greater Detroit, held May 19-23, 1972, at Wayne State University. Among the participants—including several United Auto Workers locals and the American Jewish Committee—was the Black-Polish Conference.

NEWARK'S NORTH WARD CULTURAL AND EDUCATIONAL CENTER

On a class-ethnicity scale set up to measure the influence of these two factors in the community organization movement, the Calumet Community Conference must be placed at the class end. Newark's North Ward Cultural and Educational Center, on the other hand, would fall at the ethnicity end of the scale. Italian and black cultural (or community) ties dominate the latter city's public life. There exists an ethnic polarization rooted in the demographic patterns of the past 20 years. While Irish and Jews have fled Newark, Italian-Americans have remained. Of Newark's North Ward's 100,000 residents, 70,000 are white, 20,000 black, and 10,000 Puerto Rican. More than 85 percent of the whites trace their ancestry to Italy. These Italian-Americans still retain their strong familial ties, prefer the urban enclaves originally settled by their ancestors, and persist in a distrust of those outside their extended families. Beset with many of the ills plaguing other urban minorities, Italian-Americans in Newark have turned inward and organized themselves along ethnic lines. Black and Puerto Rican expansion is perceived as an immediate threat to their life styles, values, and finally their very existence.

Newark's Italians first turned to Tony Imperiale and his North Ward Citizens Committee. This organization was the community's response to the Newark riot and the violence of the 1960s. Imperiale answered the inhabitants' demands for security. The Committee patrolled Italian-American neighborhoods nightly and made patently clear to blacks that they were not welcome there.

In the late 1960s another alternative for the Italians emerged in the person of Steve Adubato and his North Ward Cultural and Educational Center. Adubato first won the chairmanship of the North Ward Democratic Party in 1969. Two years later he beat Tony Imperiale for the same position. The North Ward Cultural and Educational Center owes its formation and existence largely to the efforts of Adubato. While he and the Center are devoted full-time to developing programs for the working-class communities of the North Ward, the primary beneficiaries are the Italian-Americans. The Center enlisted the help of 10 community aides to survey neighborhoods, identify leaders and issues, and explore program possibilities. It could easily become an ethnic organizational model because of the heavy concentration of Italian-Americans, and because it is forming a federation of local organizations. Currently, its program efforts have focused on the problems of education, drugs, and the old people in the neighborhoods. Adubato, a schoolteacher for fifteen years, supported the striking teachers during the 11-week strike in early 1971. He correctly perceived the important strike issues as a clash between certain black leaders, intent on destroying the union's power, and teacher unionists. He is concerned that Italian-Americans who have "waited their turn" in the school system of Newark will be deprived of promotions to the better jobs of administrators and principals, and asks why the rules of the game (ethnic succession) should be changed now that the Italians have earned higher positions.

THE NATIONAL HOUSING CONFERENCE: A NATIONAL
COALITION OF COMMUNITY ORGANIZATIONS

The sign covering the rear wall of the auditorium of St. Sylvester's Elementary School read "PEOPLE'S POLITICS CAN MAKE THE DIFFERENCE." Acting on this slogan, representatives of 228 community organizations from 50 cities convened the National Housing Conference in a deteriorating white ethnic community of Chicago. Held on March 18 and 19, 1972, the convention can best be characterized

as a desperate effort by these urban representatives to save their
communities. Father Ahern's invocation pleaded "We, the people, ask
for decent housing and secure homes." Gale Cincotta, a Chicago house-
wife and community organizer as well as the dominant indigenous force
in organizing and coordinating the convention, sounded the rallying cry
with her welcoming remarks:

> Chicago is my city. For others, it's Detroit or Philadel-
> phia. The city is our life. We don't want to live anywhere
> else. No one is going to push us out, whether it be gov-
> ernment, realtors, or the big money combines who think
> they are controlling our lives. What for so long have been
> considered natural phenomena—changing neighborhoods and
> deteriorating cities—are not natural. It's a plan and some-
> body is making a lot of money out of changing neigh-
> borhoods.

She concluded: "What in the hell are we going to do about it?"

Urban populism dominated this convention of over 1,000 white
ethnics, blacks, and Spanish-Americans. Committed to preserving
their neighborhoods and to reforming existing housing programs, the
three groups remained under the same roof for two days and cooperated with one another.

Delegates, while largely from the older industrial cities of the
Northeast and Great Lakes region, came from cities in 24 states and
the District of Columbia to voice their grievances against governmental
and private housing practices directly affecting their communities.
These survivors of the cities are wrestling to control their own destinies rather than abandoning them to the feeble hands of elective
officials and the greed of real estate profiteers. These urban stay-
behinds in the flight to suburban affluence are angry. Some cannot
afford to flee, others prefer to live in the city. They blame incompetent
governmental agencies and fast-buck realtors, mortgage houses, and
insurance companies for expanding slum housing and resegregating
their neighborhoods. FHA provides the subsidies, and with one hand
mortgage houses withdraw the availability of conventional loans and with
the other indiscriminately grant FHA loans. Insurance companies zone
the changing neighborhoods as "high risk" and charge prohibitive
premiums, and realtors all but steal their last asset—their home—with
scare tactics and panic peddling.

Monsignor Geno Baroni, director of the National Center for Urban
Ethnic Affairs and the emerging national spokesman for ethnic America, presented to the delegates the purposes and reasons for the Chicago
gathering—to sensitize established institutions to their problems; to
develop community organizations and leaders as an alternative to

demagogues; to bring white ethnics, blacks, and Spanish-Americans together to promote cooperation, coalition, and group action; to involve people in their own problems so that they will substitute hope and action for despair and alienation; to develop new rhetoric, strategies, and directions for urban America; and, in Baroni's words, "to get the workers and poor organized by building leadership from the bottom up and then forming a national network." Baroni's inspiration ignited his audience. He concluded: "This is our day, the people's day, let us restore our faith in ourselves and work together."

Baroni's National Center for Urban Ethnic Affairs is committed to the advancement of the ethnic movement. It co-sponsored and underwrote most of the expenses for the National Housing Conference. Baroni plans other national conferences on the problems of the urban working class, and the National Center for Urban Ethnic Affairs is providing financial aid and expertise to existing community organizations in eight older industrial cities of the North. The Center has been recognized by mainstream leaders as a legitimate spokesman for white ethnic America. The Ford Foundation has granted more than $600,000 to the Center. Baroni discussed with President Nixon urban ethnic problems and has lobbied on Capitol Hill for a bill to provide federal money for ethnic studies.

The new white ethnic minority is, in part, reacting to intensified black assertion and to economic stagnation and social and cultural disruptions that have recently affected their lives. They now demand an audience and a voice and want to influence public policy where their interests are at stake. Black successes have served to stimulate and promote emulation. White ethnic Americans are now calling for their own special programs, subsidies, and tax breaks.

Does it follow that white ethnic assertion and its black counterpart produce severe racial clashes and, indeed, intensify racial confrontations? This chapter in American history, for the most part, is unsettled, though the last decade has witnessed a certain amount of violent competition between white ethnics and blacks for jobs, schools, and neighborhoods. While racial and ethnic conflict permeated the activities of the two-day National Housing Conference, the dominant interest was in the well-being and stability of the neighborhoods inhabited by the delegates. Group styles were varied and old hostilities surfaced, but the delegates agreed that cooperation among white ethnics, blacks, and Spanish-Americans was imperative if their neighborhoods were to be saved. Despite sharp disagreement between the residents of previously stable all-white ethnic communities and the representatives of poor black and Spanish-Americans who need to expand their ghettos, no delegates walked out of the convention and majority rule prevailed.

Almost all of the delegates fell into the $5,000 to $10,000 income category and their socio-economic class, coupled with their common concern on the issues of decent housing and safe neighborhoods, held them together. The villians were FHA, HUD Secretary George Romney, and public and private housing bureaucrats. When an executive vice-president of a large mortgage bank denied that his firm profited from FHA transactions, he was nearly booed off the stage.

Given the white ethnic sponsors and setting of the convention, there seemed a distinct possibility that it would develop into a racist organization to impede black and Spanish-American residential "invasions." While the National Center for Urban Ethnic Affairs provided money and organizational assistance, it was the white ethnics of Chicago's West Side Coalition who made the convention possible. The West Side Coalition, a loose umbrella organization of 41 community organizations, claims to represent 500,000 residents of Chicago's West Side, and over the past year and a half of its existence has concerned itself with housing and real estate abuses. The Coalition is dominated by the Northwest Community Organization, Our Lady of the Angels, and Organization for a Better Austin. A major interest of these three predominately white ethnic organizations is to keep poor blacks and Spanish-Americans out of their community, for these are perceived as a threat to the stability of their neighborhoods and their life styles. Indeed, the dominant groups of the West Side Coalition called for the most critical vote of the convention on their resolution to declare a six-month moratorium on further FHA mortgage loans. Despite their legitimate complaints about FHA abuses, blacks and Spanish-Americans correctly saw that the moratorium resolution adversely affected them and allied themselves with young and poor white delegates narrowly to defeat it. No debate or vote at the convention raised the passions of the delegates to a higher level. Though implicit all along, the FHA issue became defined in racial and ethnic terms. Following this vote on the evening of the first night, the leadership of the West Side Coalition lost the dominant influence it had held over the convention. It seemed to drift toward an uncertain future. It was not until noon of the second day that leaders caucused to plan for the remaining hours of the convention and for organizational follow-up. The West Side Coalition leaders recommended a last minute idea for a follow-up committee consisting of elected representatives from each HUD region, a proposal that had not been conceived until the morning of the second day. It was negatively received by Walter Brooks of the Northeast Community Organization of Baltimore. Brooks persuasively countered with a suggestion that each delegation appoint one of its own members to meet in late April in another city, such as Baltimore. His proposal was approved at the caucus and later on the floor of the convention.

Brooks emerged as the convention's most significant leader. While he demonstrated exceptional leadership, Brooks, a 39-year-old black, also became a symbol of black and white cooperation. After taking over temporarily for the chairman designated for the first day and immediately demonstrating his parliamentary skills, he remained chairman for the duration of the convention, of whose 1,000 delegates less than 10 percent were black. He controlled the body of delegates with authority and the appearance of impartiality and handled the business of the convention efficiently, despite the frequent unruliness of delegates. When all three dominant white ethnic organizations from the West Side Coalition disputed his judgment about the negative majority for the moratorium vote, he satisfied the three groups by calling one of their members to the stage to see for herself. Brooks not only chaired the general meetings of the convention but also dominated the leadership caucus which arranged for future continuity. When a Spanish-American realtor with ties to one of Mayor Daley's political lieutenants, who is also active in real estate, arranged for 25 pickets with signs to march in front of the convention site registering their strong disapproval of the "racist" gathering, it was Brooks who reasoned with him to join the convention, air his objection, propose resolutions, and then walk out if he was not satisfied. But the picket leader's objectives were not to be served by participation or accommodation.

At the conclusion of the conference the delegates were nearly unanimous in voicing their praise of Brooks as their chairman, many giving him a standing ovation. This black leader and the black delegates had an influence at the convention that was disproportionate to their numbers. The less than 100 black delegates took more than one-third of the debate time, and were more sure of their positions and more articulate in expressing themselves. All of this indicates, as well as a genuinely open and democratic convention, their growing political sophistication and their years of experience in the assertion of their interests.

By contrast the white ethnic movement, as it has come to be called and as it expressed itself at the National Housing Conference, seemed in its infancy. Most white delegates were Polish, Italian, Irish, Lithuanian, and Ukrainian-Americans, and their limited unity was expressed in the commonality of their race, their Roman Catholicism, and a socio-economic position somewhat higher than that of the blacks and Spanish-Americans. A few Lutheran ministers attended, but the more than 20 Roman Catholic priests exerted a strong influence at the convention. Monsignor Baroni was the keynote speaker, four or five priests were among the leaders of the West Side Coalition, a priest gave the invocation, another introduced Mayor Daley, and still another introduced Senator Fred Harris. Priests moderated panels and led workshops.

Only one of the 228 community groups—the Polish-American Citizens—was explicitly organized along ethnic lines. During debates on the convention floor only one or two delegates referred to particular ethnic groups, white ethnics as a whole, blacks, or Spanish-Americans. It would be erroneous, however, to say that ethnic and racial loyalties were of minimal importance. Though difficult to assess, strong undercurrents of ethnic and racial feeling flowed through the activity of the convention. Blacks and Spanish-Americans held numerous caucuses for their own groups. However, when white delegates met, their black and Spanish-American delegation members were included. Delegations were internally segregated on the convention floor along racial lines. Most Spanish-American delegations were Puerto Rican, some Mexican-American. No all-black delegation was in evidence, and most blacks were not from Chicago. Many of the blacks present seemed to embrace a middle-class ideology and few called for black separatism. One multiracial group from a middle-class community in the Kansas City area advanced a resolution, the effect of which would be to discourage FHA support of existing homes in the community, that is, would lessen the flow of poorer blacks into their community.

The Spanish-American delegations, as a group, were insecure as participants at the convention. Though outnumbering the blacks, their insecurity and distrust surfaced immediately as they demanded that all important remarks be repeated in Spanish, a virtually impossible task given the overloaded schedule, and highly impractical besides given the small number of people actually unable to understand English. Skillfully avoiding a majority rejection, the convention tabled their motion and some key statements and resolutions were translated into Spanish. During the heated debates concerning the translation both black and white spokesmen quickly recognized and warned what a Spanish walkout would mean—the "little people" were fighting among themselves and "big business" stood to benefit from their divisions. The outburst and tacit threat of a walkout dramatized Spanish-American self-consciousness but strategically meant that for the remainder of the Convention they would not go unnoticed.

The Convention was in session for more than sixteen hours, passed more than a dozen resolutions, held seven workshops, and conducted panels on real estate abuses, insurance, FHA, and mortgages. As though to demonstrate that democracy is a messy business, delegates who wanted to speak lined up in front of the five microphones evenly distributed throughout the floor of the convention and were each allowed three minutes. With few exceptions, delegates were not interrupted as they spoke and many revealed a high level of sophistication. Too often, however, this procedure meant the mechanical recognition by the chair of a delegate, intense advocacy for three minutes, and then the recognition of another delegate and advocacy or comment on a different point. The marvel was that so much diversity, frustration, and resentment could be packed into an overcrowded auditorium and remain together for over two days without exploding.

A clever organizational stroke was the deployment of a Spanish-American high school ROTC group as ushers. In full uniform, they ushered, counted votes, excluded the uninvited, and had an opportunity to participate in an American tradition—a national convention.

The convention was deliberately scheduled three days before the Illinois electoral primary. Two Democratic presidential candidates, five senators, four congressmen, and Mayor Richard J. Daley appeared and addressed the delegates. Organizers were criticized for giving them too much time, but the politicians were generally well received. The delegates listening courteously, but by the second day of the convention they grew impatient with the politicians to whom they felt the conference had provided a forum while eliciting no specific gains. Showing his usual caution, Chicago's Mayor Daley did not commit himself to attend until one week before the convention. Daley's appeal to white ethnics was apparent. He spoke unchallenged. The delegates were honored with his presence. They knew that he had blocked scattered public housing sites in the all-white neighborhoods of Chicago and nodded with approval as he blamed the housing crisis on the federal government, thus exonerating himself.

Senator Muskie's failure to accept his invitation offended many delegates. A West Side Coalition news release said, "Muskie feels the crisis of the urban centers in Chicago and America is not a major campaign issue."

Senators George McGovern and Fred Harris were received most enthusiastically. McGovern suggested the relocation of large numbers of blacks and some whites in satellite communities in vacant areas outside the cities.

While George Wallace's name and resistance to busing school children were only mentioned by the political speakers and aroused little sympathy among the delegates, Wallace has been increasingly perceived by many as a populist alternative, in part perhaps because he is a segregationist, but more because he purports to speak for the "little people," those urban dwellers threatened by economic and social strangulation.

Specific promises and tangible concessions from the politicians were infrequent. David Borden, national Democratic Party committeeman of the Pre-Platform Committee on Housing, accepted an invitation, excused his failure to appear on grounds of illness, and sent no one in his stead. No demands have been made yet on his party's national committee.

The delegates are justified in their complaints against real estate interests and the FHA. A recently concluded study in Boston of federally subsidized housing revealed that nearly half of the subsidy money is pocketed by middlemen for their services and goes for administrative expenses. The study was conducted by the Joint Center for Urban Studies of MIT and Harvard University for the Housing Sub-committee of the House Banking and Currency Committee. In 1971 more than 500,000 housing units, about a quarter of the total housing production, were built or rehabilitated with federal assistance. Addressing the National Housing Conference, Congressman Wright Patman, chairman of the banking committee, criticized the real estate interests involved in federal housing assistance: "There's a little bit for the land speculator, the builder, the lender, the closing attorney, the title company, the insurance company and so on down the line. . . . After all these years we really don't seem to have what can be honestly regarded as a coherent national policy on housing." HUD Secretary Romney even criticizes the housing subsidy programs administered by him. On February 22, before the Subcommittee on Housing of the House Committee on Banking and Currency, he stated: "Shady get rich quick schemes have involved some real estate salesmen, some build-ers, some developers, and even some housing authorities who lined their pockets with 'sweat money' and even the food money of unsophis-ticated home buyers and renters." In January, at a meeting of the National Association of Home Builders, he acknowledged that graft exists "even in FHA."

Though the convention was conceived and organized in less than three months, it accomplished its primary purposes and was a success in the eyes of its sponsors. The need for federal reform of housing and FHA programs was dramatized. Receiving nationwide press cov-erage, the convention momentarily caught the public's attention. Two days after the convention, the HUD regional director for the Midwest announced that his office was going to require strict enforcement of FHA guidelines in the financing of existing structures.

The National Housing Conference has nationalized the housing movement by establishing a loose federation of 228 community organizations from across the nation. The convention legitimized the follow-up activities of the steering committee. During her opening remarks, convention coordinator Gale Cincotta urged, "Let's make this our corporate board here in Chicago. Let's declare war on the forces that are destroying our cities." One delegate from each organization was elected to form a steering committee authorized to act on behalf of the National Housing Convention. A meeting of the steering committee was formally scheduled for April 29 and 30, 1972, in Baltimore. This representative committee will determine future strategy. At its first meeting immediately following the adjournment of the convention, the committee proposed demands for congressional and federal grand jury investigations of HUD and FHA practices, and meetings with HUD Secretary Romney and President Nixon. Regular convention delegates had discussed the possibility of sending a national housing delegation to each of the political conventions of the two major parties.

The growing community organization and housing movements— the new urban populism—reflect the failure of existing governments at all levels, but—like populist impulses generally—their programs and goals are too vague. While the convention passed more than 12 resolutions, they were too sweeping and often contradictory, and no agreement on an agenda of goals was reached before adjournment.

6

THE EMERGENCE
OF ETHNIC POLITICS
IN THE 1960s

INTRODUCTION

The concept of ethnic politics has captured the national consciousness. The activities of the black caucus and the national
Spanish-origin coalition as well as the national debate in 1971 over
the candidacy of a black for the presidency or vice-presidency have
contributed greatly to the growing national interest in ethnic politics,
but there is much more involved than black and Latin assertion and
the reaction which it generates. Among the primary developments
have been the loosening of ethnic ties to the Democratic Party and
the emergence of ethnic leaders whose bases of power have been their
ethnic constituencies. Moreover, in the 1970s Samuel Lubell's
thesis on middle-class political assertion by nationality groups,
developed in his The Future of American Politics, became manifest.
As white ethnic groups, such as Italian and Polish, have increased
their representation in the middle class, and as their leaders improved
their political skills, they have demanded more political power and
prestige.

Lubell compared the Irish Democratic urban bosses to the
wearied heads of the British Empire, who were everywhere on the
defensive before the rising "nationality" element they once ruled.
Italian-Americans offer a good example of the unruly element. The
Irish preceded them in the United States and dominated the political
organizations of the great majority of the cities of the industrial
North. In New York City, Providence, and New Haven, Italians,
dissatisfied with their political advancement, have turned to the
Republican Party as the only alternative. In New York City the Jews
struggled for years with the Irish for control of the Democratic Party,
and many of them finally resorted to forming the Liberal Party.

The Democratic Party now appears to be the party of racial minorities rather than of the lower middle-class, organized labor, and the "forgotten" American. Moreover, Democrats suffer from bitter internal conflicts and divided leadership.

Growing prosperity has encouraged political independence. Ticketsplitting has become a mark of political sophistication among middle-class voters. Political strategists have thus grown increasingly uncertain of the ethnic vote. The Republican Party is putting forth an unprecedented effort to win the support of white ethnics and Roman Catholics, as the erosion of the old New Deal coalition gives them an opportunity to win new allies. The Republican strategy in the 1970 congressional and gubernatorial elections revealed a systematic effort to appeal to the racial resentments of urban white ethnics and the social conservatism of Catholics.

Emotions have been aroused among ethnic Americans by party rivalry for support based on cold war rhetoric and promises. The Republicans still make the "captive nations" appeal, based on Franklin Roosevelt's alleged betrayal of Eastern and Central European nations at the Yalta Conference. The Republicans have assumed a strong anticommunist posture and remind Americans who trace their ancestry to captive nations of the Democrats' failure to respond when Russia invaded Hungary and Czechoslovakia. A significant number of Americans whose native lands are under Soviet domination still blame the Democratic Party for the Yalta Agreement and believe the Republicans offer more hope for the eventual liberation of their homelands. Liberation of the captive nations is most important to the post-World War II refugees from those countries. Democrats appear to some to be "soft" on communism and tolerant of leftist radicalism.

IMMIGRANT AND NATIONALITY GROUP POLITICS

Immigrant politics was manipulative and dependent upon a non-English-speaking, docile, working class who traded their votes for petty favors, jobs, and social welfare legislation. The nationality-group politics of the 1940s and 1950s sought to "hold" or "swing" the electoral support of nationality groups "en bloc" by foreign policy promises and concessions and by nationality-group recognition. This was the period when previously weak ethnic groups gained political potency. The voting blocs of Poles, Italians, and Jews, according to Nathan Glazer, were never so important as in the 1940s and 1950s, from two to three decades after the end of mass immigration. Recognition during this period took the form of minor nominations and appointments, and token but well publicized public statements, resolutions, proclamations, and appearances. National independence days

and other nationality-group holidays were recognized by state legisla-
tures, Congress, and the president.

At the city politics level, the distribution of nominations and
appointments—the balanced ticket in its broadest sense—reflected the
gradual increase of political power among groups such as the Italians,
Jews, and Poles. When the Democratic Irish were too slow in sharing
their political power, these groups and others turned to the Republican
Party at the local and, at times, the state and national levels to demand
their share of political power. It was in Rhode Island and New York
that French-Canadians and Italian-Americans, and in New Mexico a
Spanish-American, were elected to Congress as Republicans—each
the first of his ethnic group to attain high political position. Italian-
Americans in the industrial North have turned time and again to the
Republican Party as their only vehicle for political advancement.

At the federal level politicians made an occasional foreign
policy promise in deference to nationality-group politics. President
Eisenhower's rhetoric was strongly anticommunist and in favor of
liberation of the captive nations, but the president was, incidentally,
uncomfortable in this stance and a reluctant practitioner of nationality-
group politics. Until the 1960s, the latter remained essentially an
aspect of city politics.

HISTORICAL PERSPECTIVE

Since the earliest days of the republic, American politicians
have built constituencies based in part on ethnic appeals. By 1850
almost all naturalized male citizens had the right to vote, and immigrant groups found that group solidarity at the polls put their candidates
in office. German immigrants advanced by helping to organize the
Republican Party and by contributing the votes critical to the election
of Abraham Lincoln in 1860. Most Irish stayed in the cities, joined
the Democratic Party, and soon were able by virtue of their numbers
and political skills to capture the urban political machines. In
Boston, the minority Democratic Party solicited the votes of Irish
immigrants during the 1880s and 1890s to gain power, and later the
Republicans tried the same strategy among Italian immigrants in an
effort to oust the Democrats. For the Irish and for subsequent immigrant groups, ward and city politics were the route to social, economic, and political advancement. "Excluded from society because
of their religion and class, the Irish took employment with municipal
government and identified with and captured power in the urban
Democratic parties. . . . Urban government became their preserve,
an Irish occupational enclave that gave sharper focus to their presence. . . ." (Edward M. Levine, The Irish and Irish Politicians, 1966,
p. 138).

Beginning in the 1880s, immigration from Central, Eastern, and Southern Europe—the so-called new immigration—ended the possibility that America would become a predominantly homogeneous community. Between 1900 and 1921, the years of peak immigration, more than 10 million people moved to the United States from these areas of Europe. The ethnic composition of America was massively changed. Americans of British ancestry, by the time of the severely restrictive immigration legislation of the 1920s, no longer constituted the overwhelming majority of the population, as they had before 1850. It was not until the late 1920s that the economic and political supremacy of the original settlers was seriously challenged at the national level. The newcomers had been occupied with learning the language, absorbing the culture, earning a living, and participating in local politics in their ethnic enclaves. In national politics, most of the new immigrants gravitated toward the Democratic Party. Except in the South, the Republican Party became the party of American Protestantism. It was the party which drew some strength from the nativists, opposed public aid to Catholic schools, favored prohibition, restrictive immigration, slow and difficult naturalization laws, and exclusionist election qualifications. The white population of the South, however, was overwhelmingly Democratic, of old Protestant stock, and, allied with rural voters from the North, controlled Democratic Party affairs nationally until the 1920s. But gradually the center of power within the Democratic Party shifted from the rural, southern and heartland, Protestant, and "dry" wing to the urban, eastern, Catholic, and "wet" faction, largely because the new immigration swelled the numbers of the latter faction. The shift was reflected in the political career of Alfred E. Smith.

Smith was born in New York City. An Irish Roman Catholic, educated in parochial schools, he advanced through ward and city politics to the governorship of New York State, an office which he held for four terms through. In 1924, he sought the Democratic presidential nomination and lost,.but only after he was deadlocked with William Gibbs McAdoo through 100 ballots. By 1928 he had consolidated his strength and become the champion of the newer ethnocultural groups, most of whom resided in the Northeast and in the industrial states of the Midwest. He easily captured his party's presidential nomination in that year. The positions of the two major national parties on the ethnocultural issues of the 1920s—prohibition, immigration, and the Ku Klux Klan—gave the Democrats decisive majorities.

Catholics settled in the cities and metropoli while the Protestants dispersed disproportionately throughout rural areas, small towns, and the South. Ethnic segregation characterized the large American cities and contributed greatly to the increase of ethnic politics. The

Democratic Party became increasingly the political vehicle of
Catholics, immigrants, and city dwellers and assumed a working-
class character. The large bloc of Protestant votes delivered to
Herbert Hoover in the 1928 Presidential election and the sizable
majority of Catholic votes which went to Alfred Smith demonstrated
the strength of the religious issue in American politics. Smith
symbolized the recognition, acceptance, and legitimacy that the
Democratic Party felt Catholic white ethnics deserved. Years later
the New Deal was perceived by the religio-ethnic minorities as a
program for their benefit. Catholics were, in fact, among the groups
benefiting most from Roosevelt's social welfare legislation. The
New Deal also elevated their political and social status. Ethnic groups
were brought into the American political community and, at last,
could effectively take part in national politics. The ethnic bloc vote
and balanced ticket were no longer only urban dynamics. The election
of John F. Kennedy in 1960 reflected the persistence of America's
heterogeneity. Roosevelt had recognized and vitalized religio-ethnic
group assertion and made political use of it. Kennedy made identification with religio-ethnic groups respectable. Religion, it appeared,
was a more important factor than class differences in the 1960
Presidential election. Pollsters estimated that in the East three-
fourths of the Protestants voted for Richard M. Nixon and three-
fourths of the Catholics for Kennedy. One study concluded that
Kennedy's religion cost him 1.5 million votes. In the 1968 presidential
election, in which religion was not an issue, voting patterns, for the
most part, were typical of those of pre-1960 elections. A majority
of Northern white Protestants returned to the Republican candidate,
while a majority of Catholics chose the Democrat, though some
Catholics, because of frustration over their unanswered needs, turned
to George Wallace.

SHIFTING PARTY ALLEGIANCE

The extent to which Catholic Democratic families will continue
to transmit their political allegiance is problematic. In the late 1960s
and early 1970s traditional party loyalty was greatly weakened by
intense group conflict, in which group self-interest was asserted and
advanced by means of the ballot. Various groups have begun to
perceive their best interests in terms of more concrete concessions
and gains than are offered in the traditional alliances with big business
or labor. Electoral group history and studies of political inheritance
have established that party loyalty within the family is a powerful
force in the perpetuation of religio-ethnic voting patterns. The
Republicans believe they stand a good chance of capturing a Catholic

majority in the 1972 presidential election and are actively seeking
Catholic votes. There has occurred a great change in the historical
conditions that originally led religio-ethnic minorities to lend their
electoral support to the Democratic Party. Immigration is no longer
a dominant factor. Social class is no longer so closely related to
Protestant, Jewish, or Catholic affiliations. Ethnic groups may differ
on the socio-economic scale, but the differences are much less
pronounced, and movement upwards on the scale is less difficult.
The residence of religio-ethnic groups is shifting and is now dispersed
and suburban, not segregated and urban. In the early and mid-1960s
religion seemed to have lost its salience as a source of group conflict.
Most Catholics no longer feel like outsiders. Group self-consciousness
and solidarity have diminished with lessening external antagonisms.
Some Republican strategists view these changing conditions as an
indication that the majority of voters of the religio-ethnic minorities
are no longer committed to the Democratic Party. They argue that
these Catholic white ethnics are no longer forced to rely upon the
Democrats for their economic and status needs. Their improved
socio-economic position has given them the sense of being contributors
to rather than beneficiaries of the civil rights and poverty legislation
of the 1960s. The Republicans cite the election as governor of an
Anglo-Saxon Protestant in Rhode Island in 1962, 1964, and 1966 despite
a Catholic population heavier than in any other state. Republican
strategist Kevin Phillips includes Catholic Americans as an important
segment of "the emerging Republican majority." (The Emerging
Republican Majority, pp. 83-88.) Phillips asserts that the Republican
Party has become the party of the "people—the white working-class
and middle class." The Republicans correctly perceived that the major
weakness in the Democratic majority coalition was the Democratic
position on race relations. The white South and predominately ethnic
urban North were directly affected by the black gains of the 1960s and
manifested growing disaffection with the liberal Democratic establishment. The New Deal had allied the blacks and whites from the South
and urban North to meet their common economic needs resulting
from the Depression. World War II had prolonged the coalition, as
Americans united to fight common external enemies. By the 1960s
a pattern of racial conflict was emerging. George Wallace capitalized
on the fears and resentments of the South and urban North. In 1964
he received a significantly large Democratic primary vote in Indiana
and Wisconsin, especially in the Gary and Milwaukee areas. According
to one 1968 election study, the party identification of whites and
blacks in cities of 50,000 or more in 1968 revealed diminishing
Democratic support by urban whites: Democrats 39.4 percent,
Republicans 22.0 percent, and independents 38.6 percent. White ethnic
Democrats reacted to black assertion and black political gains by

supporting such racially conservative whites as Louise Day Hicks in Boston, Mario Procaccino in New York, Samuel Yorty in Los Angeles, Charles Stenvig in Minneapolis, Ralph Perk in Cleveland, and Frank Rizzo in Philadelphia. White ethnics from urban America revealed their discontent with the Democratic Party in the presidential election of 1968. Richard Nixon won 53 percent of the white two-party vote in cities of 50,000 or more. The congressional and gubernatorial elections of 1970 demonstrated more about the loyalty of urban voters to the Democrats when an economic crisis seemed imminent, than it did about the direction of disaffected white voters from the South and urban North. The appeals of the Republican Party to these voters is still a deliberate strategy whose success has yet to be determined.

ETHNIC POLITICS

During the 1960s nationality-group politics became known as ethnic politics. The period was ushered in with the election of a third-generation Irish Catholic, a skillful practitioner of ethnic politics. John Kennedy's chief political strategist, John M. Bailey, was an accomplished ethnic politician. Bailey had mastered the art of ethnic politics as he rose through the political ranks in Connecticut. As late as 1960, more than 38 percent of that state's population consisted of immigrants and their children. Kennedy and Bailey were fully committed to rewarding and recognizing the white ethnic groups, blacks, and Latins for their electoral support. At this time also, the Lubell thesis was manifesting itself. More and more members of ethnic and racial minorities were rising to the middle classes, and this emergence together with their increasingly skillful leadership, demanded social, economic, and political advancement. The Lubell thesis may well have been one of the most influential factors in the new ethnic politics of the 1960s.

At least four books appeared in the 1960s on the subject of ethnic politics. The few previous books on the subject had been concerned with the political behavior of politicians in relation to immigrants and their children and had used such terms as foreign language groups, immigrant groups, and nationality groups.

Of course, the unprecedentedly rapid social and political progress of the blacks during the 1960s accounts, in a large measure, for white ethnic assertion in the late 1960s. Blacks were recognized as a distinct group and made substantial gains within the political structure. Such success served to stimulate and promote emulation by other minority groups. The government listened to black demands and responded with a poverty program, jobs, key nominations and appointments, neighborhood economic development programs, black history and cultural studies subsidies. White ethnics demanded a voice and similar benefits from special programs, subsidies, and tax breaks. They persuasively reminded politicians that the last legislation to benefit the working-class white ethnic was the GI Bill of Rights after World War II, which was also the first since the Social Security Act. Organizations such as Monsignor Baroni's Center for Urban Ethnic Affairs had begun to consult and petition government agencies— HUD, OEO, HEW, the Department of Commerce, and the Department of Labor—for programs for white ethnic communities. Baroni and other Catholic leaders met with President Nixon to discuss the problems of their communities.

Ethnic consciousness was formerly encouraged in the churches and social and fraternal organizations, and by local ethnic politicians. Ethnic organizations were first formed to serve the basic needs of the immigrants—for example, insurance for disability, death, and burial. These early organizations were protective, defensive, and tried to preserve cultural heritages. They have generally passed from the American urban scene, and those that remain have had to emphasize insurance programs, as well as their "influence" on American foreign policy. Membership in the Polish National Alliance and similar organizations declined considerably during the 1960s. Moreover, the number of foreign language newspapers has declined but English language substitutes are infrequent. Added to these trends, immigration has been reduced to a mere trickle compared with the waves of new immigrants who flooded the cities of the Northeast and Great Lakes states from 1880 until 1924. The percentage of United States foreign-born and foreign-stock citizenship is currently the lowest in America's history.

It is against this contradictory background that one appreciates the strength of ethnic consciousness in politics in the 1960s and early 1970s. Despite these trends, appeals to ethnic and racial groups as distinct groups at all levels of government, especially at the national level, have become more explicit and intricate. As the melting pot ideal has lost its influence and credibility, politicians have begun to recognize ethnic and racial groups in the same way they have always recognized the farm vote, labor constituency, the Chamber of Commerce group vote, the veterans' vote, and so on.

DEFINITION AND BACKGROUND

The old formula of the New Deal no longer suffices since white ethnics insist upon recognition. But a politician takes an ethnic group seriously only if he believes the group represents a bloc of votes and can be persuaded to vote as such. Building a constituency and eventually a winning coalition requires the combination of different groups. An ethnic group must regard itself as a discrete group, one composed of immigrants and their descendants. To be significant, it must have a political organization and recognized spokesmen. The organization may have specific and avowed political purposes, as does the Lithuanian Democratic League, or may be a nominally non-political organization, such as the Polish National Alliance. The test, however, of a group's thinking and acting politically as a group should not be rigid organizational criteria. Lastly, and most important from the group's point of view, it must carry enough weight to make demands upon political parties for nominations, appointments, jobs, and status recognition.

Ethnic patterns in voting behavior are, in the final analysis, an expression of the culture and traditions of the group. Samuel Lubell summed it up when he declared at the Conference on Group Life in America, held under the auspices of the American Jewish Committee in November 1965: "Ethnic groups do not now—if they every did—act simply as cohesive blocs. Rather, their influence is exerted through common group consciousness, through traditions which enable them to view developing issues from a common point of view."

ETHNIC REPRESENTATION IN CONGRESS

There is not much systematic evidence of ethnic voter behavior. But what little there is suggests that certain ethnic groups vote as such, and that it is therefore possible to influence them by appeals to their ethnicity. The factoring out of variables such as class, religion, and party allegiance is difficult, but it has been demonstrated that some white ethnic groups do vote either for or against a candidate on the basis of his ethnic or racial origin. Ethnic voters usually prefer candidates like themselves in their ethnic background and religion. Of the 50 congressmen incumbent in 1964 from districts designated by the 1960 census as highest in foreign-stock concentration, 34 had surnames associated with the major ethnic group in their district. The appeal of a third-generation Irish Catholic, John F. Kennedy, among foreign-stock voters is reflected in the 1960 presidential election, in which he carried 38 of these 50 districts while Richard Nixon carried only 12. The religious affiliation of the 50 congressmen incumbent in 1964 representing these districts mirrors the strong Roman Catholicism and Judaism of their foreign-stock constituencies. The religious affiliation of congressmen from the top 50 foreign-stock districts compares with all House members in 1964 as follows:

	Top 50 Foreign-Stock Districts	All 435 Districts
Roman Catholic	31	88
Jewish	6	9
Protestant	12	333
Others	1	5

During the 1960 campaign, a Buffalo worker was asked: "Are you going to vote for Kennedy because he is a Catholic?" He replied: "No, because I am."

Irish

Examination of specific ethnic groups reveals the same pattern of preference. Of the 30 congressional districts with the most residents of first- and second-generation Irish descent according to the 1960 census, in 1964 17 had congressmen with Irish surnames, 21 were represented by Roman Catholics, and 21 of the districts in 1962 voted Democratic. Of the 30 districts, 28 are located in the East. Nine of the 12 Massachusetts districts are among the 30 Irish districts. John Fitzgerald Kennedy was the overwhelming choice of most of the 30 Irish districts: in the 1960 presidential election 25 of these districts cast the majority of their votes for him.

Italians

The number of Italian-Americans elected to Congress and to state governorships has increased, but only in recent years. Italian-Americans had to wait until 1936 to elect their first governor, and in 1950 the same man—Rhode Island's John Pastore—was the first Italian-American to win a seat in the Senate. Italian-Americans in Chicago did not send one of their own to Congress until 1958. Of the 30 House districts highest in Italian population, 6 had elected Italian representatives in 1964. These 30 districts had 19 Catholic, 6 Protestant, and 5 Jewish congressmen in that same year. In 1960 the Italian districts voted 22 to 8 in favor of Kennedy over Nixon. The 1960 census locates all 30 of these districts in the East, with 16 in New York and 6 in New Jersey. In New York's 13th District, in Brooklyn, there were 97,240 first- and second-generation Italians, and in the city's 24th District 88,540 of Italian stock or 25.3 percent of that district's total population.

Jews

The 30 districts most heavily populated by Russian stock, overwhelmingly Jewish, were represented by 9 Jews and 12 Catholics in 1964. Of these districts, 23 were located in the East, with 14 in the New York City area. In the 1960 election the districts voted 23-7 for Kennedy over Nixon and sent 21 Democrats and 9 Republicans to Congress.

Poles

The Poles are more heavily settled in the Midwest than are the Irish, Italians, and Jews. At the end of the 1958 campaign, the Polish-American press proudly hailed the election to Congress of 13 Americans of Polish descent, an unprecedented political achievement. According to the 1960 census figures, 18 of the 30 congressional districts with the most first- and second-generation Poles are in the East. The Midwest has the remaining 12 districts, with 6 in the Chicago area, 4 in the Detroit area, and 1 in Cleveland. More than 71,180 Polish immigrants and their children live in Chicago's 8th district—nearly 15 percent of the total population of the district. Of the 9 districts with the highest concentration of Polish stock, all but 1 had Polish congressmen, five of whose names ended in -ski. Twenty-six of the congressmen representing the 30 Polish districts in 1964 were Democrats. Of these districts, 26 gave Kennedy a majority of their votes in 1960.

Other White Ethnic Groups

The congressional districts which are most heavily Czech are located in Pennsylvania, Ohio, and Illinois. Their voting behavior in 1960 and 1962 was bipartisan. The northern European immigrants and their descendants, when analyzed in terms of their heaviest concentration in congressional districts, showed no voting patterns that can be easily explained by religious affiliation as is the case with the Irish, Italians, and Eastern Europeans. The latter groups, concentrated in eastern, urban, and overwhelmingly Democratic House districts, were represented in 2 out of 3 districts by a Catholic or Jew. The 30 districts of highest Northern European stock population are largely in the Midwest, in rural areas, and they send more Republicans and Protestants to Congress.

Spanish-Americans

Voters of Spanish origin, concentrated in the Southwest, and in Florida, Illinois, and New York, are beginning to assert themselves politically. According to the 1960 census, most Mexican-Americans live in California and Texas, while Illinois, primarily Chicago, ranks third with a population of more than 63,000 Mexican immigrants and their children. The Puerto Ricans remain concentrated in New York City whence they immigrated in great numbers following World War II. It was not until 1964 that the 15th Congressional District of Texas, with the heaviest Mexican stock—nearly 70 percent with Spanish surnames—elected Mexican-American Eligio De La Garza to Congress, and not until 1963 that the heavily Mexican city of Brownsville in the 15th District elected its first Spanish-American mayor. The first Mexican-American to serve in Congress from Texas was Henry B. Gonzales, elected in 1961 to fill an unexpired term in the Texas 20th District. He served his apprenticeship in city politics in San Antonio. Gonzales was one of the leaders of the "Viva Kennedy" movement in 1960 and claimed that as many as 90 percent of the Spanish-Americans of Texas had voted for Kennedy. De La Garza and Gonzales have served continuously since their initial elections. The 30th District in California—22.2 percent Spanish—is represented by Mexican-American Edward J. Roybal, elected in 1964. He was a national leader of PASSO (Political Action for Spanish-Speaking Organizations), a group established in 1961 to persuade the Kennedy administration to appoint more Spanish-speaking Americans to influential government positions. New Mexico has had Spanish-American congressmen and senators since the 1950s. In 1972, one senator and one of the two congressmen are Spanish-Americans. Of the six Spanish-Americans in Congress in 1972, five are Democrats, one Republican.

All of the 10 districts highest in Puerto Rican population—9 in New York City and 1 in Chicago—gave Kennedy a majority vote in 1966. Puerto Ricans favor the Democratic Party partly because they identify it with the Puerto Rican Popular Democratic Movement led by former Governor Luis Munoz Marin and partly because they have a traditional disaffection with the so-called Statehood Party, identified with the Republican Party and big business. Herman Badillo of New York, elected to the House in 1970, became the first Puerto Rican to sit in Congress.

Blacks

Of the 90 congressional districts with the heaviest concentration of blacks in 1964, 64 were in the South, 14 in the East, 10 in the

Midwest, and 2 in California. Of these districts, 51 were rural, 31 urban, 7 mixed, and 1 suburban. Only five black congressmen were elected to the 88th Congress (1962-64)—four from Northern urban areas (Chicago, New York, Detroit, and Philadelphia), and one from Los Angeles. The 90 districts with the highest percentage of blacks were represented by 88 Democratic and 2 Republican congressmen. Kennedy received a majority vote in 69 of those districts.

Other Groups

So far we have been concerned with only the major ethnic groups, but other less visible groups are also conscious of their representation in government. Following the 1970 United States elections, a Lebanese newspaper noted that a third American of Lebanese extraction had been elected to the House and that two Lebanese-Americans were thus now serving in the American Congress—one from the 2nd District of South Dakota, the other from the 23rd District of Texas.

The political importance of the ethnic origin of United States congressmen can be verified by a breakdown of the 92nd Congress in terms of ethnicity. Such figures are maintained and readily accessible through the Nationalities Divisions of both parties. According to Andrew Valuchek, nationalities advisor to the Democratic Party, the 92nd Congress had the following number of ethnic Americans:

Senate		House	
Republicans	7	Republicans	32
Democrats	15	Democrats	62

Valuchek is quick to note that 25 of the 32 Republican representatives are German-Americans, as compared with 17 out of 62 for the Democrats, and that in addition to the 17 Germans, 15 Italian-Americans and 8 Polish-Americans serve in the 92nd Congress. He does not include Irish-Americans in his figures.

POLITICIANS TAKE ETHNICITY SERIOUSLY

Even without additional evidence of the persistence of ethnic voting patterns, one can find evidence of the continued influence of ethnicity in political activity. At all levels of government, politicians practice ethnic politics. It is not my purpose here to examine the ethnic tactics and strategies used by politicians at state and local levels to maintain and enhance their political power. Suffice it to say that during Mayor Daley's 1971 mayoral campaign his Ethnic Committee and the mayor himself devoted considerable time and energy to attending ethnic affairs. His staff sent letters to various ethnic groups whose business and civic leaders had already responded by endorsing him. Advertisements in ethnic newspapers announced to their readers that politicians from their own ethnic groups endorsed Mayor Daley. Governor Nelson Rockefeller of New York had used many of Daley's tactics in his 1970 bid for re-election, among other things appearing at Italian affairs and appointing an Italian-American judge. In Ohio in the 1970 senatorial race, Republican Robert Taft's campaign organization earmarked $15,000 for appeals to white ethnics, and the head of the ethnic division for Taft's campaign was rewarded for his efforts with an important appointment to Taft's regular staff.

Politicians at all levels take ethnicity seriously. They make ethnic appeals because they believe that ethnic identification is still a framework within which a large number of their constituents think and act. As Louis L. Gerson has observed:

> So long as the politican continues convinced of the ethnic vote, so long as he believes that it is not politically wise to disregard pressures from ethnic leaders, so long will the persistent belief in the voting power of nationality groups affect American political life and the ethnic leader. . . . Myth or not, it is the politician, the congressman, the senator, the President, who influences and at times executes foreign and domestic policies, often on the basis of his belief in the existence of an ethnic vote. In the continual catering to the ethnic vote by the political parties there is much that is primitive, irrational and increasingly foreboding. (The Hyphenate in Recent American Politics and Diplomacy, 1964, pp. 242-43.)

The astonishing fact about ethnic politics is that it has persisted, despite the relatively small influx of immigrants in the last 45 years, and despite the acculturation and assimilation of immigrants and their children. Nor has the character of its practice changed much. Support from ethnic leaders and groups is still sought in the traditional ways: banquets, meetings, and receptions where the candidates are honored; the formation of supporting ad hoc organizations composed of prominent businessmen, professionals, and fraternal and religious leaders; conspicuous propaganda in ethnic communications media of a candidate being endorsed by ethnic leaders; and much New Deal, Fair Deal, New Frontier, and Great Society rhetoric, coupled with

assurances that the party is committed to "self-determination" and
"freedom" for the oppressed nations of the world. Whether it be by
the balanced ticket, the distribution of patronage, the parceling out
of social services, or political campaigning, few politicians have now
or ever neglected the ethnic heterogeneity of their electorates.

THE BALANCED TICKET AND GROUP
POLITICAL PROGRESS

City politics in America has been to a large measure ethnic
politics, with the balanced ticket as the means for distributing political
influence among insiders and outsiders. The use of the balanced
ticket is still prevalent in state and local politics and has now become
a common device at the national level. Its use has institutionalized
the practice of ethnic politics. Recognition is given to ethnic groups
by politicians granting nominations, appointments, and prestige. The
balanced ticket is founded on the belief among politicians that large
groups of Americans vote on the basis of their national background,
ethnic origin, and religious ties. The ethnic candidate is slated as a
compatriot who, if elected, will represent the best interests of his
group.

The balanced ticket has been mostly integrative and has given
successive groups the means of acquiring social status and political
power. A group's political and social advancement depends on size,
distribution, facility with the language, cultural, political, and institutional adaptation, and the degree of group consciousness. At first,
immigrant groups were expected to serve an apprenticeship, but they
soon learned that they were held down so long as they accepted this
subordinate role. For the most part, immigrants themselves took
the initiative in political organization and forced their way into a
political party. Using their ethnic identity as a power resource,
immigrant leaders catered to the symbolic and actual needs of their
ethnic groups and built power bases independent of the local political
party organization.

Politically significant ethnic groups first emerged in the cities.
Ethnic newcomers typically passed through six stages: first, numerical
and electoral significance; then, communal organization and miminal
recognition in terms of party activity; followed by political benefits
and symbolic recognition; minor, then greater nominations and appointments; participation in decision-making; and finally, established
political power and perhaps political dominance.*

---

*I am indebted to Matthew Holden, Jr., for the delineation of
these stages.

THE IRISH LEAD THE WAY

Political dominance has occurred when an ethnic group's leaders take over the Democratic party organization at the state level. The Irish are the only ethnic minority to have carved out a significant niche. Their first conquest was in Massachusetts. Irish Mayor Daley has become the decisive force in Democratic politics in Illinois. John F. Kennedy's power base in the politics of Massachusetts enabled him to gain allies at the 1956 Democratic National Convention in his bid for the vice-presidential nomination and to win the presidential nomination of his party in 1960. His 1960 nomination represented the extension of the balanced ticket strategy into presidential politics. In 1956 Kennedy supporters presented him to the delegates of the Democratic National Convention as a Catholic who could win back the large number of Catholics from the key industrial states of the North who had voted for Eisenhower in 1952. In that year John M. Bailey of Connecticut, a Catholic and important Democratic strategist, issued a memorandum to Adlai Stevenson in an effort to persuade him to choose Kennedy as his running mate. Its concluding paragraph read:

> Has the Democratic era ended? Has the party permanently lost its political base among the Catholics and immigrants of the large Northern cities that made a Democratic victory possible in 1940, 1944 and 1948? . . . A Catholic Vice-President nominee could refashion this base as Al Smith did, and begin a new era of Democratic victories, without costing even the few electoral votes Smith did.

The Irish, however, are losing their dominance over the large cities as they disperse and assimilate, and as later newcomers wrest control from them. The Irish are being gradually succeeded by Italians, Poles, Jews, and the other descendants of Eastern and Central European immigrants as urban chief executives. Italian mayors began to appear in the late 1940s and 1950s. However, the succession of mayors in the major industrial cities of the North reveals two patterns: the slowness with which the Irish surrender political power and the disproportionate political velocity of the blacks. New York City has had only two non-Irish white ethnic mayors, Chicago one, Philadelphia one, Detroit one, Cleveland four, Boston none, Pittsburgh none. By 1971 blacks had won the chief executive's office in three major Northern cities—Cleveland, Gary, and Newark. But black dominance is reversible, witness the election in Cleveland in November 1971 of a second-generation Czech. Blacks will not capture control of all the city halls of the large cities of the North, for there are not enough blacks in America for this to occur in the next 30 years. It does seem inevitable that the white ethnics who remain in these cities will be confronted by formidable opposition for political dominance, especially if group orientation becomes more racial than ethnic, or if blacks ally themselves with Spanish-Americans.

THE BLACK POLITICAL MOVEMENT: LITTLE PROGRESS UNTIL THE 1960s

By 1971 blacks were regarded as a group with sufficient solidarity among its leaders to require explicit presidential recognition and the granting of substantial concessions. But their acquisition of political power has been slow indeed. It was not until 1928 that the first black since the era of Reconstruction was elected to Congress. That election occurred in Chicago's 1st Congressional District and a black has held the seat ever since. Not until 1944 was Adam Clayton Powell elected in the predominantly black 22nd Congressional District of New York City. Charles Diggs, Jr., of Detroit, the third black congressman, was not elected until 1954. In the 1960s numerous blacks won important elective and appointive offices, but by the end of that decade there was not one black governor and only one black United States senator. President Johnson appointed the first black to the Supreme Court in 1967, and when two vacancies opened in 1971 there was some pressure from blacks for another appointment. Johnson also appointed the first black to a presidential cabinet. The black caucus consisting of 13 black congressmen, formed in 1969, has been granted recognition by the president. Black political leaders from around the country met in Chicago in September 1971 and in Washington, D.C., in November of the same year to discuss strategies for 1972. They displayed a solidarity unexpected by many political observers. They spoke of maximizing political bargaining power by engaging in coalition and balance of power politics. In March 1972, over 3,000 black delegates gathered in Gary for the first black political convention in American history. The black community in all its diversity met for two days, selected a representative steering committee, and approved a national agenda of goals. Some proposed a black vice-presidential candidate and Shirley Chisholm—the first black congresswoman—declared that despite opposition from her "brothers," she would enter primaries and seek to win the Democratic nomination for the presidency. When Senator Edmund S. Muskie suggested that the American electorate was not prepared to elect a black vice-president, he created a political commotion that took on unexpected

proportions, revealing that black assertion remains a highly charged
subject. Blacks have nationalized their political movement and still
prefer to progress with the established two-party system. However,
at the Black Political Convention Mayor Hatcher of Gary warned that
the major parties have one last chance—the 1972 presidential year—
to grant blacks full participation in American political life, and that
otherwise they will form their own party.

NATIONAL PARTIES PRACTICE ETHNIC POLITICS

The Democratic and Republican national parties maintain Nationalities Divisions, and their strategists are more keenly alert than
ever before to the ethnic voter. The Republicans established their
first permanent full-time ethnic division in 1968. It was not until
Alfred Smith and Franklin Roosevelt appealed to nationality groups
in their presidential campaigns, with considerable success, that
Catholic white ethnic voters came under the influence of the Democratic
Party. The belt of industrial states from Massachusetts south to
Maryland and west to Illinois forms a critical electoral area. National party strategists are aware of the heavy concentration of white
ethnic groups in this area and have made direct appeals to them with
increasing frequency.

Before 1948 the Democratic National Committee relied largely
on local and state party organizations. The Democratic politics of
many, if not most, large northern cities were dominated by political
machines and bosses. Roosevelt and Truman respected the political
realities existing in these cities and depended upon bosses in Boston,
New York, Chicago, and Kansas City to deliver the electoral support
of the ethnic groups. This working relationship was fully accepted,
and federal investigation of the income tax returns of such prominent
public officials as Mayor Edward Kelly of Chicago was suppressed
because of the importance of these leaders in delivering the ethnic
vote. The quid pro quo for Chicago's bosses was federal welfare and
public works programs for the city, personal immunity from federal
prosecution, and the opportunity for a politically conservative municipal establishment to benefit from the progressive image of the New
Deal.

The nationality-group activities of the local Democratic organization in the Chicago area illustrates the point. Anton J. Cermak, a
Bohemian immigrant, overcame the Irish Democratic leadership to
become Mayor of Chicago in 1931 by his systematic courtship of the
immigrant vote from eastern, southern and Central Europeans. His
chief organizer of nationality-groups was Adolph J. Sabath, a
Bohemian Jew who held the distinction of being the only representative

of the new immigrants in Congress from 1906 until the end of World
War I. Sabath headed the Nationalistic Groups Organization, an arm
of the Cook County Democratic machine in 1928, and worked quietly
behind the scenes to corral the nationality-group vote. The Nationalistic Groups Organization was divided into separate sections, each
devoted to a specific major nationality group, with representatives
of each group leading and speaking for their section. Sabath worked
to make it more than an ad hoc body. His hope was to consolidate
the major nationality groups and gain control of them through
patronage. He failed, and eventually the Chicago Democratic machine
revived the old practice of establishing a Nationality Division before
major elections and allowing each group to manage its own affairs.
The leaders of each group stayed within the framework of the Chicago
Democratic machine because their continued access to party patronage
depended upon their party loyalty. Cermak's opponent in the 1931
mayoralty race was incumbent Republican Mayor "Big Bill" Thompson.
The latter underestimated the new immigrants—both the importance
of their vote and their sensitivity. He belittled Cermak's foreign
birth. "Tony, Tony, where's your pushcart at? Can you imagine a
World's Fair Mayor with a name like that?" It was clearly Thompson's
intention to appeal to the nativists, Irish, and Germans. In a bid for
Irish support he threatened to "punch the snout" of the king of England
should he set foot in Chicago. And to befriend German-Americans,
he refused to receive French Marshal Joffre. After Cermak's assassination in 1933, Democratic Party leadership in Chicago passed to
Patrick Nash and Mayor Edward J. Kelly. Franklin Roosevelt relied
increasingly on the power of these bosses. "Recognize and rule"
was the watchword of Chicago's Democratic machine throughout the
Sabath-Cermak-Kelly-Nash period (1931-47). By granting the major
nationalities a modicum of elective and appointive offices, the party
leadership won a majority of the white ethnic vote without giving up
control of local party affairs. In the late 1930s it was Kelly who
actively courted the black vote in Chicago by supporting William
Dawson, an emerging black leader, and by offering patronage; by the
early 1940s Chicago's Democratic machine was receiving black
electoral majorities.

7

THE DEMOCRATIC PARTY
FORMALIZES
ETHNIC OPERATIONS

The Democratic National Committee, the formal party apparatus of the presidential wing of the Democratic Party, established a Nationalities Division in 1936 as a special unit whose function it was to coordinate, expand and make more explicit, and direct Franklin Roosevelt's and the Party's appeals to nationality groups. The Division was established as a temporary one and operated only on a limited scale, primarily during presidential campaigns. It served as a liaison with the local bosses. The Division represented Roosevelt's political recognition of the electoral support he had received from ethnic minorities in 1932 and of the role white ethnics would play in the New Deal coalition. His chief political strategist was James Farley—an Irish Catholic.

The Democratic National Committee, to a great extent, took for granted the electoral support of nationality groups in the presidential campaigns of the 1930s and 1940s. In the 1930s the Foreign Language Citizens' Department of the Democratic National Committee appealed to the economic concerns and needs of ethnic Americans. A line from President Roosevelt's acceptance speech—"Liberty requires an opportunity to make a living"—was translated and appeared widely in the foreign language press. It symbolized Roosevelt's commitment to the economic welfare of ethnics. Such translations of presidential statements constituted important recognition for ethnic groups. In the late 1930s the Democratic National Committee, as well as its Republican counterpart, appealed to ethnic Americans through foreign policy issues. These appeals often were no more than the exploitation of emotional ties to ancestral lands that were threatened, actually or potentially, by Nazi or Fascist aggression.

It was not until Harry Truman's campaign in 1948 that the Nationalities Division was created as an elaborate addition to the

Democratic National Committee. Its formation was, in part, an effort by the Committee to capitalize on the gratitude of white ethnics in America, gratitude which had been generated by the Truman Doctrine, the Marshall Plan, the policy of containment of Russia, and Truman's program to admit thousands of displaced persons into the United States following World War II. It was realized that the enthusiasm generated by Truman's postwar programs could be converted into votes for the Democrats. Moreover, the very formation of the Division represented the Democratic leaders' awareness that the electoral support of these groups could no longer be taken for granted.

As early as 1942 and 1944 the Poles and other nationality groups grew increasingly restive. The Republicans were making inroads. On October 11 (Pulaski Day), 1944, Roosevelt was persuaded by his ethnic strategists to receive a "memorial," presented on behalf of the Polish-American Congress by its president, in order to maintain what the strategists believed to be a wavering ethnic vote. In 1948 Michael Cieplinski became executive director of the Nationalities Division with the explicit assignment to prevent defections of foreign language groups to the Republican Party. Louis Martin, associated with the Nationalities Division from 1944 until 1969, refers to Cieplinski as the "father of nationality-group politics." As a founder of the Foreign Language Newspaper Association, he relied heavily on the foreign language press and radio and on exchanges with social and fraternal organizations, notably the Polish National Alliance, Czech Sokols, and German Turnvereins. Cieplinski sought the advice of ethnic editors and publishers, business and communal leaders, and clergymen, and with the assistance of these men, organized a national committee consisting of representatives of 20 different foreign language groups. The members of this committee served as the communications link with the ethnic communities. The individual committees worked closely with local and state Democratic organizations in appointing local representatives wherever there were ethnic concentrations, and kept in close touch with the activities of these local representatives. By the end of the 1948 campaign, there were more than 930 such representatives. Party publicity, advertisements, and news releases were translated and furnished to the foreign language newspapers. An effort was made to tailor the material nationality by nationality to make it more appealing to each group. That is, a more emotional presentation was used for groups like the Italians, Slavs, and Spanish, while a more logic, rational, and concrete approach was used for Northern European groups. Before the convention of 1948, the Nationalities Division arranged for representatives of nationality groups to be heard by party officials. Convention delegates of foreign extraction were received in the Democratic chairman's office. These meetings generated much publicity for the 780 foreign language newspapers. Truman backed Cieplinski's plank for the 1948 party platform promising legislation to admit thousands of refugees. The "displaced-person" plank referred specifically to Poles and made headlines in all Polish-American newspapers. To counter the defection to the Republicans of Charles Rozmarek, president of the Polish National Alliance and the Polish-American Congress, the latter an umbrella association for all Polish-American organizations, Cieplinski persuaded Tade Styka, a popular Polish artist, to paint Truman's portrait. In a White House ceremony in October 1948, attended by the President and his entire cabinet, Styka presented the completed portrait. All 72 Polish-American newspapers printed a reproduction of the portrait and Styka's personal eulogy of the president. According to Jack Redding, author of Inside the Democratic Party: "We had the President's candidacy wrapped in the folds of Polish national patriotism as represented by one of the great Polish heroes—Styka." The Democratic platform also had a favorable Palestine plank. The Republicans included a pro-Israel plank in their platform but made no other reference to nationality groups. Italian-American precincts were flooded with campaign leaflets telling how Truman had "saved Italy from Communism." In his 1948 campaign, on "I Am an American Day" and on Columbus Day, President Truman praised Columbus and his crew of Spaniards. He recognized other ethnic groups in various ways. The Democrats had preferred to keep foreign policy issues surrounding the cold war out of the presidential campaign of 1948, that is, to continue the bipartisan unity that had lasted through the war and had resulted in the Vandenberg Resolution. But the Republicans, by their appeals to ethnic groups on the basis of foreign policy promises and rhetoric, forced the Democrats to make foreign policy a campaign issue. The expanded activities of the Nationalities Division under Cieplinski's leadership was a decisive factor in Truman's narrow victory. A critical majority of ethnic Americans voted Democratic in 1948. In his analysis of the election, Samuel Lubell singled out the ethnic vote as significant and placed particular importance on the Democratic voting of Polish, Italian, and German-Americans. Cities like Buffalo, Boston, Chicago, Cleveland, Detroit, Milwaukee, and St. Louis supported the Democratic Party more strongly than they had in 1944. In his book, Jack Redding, a former director of public relations of the Democratic National Committee, credits the expanded activities of the Nationalities Division of the Democratic National Committee with turning what had seemed certain defeat into victory. The apparent relationship between the work of the Nationalities Division and the favorable ethnic vote led to the establishment of the Nationalities Division as a permanently functioning unit of the National Committee. In 1951 Rhode Island Senator Theodore Green, senior Democrat on the Foreign Relations Committee, was

appointed the first permanent chairman of the Nationalities Division
and headquarters were established in New York City.

DEMOCRATS AND REPUBLICANS COURT
THE ETHNIC VOTE IN THE 1950s

In 1952 and 1956 both major parties operated nationalities divisions. These divisions prepared and furnished candidates with lists
of dates important to foreign language groups in order that the "proper
felicitations" could be made on appropriate occasions. Candidates
were also supplied with guidebooks which gave important information
on the history of the major nationality-groups and problems of current
interest to them. Where leaders of ethnic organizations were known
to exert political influence, they were included in campaign programs.
The divisions prepared and distributed to candidates campaign literature in various languages and worked closely with the foreign language press. The Republican division in 1952 was known as the
All-American Origins Division and in 1956 was split into three
organizational units: Nationalities (Italians, Poles, etc.), Ethnic
(Jews), and Minorities (blacks). In 1952 Dwight Eisenhower promised
to work for liberation of the captive nations, and the party inserted
this pledge in its platform. But in late 1953 White House spokesmen
advised Republican ethnic leaders that President Eisenhower opposed
"any effective organization of Nationality Groups" and did not want
to differentiate among groups within the electorate. In July 1955 the
Republican National Committee abolished its Nationalities Division.
It was not until July 1956 that a Nationalities Advisory Group, consisting of 18 ethnic leaders, was established. Indicative of the
increasing Republican effort to enlarge its electoral support by
nationality groups was the inclusion in the 1956 Republican Party
platform of the first plank renouncing restrictive immigration
policies.

The Democrats, in the campaigns of 1956, 1958, and 1960,
intensified their efforts to hold and recapture what they perceived
as the diminishing preference of ethnic Americans for the Democratic
Party. Michael Cieplinski continued his work as executive director
through the 1950s. In 1956 the Democratic Nationalities Division
attempted to influence the editors and publishers of 500 foreign language newspapers and win the support of their readers. Democratic
and Republican advertisements in these newspapers often listed the
elective and appointive public offices held by "representatives" of
their groups. In April 1958 the Democratic Nationalities Division
held a convention of representatives of 26 ethnic groups to discuss
organizational methods. In addition to developing ways in which to

appeal to groups on a nationality-by-nationality basis, organizational and operational efforts directed at geographical concentrations of nationality groups were considered. In preparation for the 1960 campaign, the Democratic Nationalities Division invited ethnic congressmen to participate in a meeting, in November 1959, to discuss "ethnic" strategy and formulate platform planks to attract ethnic voters. As it developed, the planks of both parties concerning issues of interest to nationality-groups were very much alike. In 1960 the Democrats, with a third-generation Irish Catholic as their presidential nominee, held an advantage in their competition for the ethnic vote. One of the triumphs of the Democratic presidential campaign was the parade and rally in Chicago sponsored by Richard J. Daley's Democratic machine shortly before the election. Tens of thousands, the majority of whom were white ethnics, came out to support Kennedy.

JOHN F. KENNEDY VITALIZES ETHNIC POLITICS

It is an irony of history that President Nixon's new ethnic strategy may be rooted in his defeat in 1960 by a third-generation Irish Catholic. It was John F. Kennedy's presidential victory in 1960 that opened many political doors to white ethnic Americans and formalized the practice of ethnic politics at the national level.

Before 1933 only 4 Catholics had held cabinet posts. Of the 33 United States presidents from George Washington to Dwight D. Eisenhower, 28 were of British stock and 30 were Protestants. Only 7 Roman Catholics of more than 100 appointees have been appointed to the Supreme Court since 1789. The first Jew—Louis D. Brandeis— was not named to the Court until 1916, but 4 others have been appointed since then. No non-Irish, non-Jewish white ethnic has ever been appointed to the Court.

Irish Catholic Alfred Smith was nominated for the presidency by the Democratic Party in 1928, but the country was not ready for a Catholic president. Kennedy and then Johnson opened the leadership of the national government to ethnic and racial minorities. Kennedy appointed the first Italian-American (1962) and Polish-American (1963) to the cabinet. Johnson appointed the first black to the cabinet in 1966 and to the Supreme Court in 1967. In 1968 Senator Eugene McCarthy's campaign for the presidency as an antiwar candidate, which contributed greatly to President Johnson's decision not to seek reelection, overshadowed any concern about his being a Roman Catholic. Robert F. Kennedy mounted a strong campaign for the presidential nomination, and again few raised the issue of his Catholicism. Ironically, Robert Kennedy was killed by an insane ethnic who resented his political courtship of the Jews.

The Democrats nominated a second-generation Polish-American as their vice-presidential candidate in 1968, and the Republicans had already named a second-generation Greek to seek the vice-presidency. Both nominations marked the first time in American history that non-Irish white ethnics were on the presidential ticket. One of the leading contenders for the Democratic presidential nomination in 1972 was a second-generation Polish-American Catholic. It would appear that anti-Catholic bias is no longer a major factor in presidential politics. Eugene McCarthy, Robert F. Kennedy, and Edmund Muskie were not faced with the question John F. Kennedy fielded every day in 1960: "Mr. Kennedy, as a Catholic, what would you do about . . . ?"

Realizing that heavy majorities of ethnic and racial groups had elected him, Kennedy decided that the Democratic National Committee should practice ethnic politics on a full-time basis. He requested that Louis Martin, a black newspaper executive, stay on the Committee as an ethnic advisor. Martin had spent three or four months in Washington, D.C., in 1944, helping the party enlist more of the black vote during that year's presidential campaign. He returned in 1960 for the same purpose. Kennedy credited him with decisive assistance which enabled him to win the black vote overwhelmingly.

Martin spent the next nine years working in Washington, D.C., at Democratic headquarters. Mayor Robert F. Wagner of New York City, with the assistance of Julius C. C. Edelstein, supervised the Nationalities Division of the Party during the early 1960s from his offices in New York City. Wagner was designated chairman of the Nationalities Division in 1961. In some of the old Northern cities Kennedy relied on local political bosses to manage ethnic relations. According to Martin, Kennedy told him that an appeal on the basis of ethnic origin was not the most important one in politics but became critical "when all other factors were equal."

Kennedy's election culminated the long struggle of the Irish to rise to the top in American politics. When he attained the White House, Irish Catholics ceased to be a minority group. Kennedy was Chief Executive, Irish Catholic John Bailey was National Chairman of the majority party, and local Irish Catholics, such as Richard J. Daley, Robert F. Wagner (half Irish, half German), and David Lawrence dominated the politics of many states and local governments. Mayor Daley and his wife were Kennedy's first overnight guests in the White House. Non-Irish insiders often referred to Kennedy and his chief advisors as the Irish Mafia.

The 1970s may turn out to be the period in American political history when an ethnic without an Anglicized name was first nominated to a presidential ticket. Previously the melting pot had required that ethnic names be amputated to conform to the WASP idiom. Political advancement was much more likely if "Spiro Anagnostopoulos" was

transformed into "Ted Agnew" and "Edmund Sixtus Marciszewski"
into "Ed Muskie." It was bad enough to appoint a Jew to a minor
post in the State Department, but an ethnic bearing an "impossible
foreign surname" was out of the question. Kennedy's victory shook
the foundations of WASP dominance in national politics. He had
beaten a bastion of the WASP establishment—Republican Senator
Henry Cabot Lodge—in 1952 in Massachusetts, and eight years later
was elected president. While John F. Kennedy was closer in style
to the Harvard elite and East Coast upper class than to the Irish of
South Boston, he nevertheless brought to the White House and to his
administration a distinctive style unlike the styles of previous WASP
administrations. Robert F. Kennedy developed his own political style
which matured greatly between 1960 and 1968. He was more indi-
vidualistic and independent of the WASP model than his brother John.
Senator Edward M. Kennedy is still struggling to establish a distinctive image.

But it was Edward Kennedy who championed the cause of the
Irish in Northern Ireland, in an October 1971 Senate speech, proposing
a resolution demanding that Britain pull her troops out of that country
and establish a united Ireland. He referred to Ireland as "Britain's
Vietnam." Kennedy said: "We believe that the resolution states the
only realistic means to end the killing in Northern Ireland, and to
bring peace to a land that has given so much to America, a land that
has done so much to enrich the history of our own nation." The
British press reacted angrily to Kennedy's call in the United States
Senate for the immediate withdrawal of British troops. The Sun,
noting that Kennedy's "ancestors were from Ireland," described his
speech as a "blatant piece of electioneering—aimed at America's
powerful Irish vote." The Daily Telegraph declared that the speech
would "no doubt make him a popular figure among the gunmen and
saboteurs operating in Ulster and among some of the Irish Roman
Catholic voters of Massachusetts." Because the bloodshed and
British military occupation in Northern Ireland are perceived by most
American Catholics as an oppression by a Protestant majority of a
Catholic minority, Kennedy certainly stood to benefit politically from
his speech. Republican National Chairman Robert Dole immediately
condemned Kennedy's call for the immediate withdrawal of British
troops as "oversimplified meddling" and "a blatant attempt to inter-
fere in the internal affairs of a friendly nation."

After 1960 President Kennedy and party chief John Bailey
revealed their full commitment to the further development of a
permanent nationalities and minorities division within the Democratic
National Committee. Michael Cieplinski, nationalities advisor to the
Committee for more than 12 years, assisted the Democrats in the
1960 presidential campaign, but was forced to limit his participation

since he had been appointed to the State Department. Louis Martin remained with the Committee in Washington, D.C., on a full-time basis, and Mayor Wagner headed the Nationalities Division, giving policy direction and guidance to the Division from his home offices in New York City. When Martin, a black, encountered difficulties in dealing with the leaders of nationality groups, Andrew J. Valuchek, associated with Mayor Wagner's ethnic operations in New York City and president of the Sokols (a national Czech organization), was appointed to the staff of the Committee as special assistant for nationality groups. Martin was to concentrate his efforts on racial minorities. Valuchek still serves in his original capacity with the designation of "Special Assistant to the Chairman" of the Democratic National Committee. Martin left in 1969 to return to an executive position with Sengstacke, a black newspaper chain. He was replaced by another black, also hired on a full-time basis.

According to Martin, he served during his nine years as an "expediter"; his task was to keep the nationality and minority groups informed of those activities of the national government which were of special interest to them and to inform the White House of when and how to acknowledge ethnic groups. He was in daily contact with White House aides during both the Kennedy and Johnson administrations, serving as an ethnic communications link and lobbyist. As he relates his nine-year experience on the Committee, one is struck by his openness, facility in communicating, and political sophistication. According to his comments, his dealings with Valuchek, Edelstein, and other ethnic leaders were apparently rarely disturbed by any conflict that was racial in origin. They seemed to have acted upon Kennedy's promise to open the government and Party to participation by ethnic and racial minorities, cooperated with one another, and responded to ethnic and racial group pressures whenever possible. Martin goes so far as to say "Personalities were lost in the cause." Competition for appointments and programs was vigorous, but the majority of ethnic group leaders apparently trusted Kennedy and later Johnson. Conflicts between and within nationality groups were recognized and handled as skillfully and quickly as possible. To avoid conflict during one campaign, a WASP from Texas was appointed as head of the Nationalities Division. Wagner's apparent ethnic neutrality made him an effective chairman of the All American Council (AAC) and helped skirt potential jealousies among the leaders of Eastern, Central, and Southern European groups. Moreover, Wagner had proved his skills at ethnic balancing and mediating in America's ethnic capital—New York City.

Martin emphasized that "they kept the organizational structure loose and used and changed titles frequently" as they did not want high visibility and wanted to "keep the leadership of the Republican National

Committee in the dark" as to their activities. After considerable discussion among the leadership of the ethnic and racial groups, the Committee decided "to go public." In 1963 the Nationalities Division of the Democratic National Committee was rechristened the All American Council (AAC), and headquarters were officially established at Democratic headquarters in Washington, D.C. President Kennedy gave the new Council his full blessings; Mayor Wagner, appointed as chairman, conferred status; and the New York Times ran a front-page article noting these significant developments in nationality-group politics, now beginning to be known as ethnic politics. Louis Martin was named deputy chairman of the AAC and head of the Minorities Division.

THE DEMOCRATS' PERMANENT ETHNIC DIVISION
AND ITS ACTIVITIES

In announcing the formation of the AAC, Wagner said that it would expand its program and function throughout the year, rather than only during campaigns. In April 1963 he declared that the party sought "to attract into the mainstream of our national life the maximum number of Americans who speak a second language or, indeed, whose first language is foreign. . . . Of course, we hope to induce them to express their political wills through the Democratic Party." In that year Andrew Valuchek was hired by the AAC on a full-time basis as director of nationality groups, a position he held through 1971. The AAC maintains two divisions: Nationalities and Minorities. The latter division is for blacks, the former nationality groups.

The purpose in forming the All American Council was again described by Mayor Wagner in 1967 when, as its chairman, he addressed the delegates of the Democratic National Committee: "The first mission of the All American Council is to transmit and convey the Democratic Party's message to these fellow Americans in their own idiom. At the other end, our job is to get their message about their special needs and views across to the Party organization and to office-holders and office-seekers of the Party." Wagner went on to say that the AAC was the instrument through which the Democratic National Committee hoped to maintain and develop communications and ties with ethnic groups. The AAC has sought ". . . to eliminate second class citizenship . . ." and was "organized to function both as a service arm and a fighting arm of the National Committee and of the Democratic Party." These statements overemphasized the social and nonpartisan functions and understated the political purpose— the primary one—which was to maximize the ethnic and racial group vote.

The AAC concentrates on presidential elections but also assists congressional candidates in the off-year elections. Details about the organization and its activities are not easy to find. Little has been written about it, and most politicians prefer to deny their courtship of the ethnic vote. In fact, the Nationalities Divisions of both parties operate with a minimum of publicity. When the Republican Party in June 1971 convened nearly 300 ethnic leaders in Washington to recognize officially the formation of their National Republican Heritage Groups Council, the major newspapers in the United States did not report the convention.

In 1964 the AAC submitted a proposed budget for $500,000, was allotted $125,000, but ultimately spent $600,000. The expenditure beyond the allotment resulted from last-minute fears among Party leaders, who authorized extra spending by all the divisions. Some of AAC's budget came from specifically earmarked contributions from ethnic organizations. In 1968, during Hubert H. Humphrey's campaign, much less was spent by the AAC because the Democratic National Committee was extremely short of funds.

During the national conventions of 1964 and 1968, the AAC sought favorable ethnic planks for the party platform. The Nationalities Divisions of both parties have made this a regular practice. During the months of formulation of the party platform, ethnic congressmen and leaders are consulted for suggestions. To persuade members of the platform committee to recognize racial and ethnic groups, the Nationalities Divisions arrange for spokesmen from these groups to testify before the Committee. The Democratic platform of 1964 stated that it "encouraged by all peaceful means the growing independence of captive peoples living under Communism to hasten the day that Albania, Bulgaria, Czechoslovakia, East Germany, Estonia, Hungary, Latvia, Lithuania, Poland, Rumania and other captive nations will achieve full freedom and self-determination. We deplore Communist oppression of Jews and other minorities." The platform noted the Party's determination to eliminate the discriminatory national-origin quota system and made specific reference to its assistance of Cuban and Chinese refugees. It also listed its anti-Communist achievements from 1960 to 1964. The Republican platform, on the other hand, spoke extensively of the Democrats' foreign policy failures, renewed its "longstanding commitment to a course leading to eventual liberation of the Communist-dominated nations of Eastern Europe, Asia and Latin America," and took a strong anti-Communist line.

In 1968 the Democratic platform pledged: "As long as Israel is threatened by hostile and well-armed neighbors, we will assist her with essential military equipment needed for her defense, including the most advanced types of combat aircraft." The platform revealed

the difficulty in reconciling the Johnson administration's inaction in
the face of what the platform called "the brutal and unprovoked Soviet
aggression against Czechoslovakia" and "hard-won agreement" with
the Soviet Union on the one hand, and the Democrats' commitment to
the liberation of the captive nations on the other hand. The Republican
platform of 1968 spoke primarily of the need for international cooperation and improved trade relations. Their plank concerning captive
nations was weak, promising to encourage "greater political freedom"
for these nations by "a liberalization of trade in non-strategic goods."
No mention was made of the Soviet invasion of Czechoslovakia. The
Republicans also promised "supersonic fighters" to Israel.

The major parties tacitly recognized the white ethnic movement.
However, the platform of the American Independent Party reveals a
strong appeal to the fears, resentments, and antagonisms of the white
ethnics. The Democrats, under a section of the platform entitled
"Toward a Single Society," qualified the primary recommendation
of the bipartisan National Advisory Commission on Civil Disorders.
The major goal, the Commission wrote, "is the creation of a true
union—a single society, a single American identity." According to
the Democratic platform, a "single society, however, does not mean
social and cultural uniformity. We are a nation of many social, ethnic
and national groups. Each has brought richness and strength to
America." The Democratic platform drafters in the same section
also singled out the neglect of "the abilities and aspirations of Spanish
speaking Americans" and pledged "to fund and implement the Bilingual
Education Act and expand recruitment and training of bilingual federal
and state employees." Promises were explicitly made to Indians
and Eskimos, but the section did not refer specifically to blacks,
preferring to substitute the term "victims of past discrimination."

Before the presidential campaigns of 1964 and 1968, the chairman
of the AAC summoned the nationality chairmen to workshops to discuss
strategy. Campaign issues of particular importance to ethnic and
racial groups were identified and discussed. As early as May 1967,
Chairman Wagner called a conference of all the ethnic division
chairmen to begin plans for the 1968 presidential campaign. Representatives from the Bulgarian, Chinese, Croatian, Czechoslovakian,
German, Greek, Hungarian, Italian, Japanese, Lithuanian, Polish,
Portuguese, Puerto Rican, Rumanian, Russian, Spanish-Mexican,
and Ukranian Divisions attended and spoke at the conference. Plans
were drawn up for a September 1967 convention of the AAC, and
Wagner listened to the grievances of ethnic spokesmen concerning
the National Committee and the Johnson administration. In a report
to the National Committee in 1967, Wagner outlined the programs
of the AAC: extensive coverage in foreign language press and radio,
close coordination of nationality and state chairmen, speeches by

prominent public figures, and fund-raising affairs. Particular emphasis was also placed on registration and getting out the vote. During recent presidential campaigns, nationality chairmen were expected to organize political clubs, handle the ethnic newspapers, and prepare and distribute campaign literature and news releases.

The Nationalities Divisions of both parties are less active during nonpresidential congressional elections. But representatives of these divisions do assist congressional candidates during off-year elections. Though the AAC was primarily organized for presidential campaigns, it has, when requested, assisted Democratic candidates for the House and Senate and for governorships. During the 1966 campaign, the AAC served 132 such candidates. It sent out releases to nationality-group newspapers, taped radio programs for nationality-group stations, provided candidates with nationality breakdowns of their constituencies, and furnished them with lists of ethnic newspapers, radio programs, and the ethnic leaders in their districts and states. Congressional candidates are less likely to need these services than candidates for the Senate and state governorships. In 1966 Andrew Valuchek traveled around the country offering advice, when requested, to Democratic candidates in heavily ethnic districts. He attended campaign strategy conferences and offered suggestions, but always emphasized that local organizations had to implement strategies, such as endorsements and speeches by popular and influential ethnics representative of the major groups and advertising in ethnic newspapers, and that they had the final decision-making responsibility. Sometimes in critical campaigns, the AAC will provide financial support, campaign literature, and research reports on major issues.

Until the Republicans established a permanent nationalities council in 1968, the Democratic AAC was better equipped to offer a wider variety of services, and operated a more flexible program than its ad hoc counterpart. The 1968 presidential campaign may have been an exception since the Republican Party was able to overcome its lack of a permanent ethnic organization by spending more money on ethnic radio and newspaper campaigning.

Each year the AAC publishes and distributes to Democrats a guide to nationality observances containing a calendar of the birthdays of national heroes, historic anniversaries, and religious holidays. It serves as an intelligence link between Democratic politicians and their ethnic constituencies. The All American Council maintains a list of foreign language newspapers and foreign language radio stations. When spokesmen for the Party or important Democratic officeholders want to issue statements on subjects of special ethnic interest, the AAC prepares and distributes press releases to the appropriate newspapers. Democratic congressmen cooperate with the Council by reading statements into the Congressional Record which can later be used by the AAC to its advantage in the ethnic press. The ethnic press is generally cooperative since during campaigns revenues are received from politicians from all levels of government for the purchase of advertising space. In 1967 the AAC released, at the rate of one or more a week, articles dealing with political developments significant to ethnics. The AAC keeps informed of, but systematically avoids Communist- and Fascist-oriented newspapers. It does not differentiate groups on the basis of religion. The radio and television division of the Democratic National Committee assists the AAC in its communications with foreign language radio stations. The AAC books speakers for various ethnic functions.

The activities of Andrew Valuchek since his appointment to the staff in 1963 offer in microcosm the varied activities of the AAC itself. Valuchek travels around the country exchanging information with ethnic leaders and editors. He makes speeches, attends meetings and conventions, and keeps in close touch with the chairmen of each nationality group. He reads a great many ethnic newspapers. On June 26, 1971, he appeared on a local television program in Washington, D.C., discussed "Ethnic Politics 1972," and debated numerous issues with his Republican counterpart. While the executive director of the Polish-American Congress was attending an ethnic conference in Washington, D.C., in June 1971, he talked with Valuchek. Occasionally Valuchek arranges a private meeting between an individual and a senator. On one occasion he helped a Polish mother whose daughter was about to be expelled from school. He must advance the Democratic Party but, at the same time, patiently and sympathetically listen to grievances of ethnic leaders and spokesmen. If he can assist a reliable Democrat to win the leadership of an ethnic social or fraternal organization, he does so. In June 1970 he spoke at the first conference on white ethnics at the Catholic University of America.

The AAC has distributed procedural information to apprise nationality groups of the operation of such branches of government as the State Department. If specific legislation benefits a particular group, the AAC informs the groups of the law and gives the Democrats credit for it. It stresses its initiatives in liberalized immigration laws and social welfare legislation. In 1965 it worked closely with the Department of Health, Education, and Welfare to inform the millions of Americans who speak little English and were 65 or over that they were required to register to be eligible for Medicare. Through the ethnic press Valuchek helped to promote a series of conferences in 12 major American cities. Meetings and press conferences were held with the editors and publishers of foreign language newspapers, with radio programming directors, officers of social and fraternal organizations, and the clergymen of large ethnic congregations. Medicare officials appeared, spoke to these ethnic

leaders, and distributed pamphlets in various languages. The Democratic Party was thus associated with the Medicare program and
many recipients and their families identified the Party with the
benefits received.

The All American Council, while located in Washington, D.C.,
at the Party's headquarters, operates through state, regional, and
national chairmen, many or perhaps the majority of whom are politicians with ethnic constituencies. Local and regional chairmen
coordinate their activities with the Democratic state chairmen. In
the 1968 campaign, nationality-group activities were more regionalized
than in the 1964 campaign. John Marcin handled Polish-American
activities in the Chicago area, while John Gronouski supervised such
activities in the New York City area. The chairmen maintain volunteer
staffs and, if they are government officials, their staff often consists
of public employees under their direction. In the great majority of
cases, the chairman stands to benefit from enlarging the electoral
support of his group. If he is not an elective official with an ethnic
constituency, he usually has economic interests as a businessman or
professional in his ethnic community. Each chairman, 28 of them in
1967, represented a particular ethnic group in the national Party.
During election campaigns these chairmen and their volunteer staffs
do most of the work of the council. While former New York Mayor
Robert Wagner is the official head of AAC, the permanent staff directs
most of the activities of the Council. The permanent staff has never
been large, and in 1971 consisted only of Valuchek (Nationalities),
Muse (Minorities), and secretarial help. The meager staff of 1971
does not mean that the Democratic National Committee is less interested in ethnic politics; rather it reflects the financial bankruptcy
of the party and, to a lesser extent, internal discord. The AAC had
24 ethnic divisions in 1971.

The AAC has been greatly limited in its activities since 1968
because it has had a very small budget. But party strategists are
as committed as they were in the 1960s to appealing systematically,
explicitly, and nationally to ethnic Americans.

ACTIVITIES OF ONE DEMOCRATIC SUBDIVISION
DURING ONE CAMPAIGN

According to a privately published book entitled Operations
During the Johnson-Humphrey Campaign 1964, the Polish-American
Division of the AAC was one of its most active groups. This 121-page
book was prepared by the Polish-American Division for the AAC and
gives the details of the organization, its activities, and results of the
efforts of the Division in 1964. John C. Marcin, city clerk of Chicago,

a close ally of Richard J. Daley and one of the two key leaders of the Chicago Polish-American community, was national chairman of the Polish Division, editor of the book, and administrator of the activities reported in it. The organization relied fundamentally on volunteer staff. The failure to mention its budget suggests that it was probably a limited one. The book reveals that the Division worked hard with measurably positive results. The Division operated at the state and local level through 92 Polish-Americans, all of whom were public officials and business and professional leaders in their communities. Primarily they were concerned with linking the National Committee to Polish-American voters through their immediate associates and their contacts with local Polish-American newspapers and radio programs. They constituted a channel through which press and radio releases and campaign pamphlets were distributed. Many of them were officers in local Polish-American social, cultural, and fraternal organizations, and many were elected officers in the local, state, and federal government. They hailed mainly from Hartford, Gary, Baltimore, Chicago, Detroit, Jersey City, Buffalo, Brooklyn, Cleveland, Philadelphia, and Milwaukee. Questionnaires were sent to these 92 Polish leaders to elicit much of the information required by the Division for the campaign. The permanent staff prepared 30 press releases. These releases, in the Polish language, went out to 5 daily, 23 weekly, 5 bimonthly, and 2 monthly publications. They covered the organization and activities of the Polish-American Division, listed prominent Polish-American politicians who had achieved their elective and appointive positions through the Democratic Party, reported the Republican Party's displeasure with the sale of wheat to Poland, Goldwater's stand against minority groups in America, the enactment of a Democratic-backed minimum wage law, the 1961 juvenile delinquency law, the economic frugality of President Johnson, the prosperity and nuclear strength of the United States, and the prospects for Medicare. In addition to press releases, the Division prepared four separate display advertisements which were placed in 5 daily, 15 weekly, and 3 semimonthly Polish-American newspapers. Ten one-minute radio spot announcements were broadcast on 21 stations for a total broadcasting time of 236 minutes. With the exception of one in Miami, all the radio stations were located in the industrial cities of the North. Most of the campaign budget went for newspaper and radio coverage in such cities as New York, Chicago, Milwaukee, Buffalo, and Cleveland. Thirty thousand copies of a campaign pamphlet were distributed at the Polish-American Congress convention in Chicago in 1964. The pamphlet included quotations from President Johnson at the launching of the U.S.S. Pulaski at Groton, Connecticut, in 1964, and by Vice-President Humphrey in Chicago at the Polish Constitution Day festivities on May 3, 1959.

A total of 334,000 copies of another pamphlet, in the Polish language, entitled Poland Again Will Be a Liberated Country, was distributed throughout the country. As part of the 1964 campaign and during the Polish-American Congress convention in Chicago, the Division held a luncheon reception for the Polish-American press. U.S. Postmaster General John Gronouski addressed the group. The Division also provided a hospitality suite for Polish-American delegates to the convention. On October 13, 1964, the Division participated with the All American Council and the Cook County Democratic organization in a reception for Mayor Robert F. Wagner and Mayor Richard J. Daley in Chicago. Polish folk dancers entertained. The Division operated a speakers' bureau to provide campaign speakers for Polish fraternal, social, cultural, and religious groups. A telephone address by President Johnson and a speech by Hubert H. Humphrey to the delegates of the Polish-American Congress were arranged by the Division. In his address Johnson intoned: "For a thousand years, the people of Poland have been undaunted in their fight for freedom. . . . General Pulaski gave his life that Americans might be born in freedom. . . . We will continue to devise a policy that will achieve freedom for the Polish people. . . . In the past four months, I have sent two members of my cabinet—Postmaster General Gronouski and Attorney General Kennedy—to Poland to express our continued dedication to their cause. Soon we will dedicate the magnificent new Children's Hospital at Krakow, a gift from our people to the people of Poland. . . ." The Division arranged for other prominent Polish-Americans to speak to Polish-American gatherings. The concluding three pages of the Division's book concerning its operation in 1964 notes that the "Polish ethnic ticket" presented by the Republican Party—Polish ancestry of Barry Goldwater (Polish-born grandfather) and the Polish ancestry of William Miller's wife—was unconvincing to Polish-American voters. In Miller's last television appeal, on the eve of the election, his wife, Stephanie, referred to her Polish background. In the same concluding pages, the editor also mentions that the supposed "white backlash" among "middle-European nationality groups" did not manifest itself in the election returns to the advantage of the Republicans.

8

**REPUBLICAN PARTY
REACTION**

INTRODUCTION

The Republicans took seriously each national meeting of ethnic leaders sponsored by the Democratic National Committee, the expansion of the staff and activities of the Democrats' Nationalities Division, and the creation of the AAC. Nixon pushed the captive nations appeal in his 1960 campaign. On October 17, 1960, he spoke to a predominantly Polish-American audience in Buffalo's Polish Union Hall, promising liberation of the captive nations and support of Polish claims to former German lands by recognizing the Oder-Neisse line as Poland's western frontier. While in Chicago in 1964, Republican presidential candidate Barry Goldwater visited the then heavily Polish Milwaukee Avenue area, was photographed at a Polish museum, and referred to his Polish ancestry in an effort to win Polish-American votes. His vice-presidential running mate, William E. Miller, touted the Polish background of his wife and often took his Polish-speaking mother-in-law on tours with him. But when Miller attacked an immigration bill sponsored by the Democratic administration which would have made it easier for Europeans to emigrate to the United States, Polish Democrats seized the opportunity to publicize Miller's opposition to the more liberal entry laws which were an important goal of most nationality groups.

Since the Party was out of national power, divided on the question of whether or not it was important for an organization to court the ethnic vote, and devastated by the 1964 presidential defeat, it took Nixon until 1968 to consolidate Party power and convince the Republicans to devote substantial financial and leadership support to attracting more ethnic voters to the GOP. Following the 1964 election, the Republican leadership and the ranks of Republican partisans were overcome by despair: not only had they failed to gain the presidency, but 33 of the nation's 50 governors, 68 of the 100 senators, and 295 of the 435 congressmen were Democrats. The commitment of Nixon and Mitchell was largely reactive. Ethnic and racial minorities had elected Kennedy in 1960, but by 1968 the policies of Kennedy and Johnson had created resentment among white ethnics. The GOP leadership had an opportunity to gain new votes. The record shows it to be doubtful indeed that the Republicans have a permanent, long-run ideological commitment to the shared interests of ethnic Americans.

NIXON'S ETHNIC STRATEGY

Richard M. Nixon, as political head of the Republican Party, and his political strategists are aggressively committed to win the electoral support of ethnic Americans. The commitment, made during the 1968 presidential campaign, was developed during the next two years and by 1971 had reached maturity. Nixon and his strategists believe strongly that to win in 1972 the Republicans must capture a majority of the white ethnic vote. The 1972 presidential campaign may well produce the most aggressive and explicit effort by both parties to win the ethnic vote in the history of presidential politics. In 1948 and 1952 both parties actively courted ethnic Americans, but the record as of October 1971 suggests that the 1972 presidential campaign will press with unprecedented effort for the ethnic, racial, and religious vote. President Nixon is an uncompromisingly political animal, and the Republicans under his leadership have appealed to white ethnics on two bases: class and ethnicity.

SOCIAL AND ECONOMIC CLASS

The appeals to ethnic Americans in terms of socio-economic class take two directions: "silent majority" and blue-collar strategies. Strategists invented the term "the silent majority," and Vice-President Agnew was assigned the task of courting this vaguely defined group, primarily by appealing to its fears, resentments, and hostilities. Their only commonalities appear to be class and race—mostly lower-middle and middle-class whites—social conservatism, and a distaste for student and black outspokenness, demonstrations, disruptions, and riots. White ethnics probably account for the majority of this group, but it is so broadly delineated as to include the white Protestants of the South and Midwestern heartland.

The determining factor in the selection of Spiro Anagnostopoulos (Agnew) for the vice-presidency and his assignment to court the silent

majority was not that he is the son of a Greek immigrant. Agnew
mentions his Greek parentage to lend credence to his statements on
the problems of minority groups, but he is not an ethnic politician.
Many Maryland Greeks scoffed at his references to his Greek ancestry.
His father had Americanized his name; he himself prefers the nickname
Ted to Spiro; he did not marry a Greek woman and does not speak
Greek. Nixon selected him as his running mate because, as Maryland's
favorite son candidate, he committed the Maryland Republican delegation to Nixon before the 1968 convention, and because Agnew was
apparently acceptable to Southern voters for his confrontation with
black leaders two weeks after the Baltimore riot. He received national
attention for his chastisement of the blacks. Some political commen-
tators urged that following his dressing-down of the black leaders,
Agnew be referred to as "Mr. Backlash" and "Mr. Law and Order."
His ethnic background was undoubtedly regarded by Nixon as an asset.
His selection as wooer of the silent majority and as the Republicans'
practitioner of the politics of resentment was intended to keep the
president above such conflict. While Agnew traveled the low road,
Nixon could insulate himself from charges that he was systematically
engaging in divisive political tactics—pitting region against region,
race against race. In the simplest and crudest terms Agnew could
"out-Wallace Wallace." Agnew has talked little about the Yalta
"betrayals" or Democratic softness on Communism. In Polish or
Italian neighborhoods in 1970, he talked of neighborhood schools,
permissiveness, radical liberals, and pornography. Universities,
according to Agnew, were "a whole zoo of dissidents." On the subject
of captive nations, Agnew charged that Averell Harriman sold out
Poland to Stalin "for two riding horses." In his defense of the Nixon
administration's policy late in 1969, he referred to critics of the war
in Vietnam as "an effete corps of impudent snobs." Agnew has been
implementing the Republican strategy as outlined in Kevin Phillip's
The Emerging Republican Majority. The Democratic Party had tied
its fortunes to the plight of racial minorities and the poor. The eight
Democratic years of the 1960s produced the major civil rights bills.
"The colored began acting up after those laws were passed" was the
view expressed by many members of the silent majority. The Democrats were blamed for high taxes, rising welfare costs, and disruptions
by blacks and students. Growing black political power seemed to be
at the expense of white ethnics. Moreover, white ethnic resentment
against WASP culture could be transformed into resentment against
liberals, intellectuals, the media, and the Northeastern establishment.
Agnew's rhetoric played heavily on the potential of these divisions.

The other appeal in terms of class was to white blue-collar
workers, who probably constitute a majority of the silent majority.
They live closest to the black and Spanish-speaking minorities and

feel the most competition from these minorities for the diminishing
number of jobs in the urban centers. They are also disproportionately
squeezed by inflation. In the summer of 1969 President Nixon directed
a White House panel to study blue-collar workers. The panel was
headed by George P. Shultz, then Secretary of Labor, and the report
of the study was written by Jerome M. Rosow, Assistant Secretary of
Labor for Policy, Evaluation, and Research. In June 1970 the Rosow
report, in the form of a memorandum to the Secretary of Labor and
described as "a confidential study," was submitted to the president
and shortly thereafter "leaked" to the public. The report dealt with
the approximately 70 million people in blue-collar families who live
on incomes of between $5,000 and $10,000. The memorandum was
intended to reflect the White House's commitment to improving the
plight of these families. Blue-collar families, according to the report,
are trapped by inflation, limited earning capacity, inadequate education,
regressive state and local taxes, poor recreational facilities, and
lack of child-care facilities, and fall victim to the general discrimination against people who work with their hands. "To a considerable
extent," the report said, "they feel like 'forgotten people'—those for
whom the government and the society have limited, if any, direct
concern and little visible action." The report failed to mention the
Vietnam War and the pervasive climate of divisiveness and limited
hope that now in the 1970s afflicts large groups in the country, but it
did note that blue-collar workers are "overripe for a political response."
It recommended few concrete programs and no time-schedules for
implementation. Since the publication of the report, little has been
done for blue-collar workers, though Nixon in his speeches has praised
hard work and the contribution of America's workers and has condemned welfare freeloaders. Nixon Republicans reasoned that if
they could attract a substantial number of previously Democratic
blue-collar votes they could win a number of House and Senate seats
in the November 1970 elections. The hard hat of the construction
worker became the symbol of these voters, and both Republican and
Democratic candidates donned hard hats to demonstrate their identification with them. Vice-President Agnew appealed to blue-collar
workers' fears of school busing, violent crime, drugs, and subversive
bombings, and to their suspicion of intellectuals and the news and
electronic media. After President Nixon and AFL-CIO President
George Meany had a cozy chat "to discuss foreign policy" in 1970,
Republicans used pictures of the meeting in working-class neighborhoods.

The Republican blue-collar strategy in 1970 was a failure.
Organized labor was not persuaded by the diversionary tactics of
Agnew and Nixon. AFL-CIO President George Meany kept the issues
in clear focus: the "gut issues" for him were rising unemployment

and inflation. The Republican rhetoric was "an attempt to smokescreen the real issue—the pocketbook." An article, "Nixon-Agnew Think They Have Your Vote," in the October 1970 issue of the United Steel Workers' monthly newspaper, Steel Labor, stated:

> The Nixon-Agnew tactic is really the utilization of one of
> their own allegations: the assertion that the working man,
> and particularly the union man, is a boob who votes his
> emotions and cannot think for himself. It is the worst of
> both men and their low-road politics: talk of fear, threats,
> conspiracies, crime in the street, violence on the campus.
> But they don't talk about rising unemployment, spiraling
> inflation, increased interest rates, the contempt of the
> Administration and its agencies for the consumer, the bad-
> gered taxpayer and the parent who is witnessing the finan-
> cial destruction of the nation's public education system.

The article went on to analyze and report the voting records of the senatorial candidates, to insist that labor's friends were Democrats, not Republicans, to emphasize that "There is not one country for whites and one country for blacks," and concluded that the steel workers should call Nixon and Agnew's bluff: "Demonstrate that 'the blue collar vote' is not for sale to political hucksters whose men in Congress have voted against everything of vital interest to workers and their families."

Despite the disappointing results in the November 1970 elections, Nixon continued to woo blue-collar workers. At the annual meeting of the Teamsters Union in 1971, Nixon made a surprise appearance, bestowing the prestige of the president's office on the 2-million-member union.

ETHNIC APPEALS: RECOGNITION AND THE ESTABLISHMENT OF A PERMANENT ORGANIZATION

Nixon's Republican strategists have used the ethnic framework to appeal directly to white ethnic and racial groups. This has been done in two basic ways: grants of recognition and formation of a permanent nationalities division known as the National Republican Heritage Groups—the latter the largest and most aggressive under-taking by any national party in American history. Recognition is the prestige that accrues to an ethnic group when one of its members is nominated or appointed to public office. It may also take the form of acts and statements by government officials which benefit or honor ethnic groups as, for example, foreign policy concessions to Israel, an appearance at an ethnic parade, or a public utterance supporting the liberation of a captive nation.

As leader of the party, Nixon uses, to a limited extent, the mechanism of the balanced ticket. But, of course, presidential politics are different from city politics because in the former the constituency is spread over thousands of square miles, is more diverse, and consists less of ethnic and racial minorities. Ninety percent of America's voters are white, 9 percent black. All other racial groups constitute 1 percent. Only 1 out of 3 Americans is Roman Catholic, 1 out of 6 is first- or second-generation, and only 3 out of 100 are Jewish. Less than 1 out of 4 Americans is likely to be influenced by ethnic appeals in presidential campaigns, though white opposition to the election of a black man to the White House may be the exception. A mayor of a large Northern city, on the other hand, would not survive for long unless he practiced ethnic politics, as the great majority of his constituency belongs to some ethnic or racial group which competes for limited political power, public offices, and jobs.

At the national level, the party slates only two candidates. While Agnew's heritage was not vital to his selection as Nixon's running mate in 1968, it would have been in 1972 if second-generation Polish-Catholic Edmund Muskie had won the Democratic nomination. The best possibility at the presidential level for application of the "balanced ticket" strategy is in the appointment of the cabinet. Nixon's cabinet has contained white ethnics: former Attorney General John Mitchell, an Irish-Catholic, and Transportation Secretary John A. Volpe, an Italian-American and former governor of Massachusetts. The former cannot be construed, however, as an ethnic appointment—Mitchell was Nixon's campaign manager and former law partner. The latter was very much a part of Nixon's ethnic strategy. In fact, Volpe, a Catholic, "will play a very major role" in the 1972 campaign, according to a Nixon administration insider. He will spearhead strategy to win the white ethnic vote. Having alienated many blue-collar workers and unionists with the wage-price freeze, and having apparently reaped few white ethnic votes through Agnew's rhetoric of resentment, Nixon now plans to appeal to white ethnics as Catholics. In 1972 Volpe will speak widely to Catholic groups, but the extent to which the Nixon administration is prepared to make concrete promises is still unclear. Daniel Patrick Moynihan, an Irishman, and Henry Kissinger, a Central European immigrant, were also appointed by Nixon as key aides, but neither of these academicians are associated with ethnic communities or constituencies.

In October 1971 GOP National Chairman, Robert J. Dole, spoke to the Illinois Republican Nationalities Council at a dinner in suburban Chicago and emphasized that in the last two months Nixon had appointed

17 ethnic Americans to office, including persons of Polish, Cuban, Mexican, Hungarian, Latvian, Filipino, Chinese, Italian, Puerto Rican, and Greek ancestry. Many political analysts reason that Nixon lost in 1960 because he failed to win Illinois by less than 10,000 votes. The Republican nationalities chairman in Illinois in 1968 spent more than $40,000 to win the state's ethnic vote. He and Agnew came to Illinois shortly before the November 1970 elections to bolster the campaigns of Illinois Republican candidates. Ten days before the 1970 November elections, Illinois Republican senatorial candidate Ralph T. Smith attended numerous ethnic meetings and receptions— an Italian breakfast, a Latvian brunch, a Puerto Rican luncheon, a Hungarian reception, a Polish polka party, a Ukrainian banquet, and a German reception. In a Puerto Rican community center in Chicago, youngsters jammed scores of "Ralph Smith Coloring Books" into "Edmund Kucharski for Treasurer" shopping bags. Smith received a standing ovation at a Hungarian liberation meeting in the Saint Alphonse Athenaeum, where Hungarian-Americans were mourning the unsuccess- ful Hungarian uprising. "I hope your nation behind that wall of Com- munism will again see the light of freedom we all love so dearly," Smith said. The Latvian immigrants assured Smith that 95 percent of them were Republicans. Voldemars Korsts, chairman of the Latvian-American GOP National Committee, explained, "Most Latvians came here around 1950—still bitter about former President Roosevelt who sold out Latvia after World War II to slavery under the Russians." Smith replied, "I hope the revolutionaries who would destroy America would someday come to love the country as much as Latvian immigrants have." Smith, state treasurer candidate Edmund Kucharski (first Polish-American with a -ski surname to run statewide in Illinois), and other leading Republicans spoke at an "old time Lithuanian political rally" sponsored by the Lithuanian Republican League of Illinois and held in a Lithuanian neighborhood.

Italians

Nixon concentrates his ethnic recognition on the major groups. Three New England Italian-Americans have major leadership roles in the United States Department of Transportation. In addition to Secretary John A. Volpe, there are Rhode Island's Herbert F. DeSimone, Assistant Secretary of Transportation, and the department's new Director of Consumer Affairs, the former mayor of Hartford, Ann P. Uccello. The recognition of Italian-Americans in the transportation field seems to be coordinated by Nixon strategists. In Illinois Republican Governor Richard B. Ogilvie appointed an Italian-American to head the state's Department of Transportation. In December 1970

Nixon named Frank Carlucci as director of the Office of Economic
Opportunity. Months later Carlucci was moved to the third highest
position in the Office of Budget and Management. The Italian-American
press ran front-page stories on the appointments, comparing their
prestige and influence to the positions held by Volpe and Joseph J.
Sisco, Assistant Secretary of State for Near Eastern and South Asian
Affairs. Nixon observed Columbus Day in 1971 by meeting for nearly
an hour with Italian Foreign Minister Aldo Moro. He received the
annual Marconi Award from the Order of Sons of Italy, honoring his
"great leadership for permanent peace in the world." Presenting the
award to the president was the group's Supreme Venerable, Amerigo
Cortese of Philadelphia. During the ceremony in the Oval Room,
Nixon declared that he was "grateful and very honored" to be selected
as the sixth recipient of the award. In Chicago Republican Senator
Charles Percy marched with Richard J. Daley in the front line of the
1971 Columbus Day parade. Republican Governor Ogilvie apparently
does not march with Daley and vice versa. But Ogilvie had his turn.
The Sons of Italy arranged a banquet shortly thereafter with him as
the guest of honor.

Irish

        When Nixon went to Europe in 1970, he traveled out of his way
to reveal that his and his wife's ancestral homes were in Ireland.
Nixon is Protestant Irish, sometimes referred to as black Irish;
Nixon ancestors hail from Cork, the Milhous family from Kildare.
His great-great-great-great-great-grandfather, he announced, had
been born in Ireland, though he had immigrated to America more than
200 years ago. Nixon, like John Fitzgerald Kennedy, sought and found
his ancestral roots, and, like Robert Fitzgerald Kennedy, stood on the
trunk of his car embracing the mayor of Limerick and shaking hands
with fellow Irishmen. This was for the benefit of Irish-Americans
back home, and a striking example of the new ethnic politics.

Poles

        Appeals by national politicians to Polish-Americans are usually
made in Chicago, where there are more Polish-Americans than in
any other American metropolitan area. Chicago is the center of
Polish-American organizational activity in the United States. In 1970
President Nixon went there to bolster the senatorial campaign of
Ralph T. Smith and other Illinois Republican candidates. During his
visit he met with a delegation of Polish-American leaders: the editors

of the two Chicago daily Polish-language newspapers and the heads
of the four national fraternal organizations, all based in Chicago and
with a combined membership of nearly 2 million. Nixon, as leader of
the Republican Party, did not meet with the representatives of any
other ethnic or racial groups during his 26-hour stay in Chicago.
The meeting in the president's suite was prearranged by Republican
Congressman Edward Derwinski for the publicly declared purpose of
obtaining assurances from Nixon that he would appoint more Polish-
Americans to federal positions. During the meeting with these Polish-
American leaders, the president of the Polish Women's Alliance of
Americans advised Nixon of the Alliance's program for American
relief to Poland. It was a grand and explicit display of ethnic politics
and recognition. At least one major Chicago daily showed Nixon
shaking hands and smiling with eight Polish-American leaders. Similar
pictures appeared in the Polish press. The only Democratic politician
in the group was a trustee of the Chicago Metropolitan Sanitary District,
included only because he was president of the Polish Alma Mater.
Aides to Democratic senatorial candidate Adlai Stevenson III objected
to Nixon's special meeting, declaring it was simply an effort to diminish the ethnic attraction of Senator Muskie, of Polish descent and at
the time an aspirant to the presidential nomination in 1972. In fact,
Nixon, a master politician, was only following the tactics established
by Daley and his Irish predecessors, who for forty years had dealt
successfully with ethnic and racial groups in Chicago. While appearing to give much, they, in fact, gave only as much recognition to non-
Irish groups as was absolutely necessary. And though Nixon's appearance with these Polish leaders may have enhanced their careers, few
Polish-Americans have been appointed to federal office. During the
1968 presidential campaign, Polish-American leaders meeting with
Nixon had submitted the names of qualified Polish-Americans they
wanted to see appointed to federal posts. But between that meeting
and a September 1970 meeting, some of these leaders had complained
that the Nixon administration was not giving Polish-Americans their
fair share of appointments. Significantly, however, most of these
leaders have not publicly called Nixon to account, nor have they made
explicit demands upon him. His 1970 conference in Chicago was cor-
dial; he got the exposure he wanted, and he lent prestige to the Polish
leaders who were present. After all, the president of the United States
had taken time to talk and be photographed with them. Congressman
Derwinski, the leader of the delegation, when asked about Nixon's
response to the request for federal appointments, said the president
had "tossed the ball" back to him and told him "to recommend more
qualified Polish people and when I did so, there would be more
appointments."
     One important appointment made by Nixon was of Aloysius
Mazewski as an alternative United States delegate to the 25th United

Nations General Assembly. It was no accident that he was and remains
the most influential Polish-American leader in America. He has been
since before his appointment president of both the Polish National
Alliance (PNA), a national fraternal organization with 328,000 members
in 1971, and the Polish-American Congress (PAC), an umbrella for
Polish organizations. Some Democratic Polish-Americans believe
that Mazewski "was bought cheaply." (President Kennedy had appointed
a Polish-American to his cabinet as postmaster general, the first
Polish-American to receive a cabinet appointment.) Leaders of the
PNA have historically played an active role in local and national
politics. Charles Rozmarek was its president for 28 years and
actively supported the Republicans nationally in the late 1940s and
in 1952 and 1956. In 1967 he was deposed in a surprise coup by
Mazewski at the quadrennial convention. Mazewski defeated Rozmarek
by 20 votes out of the 450 cast by delegates representing local chapters
of the Alliance throughout the country. In the 1960s Rozmarek leaned
slightly toward the Democratic Party, but his presidency of the PNA
and PAC inhibited his political activities since these organizations
are ostensibly nonpartisan. At the 1967 convention Chicago Democratic Congressman Roman C. Pucinski, who had often worked with
Rozmarek in wooing Polish voters on Chicago's northwest side, was
also defeated in his bid for the chairmanship of the convention. At the
time of his election as president of the PNA, Mazewski was the elected
Republican committeeman of Chicago's 41st Ward and influential in
local Republican Party councils. Though Rozmarek's advanced age
was undoubtedly a factor in his defeat, some political observers in
Chicago interpreted Mazewski's election as president of the PNA and
PAC as a reflection of the increasing number of members of these
organizations who are drifting from their Democratic moorings to the
Republican Party. Rozmarek's accommodation with both the local
Democratic organization and Party boss Daley is partly traceable to
the appointment of Rozmarek's daughter by the Democrats as a Cook
County magistrate.

Nixon has wooed Polish-Americans in other ways as well, and his
efforts have not been in vain. In 1970 he sent Elliot Richardson, then
Undersecretary of State, to the celebration of Polish Constitution Day
in Chicago. His appearance, and designation as principal speaker,
may explain Mayor Daley's failure to appear. Richardson criticized
the Russian intervention that crushed Czechoslovakia's program of
liberal reforms. He also played down the Soviet Union's proposal for
a European security conference by saying: "We seek to deal with
concrete issues and try in concrete ways to resolve them, avoiding
meetings for their own sake which can raise unfounded hopes."
Republican Senator Charles Percy noted at the same ceremonies that
the Polish people "have never given up the fight for freedom and

never will. All Americans support you in your desire for a free Poland."

As part of the Constitution Day celebration, Mazewski publicly declared his support of Nixon's invasion of Cambodia. "We may have differences of opinion as to the justification of our initial involvement in Vietnam. . . . However, the time for debates has ended with the entry of our gallant fighting men into Cambodia, to deny the enemy privileged sanctuaries. . . . We do not subscribe to the cries for bug-out raised by far-out dissenters," he said, "but we strongly subscribe to Stephen Decatur's injunction: 'Our country, right or wrong!'"

Many Polish-American groups have passed resolutions declaring their support for Nixon's actions in Southeast Asia. Thus he has not only gained votes, but support for his foreign policies. Congressman Derwinski marched in the 1970 Constitution Day parade in the costume of a Polish Highlander, and he occasionally speaks Polish in campaign speeches. Governor Ogilvie compared the Polish Constitution of 1791 to the United States Constitution "as a beacon of hope for people all over the world . . . a reminder to us that the spirit of liberty, however restricted, never really dies." In 1970 President Nixon designated October 11 as General Casimir Pulaski Memorial Day. The famed Poznan Boys' Choir of Poland were guests of President and Mrs. Nixon at the White House in June 1971. Edward J. Piszek, president of Mrs. Paul's Kitchens, Inc., sponsor of the Poznan Choir's tour in America, presented the boys to President Nixon and his wife.

Lithuanians and Slovaks

When in November 1970 a Lithuanian sailor seeking political asylum jumped from a Soviet fishing boat to a United States Coast Guard cutter off the East Coast and was returned to the Russians 10 hours later on orders from Coast Guard headquarters in Boston, Nixon publicly declared his regrets, denounced the action of the Coast Guard and ordered an investigation. The Coast Guard officers responsible for the return of the sailor were forced to retire in December rather than face court martial for their roles in the incident. Nixon was not only concerned with the adverse reaction among Lithuanian-Americans, but with the passions aroused in all Americans who trace their ancestry to captive nations and might seek to retaliate in 1972. When the Slovak World Congress met in Toronto in June 1971, Senators John Tower (R-Tex.), Strom Thurmond (R-S.C.), Roman Hruska (R-Neb.), and others sent warm greetings, and Senators Robert Taft (R-Ohio) and Claiborne Pell (D-R.I.) were on hand to address the meeting. The Congress had been organized with the aid of the Slovak advisor to the Republican National Committee.

Catholics

Besides appealing to white ethnics on the basis of their ties
with captive nations, Nixon reaches out to them as Catholics. On
August 17, 1970, he met with seven representatives of the United
States Catholic Conference (USCC) for one hour at the White House.
These representatives told the president that "America cannot afford
to neglect the needs of its white ethnic minorities . . . because to do
so would further polarize society and might lead to more hostilities
between blacks and white ethnics." The USCC group emphasized the
need to give white ethnics, many of them working-class Catholics in
Northern cities, a sense of fuller participation in American life.
Bishop Bernardin, USCC General Secretary, said the group pointed
out that "ways must be found in which ethnic whites and blacks can
work together to build communities in urban America in the 1970's.
We cannot afford to emphasize one group at the expense of another,"
he said, "but instead must seek to give all a fuller sense of participation
in national life." According to Bernardin, too many "white ethnic
groups feel left out, unappreciated, neglected by government, unfairly
stereotyped as bigots and reactionaries. The potential consequences
for society are tragic." President Nixon, according to Bishop
Bernardin, was receptive to the group's proposals and "shared the
hope that viable programs can be developed to counteract these
tendencies." "The President was sympathetic and informed on the
subject of the 'forgotten' American who belongs to an ethnic minority,"
the bishop said. "He made it clear that the administration is anxious
to work with others in developing meaningful solutions to the problems
of ethnic Americans and in finding ways in which all minority groups
in our society can cooperate to build viable communities."
During the White House meeting, Monsignor Geno Baroni of the
USCC's Task Force on Urban Problems reported to the president on
the Workshop on Urban Ethnic Community Development, sponsored in
June 1970 by the Conference's Urban Task Force and the Catholic
University of America. He told Nixon of the recommendations of the
Workshop, including a proposal for a federal interagency task force
to review possibilities for assistance to ethnic communities under
existing federal programs.
Nixon also saw ethnic study leaders and was briefed by them
on the renewed interest by ethnic groups in their own heritage and of
their desire for more participation in the national government. When
the Reverend Paul J. Asciolla ventured to remind President Nixon
that Italian-Americans want more federal jobs, Nixon was quick to
respond that John Volpe was continually telling him the same thing.
Nixon thereby acknowledged Volpe as chief lobbyist for Italian-
Americans. A photograph in the Italian-American newspaper Fra Noi

(March 1971) showed Nixon smiling at the editor, Father Asciolla, while Michael Wenk of the Migration and Refugee Services Committee of the USCC and the Reverend Silvano Tomasi, Director of the Center for Migration Studies in New York, looked on. In the picture Nixon displayed Father Tomasi's new book The Italian Experience in the United States.

This bid for votes from white ethnics as Roman Catholics was indicated in 1971 when Nixon addressed the Knights of Columbus and pledged support to financially-troubled parochial schools. Nixon has established the first federally-sponsored Panel on Non-Public Education, which will consider tax concessions for parents of children in private schools. However, given the 1971 Supreme Court decision striking down a state scheme to provide financial aid to parochial schools because of "excessive entanglement" between church and school, it is not clear in what way the president will be able to honor his pledge. It is significant that Kennedy, before being elected in 1960, was virtually forced to promise not to side with his coreligionists in pleas for aid to parochial schools.

Nixon's widely publicized campaign to combat narcotics traffic and addiction has a strong appeal to family-oriented Catholics. During the first two years of his administration, he introduced anticrime and anti-obscenity legislation in Congress, appointed the first ambassador to the Vatican since the time of Franklin Roosevelt, and filed a "friend of the court" brief before the Supreme Court on the constitutionality of certain forms of aid to parochial schools.

When the leadership of the medical staffs of the military directed that abortions should be performed if requested, Nixon intervened and rescinded the order. His action has generally been interpreted as a pro-Catholic move. Nixon's efforts to influence the deliberations, findings, and recommendations of the Presidential Commission on Obscenity, and later to prevent publication of the Commission's report by court action of his appointee to the Commission, were strongly motivated by American Catholic attitudes toward pornography. But while Nixon is actively courting Catholics, he is not neglecting Protestants. Like his predecessor, President Johnson, he invites highly visible Protestants, such as the Reverend Billy Graham, to the White House. In October 1971 Nixon traveled to Charlotte, North Carolina, to lead a hometown tribute to the evangelist preacher. The two rode in a motorcade through the business district, waving to cheering crowds. Schools were closed to allow students to honor the evangelist whose "Crusades for Christ" over the last 25 years have reached an audience estimated at 42 million. In the fall of 1971, President Nixon also received the 100-millionth Gideon Bible from W. R. Davenport, president of Campbellsville College in Kentucky, who is president of Gideons' International.

Spanish-Americans

Nixon has aggressively pursued the electoral support of racial
minorities. His racial group strategy has concentrated on Mexican-
Americans in California, Texas, New Mexico, and Arizona, and, to a
lesser extent, the Mexican-Americans and Puerto Ricans in the Chicago
area. A March 1971 population survey by the Bureau of the Census
found 9 million Americans who identified themselves as being of
Spanish-origin, 5 million Mexican-Americans who did likewise, 1.5 million Puerto Ricans, and 626,000 Cubans. With the exception of the
Puerto Ricans and Cubans, most Americans of Spanish descent live in
the Southwest. In 1970 Texas had more than 1.5 million Chicanos,
and California's Mexican-American population was approaching 2
million. In the 1960s the Republican Party began to make inroads
into this group of voters at local and state levels through the use of
patronage. The active campaigning of Republican John Tower in
Mexican-American areas of Texas in 1966 revealed possibilities for
capturing the Mexican-American vote. There was a substantial
defection by Mexican-Americans to Tower, successor to Lyndon B.
Johnson's seat and the first Republican to be elected to the Senate
from Texas since 1870. The disenchantment of Mexican-Americans
in the Southwest in the 1960s also led to the formation of independent
splinter organizations and third parties. Such third parties as La
Raza Unida have been able to elect entire Mexican-American slates
in local elections. In 1969 its school board ticket in Crystal City,
Texas, won all the seats on the board. In such large cities as Los
Angeles and San Antonio, the Chicano vote can be decisive. Protest
demonstrations, school boycotts, police confrontations, and riots by
Mexican-Americans have erupted in the last few years in East Los
Angeles. La Raza Unida, other splinter organizations, and youth gangs
show increasing followings. In November 1971 Edmund Muskie, campaigning for a Mexican-American Democratic nominee for the state
Assembly in Los Angeles, was picketed and eggs were hurled at his
group by members of La Raza Unida, which was supporting another
candidate.

Nixon's strategy is to swing enough of the normally Democratic
Latin votes from these groups to win majorities in Texas, California,
and Illinois in 1972. To that end, he appointed Philip V. Sanchez of
Fresno, California, as Director of the Office of Economic Opportunity—
the highest position ever held by a Mexican-American in the United
States government. The Sanchez appointment, in the summer of 1971,
was atypical because, contrary to public statements by his two Nixon-
appointed predecessors, Sanchez at his first press conference declared
that he did not believe that the poor, especially in the community action
agencies, should be prohibited from having confrontations with local

government. In the fall of 1971 Nixon nominated Mrs. Romana Banuelos of California as United States Treasurer. She had founded a $5-million-a-year food business, a bank, and a scholarship program to assist students from East Los Angeles schools. Nixon, in introducing Mrs. Banuelos at a ceremony in the White House, noted that she was the first Mexican-American woman to be named to such a high government post. He said it was "significant" that Mrs. Banuelos's appointment came at a time when the president is from California and the Secretary of the Treasury from Texas—the two states with the largest number of Mexican-Americans.

The Nixon administration revitalized the Cabinet Committee on Opportunities for Spanish Speaking People and nominated Henry M. Ramirez, a Mexican-American, as its chairman. President Johnson had originally organized the Committee, but it had been limited to Mexican-American affairs. Under Johnson, the Committee had held hearings and issued reports. In October 1971 Ramirez went to Chicago with Sanchez and high-ranking administration officials for conferences with Midwest Latins. The Chicago conference had not originally been scheduled, but when conferences were held in the Southwest, Midwest Latins complained loudly that they had been overlooked. The federal conferences coincided with workshops for local Latin organizations sponsored by the state of Illinois and its Republican governor. A small and carefully selected group of Spanish-origin professionals and businessmen—but few indigenous leaders—was invited. Basic economic problems, such as the high unemployment rate among Spanish-origin Midwesterners, were not on the agenda. Nearly 50 grass-roots leaders and their followers attended at least one closed meeting. The conferences were stormy as Chicago Latins demanded formal meetings and sought, without delay, concrete programs, jobs, and federal appointments. They loudly protested that Midwestern Latins were ignored by Washington. Following the conferences, the president of the Spanish-American Businessmen's Association commented: "Ramirez and Sanchez got roasted; they were punching bags for our problems. . . . I do not see any purpose in top officials coming out the way they did—arousing expectations and delivering nothing. It was O.K. sending scouts, but they should not have come without something concrete." Some Puerto Ricans were irritated that Ramirez, a Mexican-American from the Southwest, did not commit himself to appointing a Puerto Rican as his single executive director. "This is the first time a President has really addressed himself to this [Latin] problem," said George Vavoulis, a Nixon-appointed regional administrator of the Department of Housing and Urban Development and a participant in one of the meetings. The president, according to Vavoulis, has a 16-point program (November 1970), to have more Latins hired by federal agencies and to reach them with training and other

programs. Earlier in 1971 as part of the program, the director of
the Office of Spanish-Speaking Affairs for the Department of Health,
Education, and Welfare went to Chicago to discuss with Latin representatives opportunities for improving education in the city's Spanish-
speaking communities. At two public meetings arranged by the director
there were discussions of bilingual education, programs for teaching
English as a second language, and the possibility of bringing education
specialists to Chicago from other parts of the country to improve the
curriculum.

Blacks

Nixon has now written off the black vote, but he limits his visible
appeals to the black electorate—to appeal to blacks directly would be
to risk antagonizing white ethnic Americans. He did recognize and
meet with the black caucus, and formally answer their demands. He
did not appoint any blacks to his cabinet and has not appointed blacks
to many influential positions in the federal government. He did appoint
Walter Washington as mayor of the District of Columbia. A few of his
black appointees have resigned, and some of those resigning have
been highly critical of the Nixon administration and its minorities
programs.

During the first two years of his administration, he continued
the school integration program, supported low-income housing, and
filed a federal suit to open the suburbs in Black Jack, Missouri. In
October 1971, in a special message to Congress, he requested a 20-
fold increase over two years in federal spending to help minority
businessmen, and thus, three years after his election, Nixon appeared
to be making good on his campaign promise to promote black capitalism.
Noting these lukewarm efforts, and the strong possibility of Nixon's
reelection, the National Association for the Advancement of Colored
People, the largest and oldest civil rights organization in the country,
stated through its board chairman at its 1971 convention that the Nixon
administration had earned "cautious and limited approval." The leaders
of the NAACP apparently had decided to accept President Nixon, at
least tentatively. Whether Nixon will reward the black community for
the easy-on-Nixon approach of the NAACP remains to be seen. Despite his pledge not to talk politics in 1971, Nixon did not miss any
opportunities to court the blacks. Citing the election of President
John F. Kennedy, a Roman Catholic, and Senator Edward W. Brooke,
a black, President Nixon rebutted Senator Edmund S. Muskie's view
that a black could not be elected vice-president in 1972. "I believe
it is frankly a libel on the American people to suggest that the American
people . . . would vote against a man because of his religion, race or

color," he piously declared. Gary Mayor Richard Hatcher charged in early October that the Republican National Committee submitted to Ebony magazine an editorial condemning Democratic Senator Edmund Muskie, because of the latter's statement over his dubiousness of the chances of a black running mate. The editorial, which Ebony turned down, charged that Muskie's statement had caused "increased polarization" and "may have doomed Muskie's presidential chances in 1972." Hatcher called the editorial "an attempt by a Republican to pretend he was doing the black people a favor."

REPUBLICANS ESTABLISH PERMANENT
ETHNIC DIVISION

In addition to granting recognition to white ethnics, the Republicans have formed a permanent Nationalities Division as part of the Republican National Committee. All previous efforts to attract ethnic Americans had been on a campaign-by-campaign basis. During the campaigns of the 1930s, the Republican National Committee's Division of Nationalized Citizens exploited ethnic concern with economic issues. By concerted efforts in the presidential campaigns of 1948 and 1952, the Republican Party challenged the majority electoral support which ethnic minorities had traditionally given the Democratic Party. The Republicans referred to this effort as their "foreign language group activity." The Party's pursuit of the ethnic vote during these two elections was as vigorous as the campaigns waged by the Democrats. But the Nationalities Division of the Republican National Committee ceased all activity between presidential campaigns.

In 1968, however, Nixon authorized a systematic courtship of the white ethnic vote. Laszlo Pasztor, a Hungarian freedom fighter in the 1956 uprising, had been brought to the Republican National Committee by Robert Dole's predecessor and was hired as a full-time advisor on ethnic affairs. He had previously campaigned for Richard Nixon in 1960 and Barry Goldwater in 1964, and had been a member of United Citizens for Nixon-Agnew. Pasztor spent two years traveling around the country, talking and listening to ethnic Americans. He determined that a formal ethnic organization within the GOP was feasible and would be politically profitable. Nixon and the GOP leadership were already committed to an aggressive ethnic strategy. Pasztor was designated Director of the Nationalities Division of the Republican National Committee and given a staff—which by June 1971 had grown to five. It was the nearly two years of preparation by Pasztor that made the May 1971 organizational convention a success and the new permanent GOP ethnic council a reality. By the fall of 1971 Pasztor had assisted in the organization of more than 15 state Republican Nationalities Councils and had established contacts with many ethnic communities.

The Nationalities Division is staffed with white ethnics. During Nixon's 1960 presidential campaign, however, the Nationalities Division of the Republican National Committee was heavily staffed with nonethnic personnel who apparently had little know-how and provoked resentment among the ethnic leaders who were being wooed. This mistake was corrected. The Committee is prepared to spend a considerable amount of money to organize an ethnic council, and Pasztor has been assured the necessary funds.

In May 1971 Pasztor invited some 300 ethnic Americans to Washington, D.C., to formalize their permanent organization. More than 250 attended the May 21-23 convention. The delegates to the convention were representatives of major ethnic organizations, nationality clubs, and observers interested in establishing a formal ethnic organization within the GOP. Delegates from 27 states and the District of Columbia, representing 31 nationalities, officially formed the National Republican Heritage Groups (Nationalities) Council, supposedly autonomous, but actually no more than an arm of the Republican National Committee, which had convened these white ethnics to legitimize their new ethnic strategy. The first newsletter claimed that the Council was "the first permanent ethnic auxiliary of a political party."

The convention was organizational. A constitutional framework was established and 13 officers, representing 12 nationalities and 10 states, were elected at the Council's first meeting. Laszlo Pasztor was named chairman. Workshops were held and resolutions adopted. The goal of the Council's leadership was to build a nationwide grass-roots organizational network consisting of local ethnic clubs in every state. Tactics for an all-out effort to attract ethnic American voters to the Republican Party were discussed at the convention. "The formation of this permanent auxiliary to the Republican Party represents a major landmark in our party's history," President Nixon informed the delegates through a letter to Pasztor. "To bring together the best of our rich and varied traditions and talents and direct them to the fulfillment of our common hopes is in the finest spirit of Republics." It was agreed that the organization's fundamental purpose was to consolidate the efforts of GOP ethnic groups in order to bring about increased ethnic participation on a national scale. The first newsletter read: "Its chief goals: to attract the more than 40 million Americans of ethnic background to all levels of GOP activity; provide a sounding board for ethnic problems and opinion; and to formalize the already substantial support among ethnic Americans for President Nixon's domestic and foreign policies." At the convention Pasztor announced that for the next 18 months the Council would conduct workshops to prepare for the 1972 presidential election.

Keynoting an evening banquet at the convention, Kansas Senator Robert Dole, chairman of the Republican National Committee, predicted a heavy Republican turnout among ethnics in 1972. "They [ethnic Americans] are weary of years of political promises without performance. . . . Today more than any time in this century, millions of traditionally Democratic ethnic voters are restless. Today, more than ever before in this century, they are looking for a political alternative to bankrupt Democrat leadership." Dole told the ethnic delegates that they represented those Americans who brought a new appreciation for the things that some Americans take too much for granted. "If we succeed in building a new coalition of Americans from different backgrounds and different parts of the country," Dole said, "more progress on the domestic and international fronts is possible." He invited them to join Nixon and the Republican National Committee in broadening the base of the Republican Party.

Republican Illinois Congressman Edward J. Derwinski, special representative for nationalities affairs on the Republican National Committee, spoke to the ethnic delegates on behalf of the sponsors of the proposed Ethnic Studies Center Act. Under the bill's provisions, $50 million would be allocated over a two-year period to enlarge school curricula to include the study of the heritages of America's immigrants. Derwinski symbolizes the emerging middle-class white ethnic. His father was a Democrat. He himself worked hard to enter the middle class, moved to a Chicago suburb, and was elected to the House of Representatives in 1958 by the southwest suburbs of Chicago. "By the time my father passed away in 1947," says Derwinski, "he was disillusioned with FDR." Derwinski has served as chairman of the Nationalities Division of the Republican National Committee and has read material favorable to the Republicans into the Congressional Record in order to attract ethnic votes.

Pasztor and the Republican National Committee also arranged for other prominent white ethnics in the Party and the federal government to address the delegates, among them the Committee's deputy chairman for communications, a special counselor to the president, a White House staff assistant, the assistant secretary of the Treasury, and the assistant secretary of the Transportation Department. Blacks and Jews were not invited to participate in the formation of the GOP ethnic council, but the executive board included a Chinese co-chairwoman, a Mexican-American vice-chairman, and a Cuban treasurer. The executive board was selected to provide not only the widest possible distribution of the major nationality groups, but also to encompass the widest geographical distribution. The Council held a second major conference and banquet in November 1971.

When Laszlo Pasztor contacted the nation's ethnic leaders, he endeavored to enlist the support of those recognized as bona fide leaders and spokesmen by their respective groups. Officials of national organizations and editors of ethnic newspapers were given

top priority. The man designated to head the Ukrainian division was
the Supreme Advisor of the Ukranian Association. With status as a
duly elected national officer, and with a local Ukrainian following in
Chicago and some influence over other Chicago ethnic leaders, he
was well qualified to serve as the Ukrainian representative. Nixon
named him to an administration advisory council on education, and
then elevated him in November 1971 to the important post of regional
deputy director of ACTION. The editor of the weekly newspaper
Slovak v Amerike was appointed by the Republican National Committee
as chief Slovak-American adviser to the Republican Heritage Group
Division, and Nixon subsequently appointed him to the Small Business
Administration advisory council.

Pasztor encouraged these leaders and others to establish state
nationalities councils, federations of nationalities groups, and local
clubs. Republican assistance was promised in terms of presidential
messages, advice, appointments, guest appearances by prominent
Republicans, and, where possible, financial support. These tactics
were intended to enhance the prestige of these leaders and editors,
who would then wield more influence for the Republicans in their
efforts to capture ethnic votes. The organizational network was pro-
jected to resemble that of the Young Republicans and the Republican
Women's Federation. By November 1971 the National Republican
Heritage Group Council had assisted in the establishment of 20 state
councils. The October 1971 newsletter announced the formation of two
new Republican Nationalities Councils: the Republican State Nationalities Council of Arizona, and the National Chinese-American Republican
Federation, with Senator Hiram Fong as honorary chairman.

Indicative of the importance of this organizational effort at the
national level was the pressure on Republican leadership at the state
level, as applied by the Republican National Committee. In Illinois,
for instance, the heads of the Republican Party, the governor and the
Republican state chairman, favored a Polish-American as head of
the state nationalities council and preferred a loose and informal
organization that would remain completely under their control. The
governor's preferred appointee had directed his statewide ethnic
campaign in 1968. Pasztor supported an aggressive Ukrainian, who
was prepared to build a formal, active and elaborate state nationalities
council. The heavy influence of the national Party was evident in its
grant of recognition to an ethnic leader who did not have the blessings
of the heads of the Illinois Republican organization, and in its support
of the council which that leader and a few others organized. In October
1971 the chairman of the Republican National Committee, along with
three Illinois Republican Congressmen, took the time to appear at a
banquet attended by more than 1,000 ethnics. Any indifference or
resistance the governor may have had to the Republican State

Nationalities Council of Illinois and its independence was considerably reduced in the face of this impressive affair within his supposed sphere of influence. The leaders of the Illinois council insisted that the governor's former ethnic advisor not be placed at the table of honor where the most important guests would be located. Their insistence was honored by Pasztor and the governor.

The Illinois experience was not exceptional. When Nixon took office in 1969, 30 Republicans held governorships. These men were by-and-large WASPs with little interest in establishing state national-ities councils. The Republican National Committee, on occasion, found it necessary to persuade them to do so.

An Ethnic Council in Illinois

The formation and activities of the Republican State Nationalities Council of Illinois illustrate the nature and extent of the Republican Party's commitment to attract the support of ethnic Americans. The 1960 census reveals that Illinois had a foreign-stock population (immigrants and their children) of 2,449,098, or 24 percent of the total population. In October 1969 representatives of four active Republican nationality associations, eager to continue and perhaps enlarge the efforts of earlier ethnic GOP leaders who had worked with this sizable minority, met to discuss future organizational needs. An ad hoc committee was formed to establish a permanent and viable Republican nationalities council which could coordinate and broaden the Republican base in the ethno-national communities of Illinois. With the full support, advice, and cooperation of the Heritage Groups Division of the Republican National Committee, such a council was organized. By the end of the year, 10 Republican nationality groups had joined it. Each group had to pay a $50 initiation fee and $50 in annual dues to obtain and keep its membership. But most of the financial support for the first two years of operations came from two wealthy sponsors. Late in January 1970, at the first full meeting of interested groups, a constitution was adopted, an executive board elected, and the newly created Republican State Nationalities Council of Illinois became a reality. Representatives of 13 nationality organiza-tions signed its bylaws. The following month, the Council, with the blessing of both the Republican State Central Committee of Illinois and the Cook County Central Committee, received its state charter and was formally welcomed by Governor Ogilvie into the Illinois Republican family.

The new nationality arm of the Republican state organization demonstrated its value in November 1970, when the Council, expanded to 19 member organizations, actively participated in the campaign.

The nationalities were: Albanians, Assyrians, Bulgarians, Byelorussians, Chinese, Croatians, Czechoslovakians, Estonians, Germans, Greeks, Hungarians, Italians, Japanese, Latvians, Lithuanians, Poles, Puerto Ricans, Slovaks, and Ukrainians. There were no Jews and no blacks. Each group contributed financial support. Member organizations sponsored radio and newspaper ads, opened and staffed ethnic campaign headquarters, printed and distributed ethnically relevant literature, organized rallies, supplied precinct workers and poll watchers, and, for the first time in recent Illinois GOP history, organized two highly successful "Republican Nationality Days" for all candidates. Fifteen separate and widely publicized breakfasts, brunches, luncheons, receptions, teas, and banquets were held in as many ethno-national communities during two days. The Council and member organizations absorbed the 1970 campaign expenses. In May 1971 the Council received a "Recognition of Outstanding Service Award" from Senator Robert Dole, Republican Party chairman. In December 1970 the groups held a Christmas party at which 12 different dishes (representing the 12 apostles) and 12 different wines were served. The formation, growth in membership, and extensive activities of the Council in less than two years represented an impressive accomplishment.

A Banquet

In October 1971 the Republican National Committee extended further recognition of the Council's accomplishment. Chairman Dole attended a banquet for Illinois ethnic Republicans. His appearance assured the participation of the Republican governor and other prominent Illinois Republicans, including three congressmen. The largest Republican contributor in Illinois—W. Clement Stone—footed the $12,000 bill for the banquet, which was designated "The Annual Man of the Year Banquet." Held at the Grand Ballroom of the Marriott Hotel near Chicago's O'Hare airport on October 10, 1971, the banquet honored Illinois Congressman Edward J. Derwinski, a former chairman of the Nationalities Division of the Republican National Committee, who was presented with the Man of the Year Award by the Ukrainian-American president of the Illinois Council. The governor, W. Clement Stone, and Laszlo Pasztor spoke briefly. Chairman Dole delivered the main address and emphasized that the Republican Party had displaced the Democratic Party as "the true party of the people." "Radical liberals, labor bosses and irresponsible politicians," he charged, had taken control of the Democratic Party and driven out the ethnic groups. He added that these groups had formerly given the Democrats their strength. The Democrats, according to Dole, had

once claimed to be the "melting pot party" but, "now some of the
more radical members of its youth wing seem more interested in
'pot' than in melting pots, and the solid mass of religious, patriotic,
hard-working ethnic Americans who once identified with the Democratic Party find themselves in search of a new political base." The
Republican National Chairman accused the Democratic leadership of
"failures and disasters." "Divisive Democratic politicians," he said,
"have turned on their own elected leadership and thus prolonged the
war by sowing discontent at home and—whether they wished it or not—
boosting enemy morale and demoralizing our own fighting men. The
Republican Party that was once thought of as the party of the privileged
elite—the so-called WASPs—is now the true party of the people."
President Nixon has "opened the door" for ethnic groups to join the
Republicans. Dole was well received by an attentive audience of more
than 1,000 guests. Each nationality group was expected to sell a
minimum number of tickets, and the Council made $4,700. The New
York Times, two of Chicago's dailies, and a number of local ethnic
papers carried news reports of the banquet. Ethnic leaders sat at the
head tables, identified by the flags of their ancestral lands. Everywhere else American flags were in prominent view. An American
flag decorated the program cover. The banquet opened with a "parade
of national flags" consisting of girls and boys in the traditional costume
of their ancestral homelands, followed by recitation of the pledge of
allegiance and the singing of the national anthem. "Dessert à la Nixon"
consisted of apple pie replete with an American flag. The tiny flag
was stamped "Made in Japan."

A Routine Meeting

An observer of the regular monthly meeting of the Illinois
Republican Nationalities Council held in February 1971 would have
noted the proceedings of a vital organization that took itself seriously
and was taken seriously by politicians. Opening with the pledge of
allegiance and conducted on an orderly and democratic basis (10 votes
were required to pass motions, resolutions, etc.), almost all the 19
member nationalities were represented. The three guest politicians
were an officer of the Illinois Republican Central Committee, a
representative of the Republican candidate for mayor of Chicago
seeking the support of the Council, and an aide of Senator Charles
Percy. While the ethnic representatives were generally in their fifties
and sixties, the chairman of the meeting was in his thirties. The
minutes of the last meeting were read and approved. It was noted that
Nixon had given Director Pasztor a list of federal vacancies and had
requested recommendations of qualified white ethnics. The president

of the Council indicated that he had communicated four requests to the State Central Committee and expected favorable responses. The requests were for: 1) regular representation on the Central Committee similar to that afforded the Young Republicans and the Republican Women's Federation; 2) inclusion in the Central Committee budget of an allowance of funds for the Council; 3) the cooperation of the Central Committee and the governor in a state nationalities' banquet dinner; and 4) one important appointment in state government.

There were few questions, and the few representatives who spoke did so at some length and in theoretical and philosophical terms. The main concern which arose from the floor concerned the naming of an American ship after the Lithuanian sailor who had attempted to find asylum in the United States and been returned to the Russians by the American Coast Guard. One representative noted that at a large meeting of Lithuanians called to discuss the sailor incident, only Congressman Roman Pucinski, a Democrat, appeared and offered help. A resolution directed to President Nixon was adopted, recommending that a ship be named after the sailor. It was mentioned that the governor had been advised of important national holidays so that he might acknowledge them by proclamation or otherwise. It was also suggested that the Republican State Central Committee be given a list of all occasions on which important elected Republicans should appear. Possibilities for a statewide Nationalities Day during the annual Republican Day celebration at the state capital were discussed. The officer of the Central Committee told the representatives that their requests would probably all be granted and that they could expect more jobs. He did stress, however, that ethnic identification was only one factor and noted that he—an Irishman—had recently beaten a Lithuanian nominated by the Democrats. Senator Percy's aide, urbane, articulate, and well prepared, listed in specific detail the senator's efforts to help ethnic groups: he had replaced Senator Dodd as the senatorial spokesman for the Committee for a Free Lithuania; had backed Congressman Pucinski's bill to name a ship for the Lithuanian sailor; supported the ethnic studies centers bill; been instrumental in admitting numerous cadets from ethnic groups to military academies; supported the national observation of Ukrainian Day; assisted families in their efforts to pay lawyers for the defense of political prisoners in Czechoslovakia; helped the Germans with a compensation claim; publicly supported Poles on economic and church-state issues; was involved in Greek church relations; intervened in negotiations to release Soviet Jews from Russia; assisted in getting letters into Albania; and so on. The meeting lasted for more than two hours.

A Second Regular Meeting

The first meeting of the Council following the banquet of October 27, 1971, praised it as a total success. The meeting, in most respects, was similar to the February 1971 meeting, though no political guests were included, and representatives ranged in age from 25 and 45. Because of the expense and varied quality of the flags used at the banquet, the representatives agreed that the Council buy a flag of uniform quality for each group. The flags would become the property of the Council. The president reported on the progress made toward obtaining state charters for each of the groups.

Two days before the meeting, Communist China had been admitted to the United Nations. The representative of the Albanian group, seated directly behind the Chinese representative, moved that a letter from the Council be sent to Illinois United States senators and key Republicans expressing the Council's disapproval of the U.N. action and the recommendation that the American government sharply reduce its financial contributions to the world organization. The motion was unanimously passed. Plans for a winter concert were discussed—this would consist of a competition between ethnic choirs and dance groups for cash prizes and be primarily a fund-raising affair. The president mentioned his hope that the Council would be able to raise $50,000 for the 1972 presidential campaign. Another nationalities conference set for November 19-21, 1971, in Washington, D.C., was discussed and six representatives announced that they planned to attend the conference sponsored by the Republican National Committee. A newsletter stated that the November conference was the third annual Republican conference on ethnic politics and would include as speakers: Republican Chairman Senator Robert Dole, Senator J. Glenn Beall, Department of Transportation Secretary John Volpe, OEO Director Philip Sanchez, and Congressman Derwinski. Plans for the Illinois Council to host an annual national meeting of all nationality groups in May 1972 were also discussed. While this annual meeting would be similar to the first one, held in May 1971, it would demonstrate and emphasize that considerable progress had been made since that first conference and stress the commitment of the Republican National Committee to make the Nationalities Division a permanent, regular, and continuing operation. The representatives at the meeting also voted in favor of a second Christmas party and to continue the monthly practice of allowing one nationality group an hour-long presentation on some aspect of its culture. During the meeting Laszlo Pasztor telephoned from Washington, D.C., and spoke with the president of the Council. The president then advised the representatives that Pasztor had asked them to support William Rehnquist whom Nixon had nominated to the Supreme Court. The representatives were told that Rehnquist was a second-generation ethnic and strong on law and order. It was suggested that their support be expressed in individual letters to the United States senators and to Chicago newspapers. No one dissented and the request was generally acknowledged as an opportunity to assist President Nixon's drive to win confirmation for his nominee.

NATIONAL ETHNIC NEWSLETTER

In October 1971 the Republican National Committee published the first ethnic newsletter, GOP Nationalities News, "a monthly publication of the Republican National Committee." Pasztor was listed as director of the Heritage Groups Division, with a member of his staff listed as editor. The first page of the four-page newsletter featured, under a picture of the executive board of National Republican Heritage Groups Council (including Republican Chairman Dole) and under a headline reading "Nationalities Unite Behind GOP," a long introductory article which began:

> With an increasing number of Democratic Presidential candidates leaning to the left of the political spectrum, many tradition-minded Americans are beginning to wonder what happened to the ethnic coalition that was once the bastion of the Democratic Party in the Northeastern and Great Lakes states. Ethnic voters, disillusioned with radical chic politics, with being "taken for granted," and ignored are beginning to fight back. . . . The National Republican Heritage Groups Council is out to fill this leadership vacuum, and to prove that ethnic awareness is very much alive in our society and is a positive force in American political life.

The second page was devoted almost entirely to the Republican mayoralty candidacy of Cleveland's Ralph J. Perk, a second-generation Czech. The Perk article was designed to show that ethnic Americans are interested in the Republican nationalities movement and that Nixon and the Republican National Committee are their friends. It was intended also to assist Perk in his campaign by suggesting that he was well-qualified and influential in Washington, D.C. In the picture accompanying the article, Perk was shown shaking hands with President Nixon at the White House. The article predicted: "The mayoralty race in Cleveland, Ohio, this year is shaping up to be a showcase of what ethnic politics means to big city America. . . . The mosaic of Hungarians, Germans, Poles, Italians, Slovaks, Czechs, Slovenes and

Irish in the Cuyahoga County area could well be the determining
factor in electing the first Republican mayor of Cleveland in 30 years."
A three-column article noted that Perk is vice-chairman of the National
Republican Heritage Groups Council and was honored by the Diocese
of Cleveland as "Catholic Man of the Year." It listed Perk's political
endorsements, achievements, and honors and concluded that he "is a
good example of what syndicated columnist Kevin Phillips calls looking
'at middle America as society's new constituency of forward motion,
not reaction.' "

On the third page a calendar listed the twelve ethnic holidays
occurring in October and November 1971. On the same page an article
entitled "Nixon Recruits Top Ethnic Talent" stated that the Nixon
administration had appointed more than 300 ethnic Americans to
offices since 1968 and listed some of the more recent appointments,
including the president of the Italian Historical Society of America to
the National Advisory Council on Adult Education, the president of
the American Latvian Association to the National Highway Safety
Advisory Council, an educator credited with the introduction of
Japanese into American secondary schools to the National Advisory
Council on Education of Disadvantaged Children, and a Cuban architect
to the Fine Arts Commission. Thirteen others mentioned in the article
had all been appointed to national advisory boards and commissions.
The article concluded that these appointments were "one more indication of President Nixon's commitment to bring government to all the
people, and to ensure that those who often pay the bills for federal
programs—and until now were never consulted—have a say in how
government works."

Another article on the same page explicitly appealed to the sentiments of peoples of captive nations and to Polish-Americans. It
noted that Republican Congressman Derwinski had been appointed a
delegate to the 26th Session of the United Nations General Assembly
and called him "the Number One friend of the Captive Nations,"
saying he "has made a name for himself as a spokesman for ethnic
Americans" and "is the second Polish-American to be chosen by
the President for a UN diplomatic post." The article concluded:
"His appointment is a boost in the arm to millions of foreign policy
conscious ethnic Americans, and a warning sign to those who may
take the President's two-China policy lightly."

The last page of the newsletter outlined the fund-raising activities
of the National Republican Heritage Groups (NRHG) Council. The
Council's Finance Committee is headed by Steven J. Skubik, the GOP
nationalities director during the Eisenhower administration, and is
co-chaired by Secretary of Transportation John M. Volpe, Congressman Silvio Conte, and others. The NRHG Finance Committee is the
first permanent committee of its kind within the Republican National

Committee. The last page also listed seven ethnic affairs which were to take place between October 15 and November 14 in different cities throughout the country. Two were local Republican ethnic banquets, and five were national meetings of nationality organizations.

LIBERATION OF THE CAPTIVE NATIONS

Appeals by the Republican Party to ethnic Americans on the basis of Russian oppression of their ancestral homeland is still a conscious strategy, but, as the Party's platform in 1968 shows, the strategy had to change. The GOP, to a large extent, is trapped by its strong liberation and anti-Communist rhetoric, which began as early as 1948. Following World War II and the Yalta and Potsdam Agreements, Republican strategists accurately assessed that a large portion of the traditionally Democratic foreign-language groups were dissatisfied and restive. German-Americans and, to a lesser extent, Italian-Americans were alienated as a result of two world wars and ready to avenge themselves on the Democratic Party. Poles and other Slavic-Americans believed that the Yalta and Potsdam Agreements had set the stage for Communist control of Eastern and Central Europe. In 1959 Congress unanimously passed Senate Joint Resolution 111 asking that the president issue a proclamation "designating the third week in July 1959 as Captive Nations Week" and "issue a similar proclamation each year until such time as freedom and independence shall have been achieved for all the captive nations of the world." On the same day that the resolution was passed by Congress—July 17— President Eisenhower issued the proclamation declaring the week of July 19 Captive Nations Week. Less than three weeks later Eisenhower initiated an exchange of visits with Soviet Premier Nikita Khrushchev. The resolution and proclamation may have been an attempt on the part of the Republican leadership to counter the antici- pated opposition among many ethnic Americans to Eisenhower's exchange with the Russian leader.

Nixon faces the same dilemma in his initiatives with Communist China and the Soviet Union. Republican Congressman Derwinski, "the Number One friend of the Captive Nations," was guarded in his remarks following the ouster of Nationalist China from the United Nations in October 1971. He said that despite disillusionment of Americans with the United Nations, it is not the time to "meat axe" the contribution of United States funds to the world organization. Nixon enjoyed a strong anti-Communist image during the years of the Eisenhower administration. Shortly after the 1959 Captive Nations Proclamation, Khrushchev taunted Nixon during the latter's Russian tour. But Nixon stood up to him in the famous kitchen confrontation.

While in those years Nixon was regarded as an anti-Communist cold warrior, in the 1970s he knows that international cooperation and disarmament require recognition of and negotiation with Communist China and the Soviet Union. The old captive nations rhetoric and promises are incompatible with the requirements of international affairs. The Republicans did not make a major issue of the invasion of Czechoslovakia in 1968 by the Russians. Not one Republican politician appeared at the Captive Nations Parade in Chicago in July 1971. Moreover, the post-World War II immigrants from Soviet-dominated countries have grown older, and the brutal oppression of the late 1940s and 1950s which brought them to the United States has grown remote for them. But the passion for their homelands is still alive in many of these transplanted persons. The majority of them were the elite of their country—professionals, intellectuals, editors, government officials, and businessmen. An incident which occurred during the United States senatorial campaign in Illinois in 1970 is indicative of their attitude. The liaison aide with ethnic communities for incumbent Republican Senator Smith attended a meeting of the Illinois Republican Nationalities Council and, despite advice to avoid such pleas, told the ethnic representatives that his candidate deserved to have them knocking on doors on his behalf. The Latvian representative, a former member of the Latvian Senate, disagreed. He rose, announced his former high office, commented indignantly on who needed whom, and stomped out of the meeting, followed by other Latvians. These post-World War II refugees have recently been joined by many Jews whose concern for the plight of their coreligionists in Russia has encouraged them to organize and press for intervention by the United States government.

The immigrant experiences of these refugees is different from the experiences of those who came from Southern, Central and Eastern Europe between 1880 and 1924. The earlier immigrants had been mostly unskilled and uneducated. They came from rural areas, as permanent settlers, and their concerns were economic. It was the Democratic Party that opened its doors to them, maintained them through the Depression, and supported their efforts to unionize. The displaced persons who arrived after World War II took America's economic progress for granted. Jobs were available and unions protected them. They felt no particular loyalty to the Democratic Party. Their lives had been drastically altered by the war and Communist oppression. They were driven from their homelands, but hoped they would be able to go home when their ancestral lands were liberated from Communist domination. Consequently, they have intense interest in American foreign policy, and the majority of them in the 1950s believed that the Republican Party offered the more promising possibility of liberating their homelands.

The Democratic Party did not ignore the foreign policy concerns of these postwar refugees; while less willing to take a hard line on Communism, it tacitly promised liberation of their homelands. The Democrats have traditionally concentrated on the bread-and-butter concerns of the earlier European immigrants. Astute Democrats like Richard J. Daley, however, always recognized groups such as the Council of Oppressed Nations. Chicago Republicans complain that he dominates the Council, and that he or one of his top lieutenants appears at all its affairs.

The presidential campaign of 1964 seemed to underscore the diminishing importance of the captive nations appeals. Republican Barry Goldwater took a militant anti-Communist stance. He opposed trade with Communist countries and the admission of Red China into the United Nations, but did not attract the electoral support of the great majority of ethnic Americans. But the captive nations image of the Republican Party survives, and its influence was certainly reflected in the appointment of Laszlo Pasztor, a Hungarian freedom fighter, as director of the Nationalities Division of the Republican National Committee. Moreover, the makeup of the Executive Committee of the Heritage Groups Council is disproportionately weighted with post-World War II refugees rather than pre-Depression settlers. But it seems increasingly clear that as the Republican nationalities movement develops, the emphasis is shifting from the empty rhetoric of liberating the captive nations to a recognition of the domestic concerns of ethnic Americans—such social issues as law and order, grants of patronage to ethnic leaders, and so on. While the more passionate postwar refugees are now in their fifties and sixties and still dream of the liberation of their homelands, their children view the new Republican "open-door" policy for ethnic Americans as an opportunity for advancement. Besides their diminishing numbers, the post-World War II immigrants were never numerous enough to constitute a major electoral bloc. Furthermore, the captive nations strategy offers little to restive Mexican-Americans and other nationality groups not oppressed by the Russians. It was always the predominantly Catholic immigrants who came to America between 1880 and 1924 who have given the parties a considerable electoral opportunity. As these voters merge into the middle class, and if the Democratic Party remains fixed in its identification with racial minorities and the poor, the Republican Party will indeed continue to seize the occasion to win over ethnic Americans by addressing itself to their concerns.

9

**IMMIGRATION LAWS
AND FOREIGN POLICY:
RHETORIC
AND INACTION**

American immigration laws and foreign policy have provided politicians with opportunities to exploit the hopes, fears, and loyalties of ethnic Americans but have not been markedly influenced by pressures from ethnic groups. Since the 1930s the Democrats have promised liberalization of the restrictive immigration laws of the 1920s, and they finally lived up to many of their promises by enactment of the 1965 Immigration Act. It was a third-generation Irish President and his skillful political successor—Lyndon Johnson—who obtained the new immigration law which eased entry for Eastern, Central, and Southern Europeans, and Orientals. The Republican Party has never expended much political effort to ease immigration restrictions.

American foreign policy has been a deep concern of European immigrants and their children since 1860. Until World War I America maintained a strong isolationist posture, despite the pleas of many immigrant groups for her intervention in the political and economic events affecting their homelands. The major cause of Irish-Americans until 1921 was the independence of Ireland, and they encouraged Anglo-American conflict whenever possible. The politicians, of course, focused on British-American relations, and some of them went so far as to encourage the Irish to think that they favored designs for a military attack on Canada. Irish-Americans came to believe that anti-British feeling in the United States was synonymous with pro-Irish sentiment. On the eve of the Boer War, Secretary of State John Hay, in emphasizing the American "duty of neutrality," noted: "Whatever you do, Bryan will attack us as a slave of Great Britain. All their State conventions [Democratic] put an anti-English plank in their platform to curry favor with the Irish (whom they want to keep) and the Germans whom they want to seduce. It is too disgusting to have to deal with such sordid liars."

World War I and President Wilson's policy of self-determination aroused the oppressed nationalities of the Hapsburg, Russian, and Prussian empires and their first- and second-generation compatriots in the United States. In his book The Hyphenates in Recent American Politics and Diplomacy, Louis L. Gerson has observed that "for many decades before the war American politicians had catered to the 'foreign vote' and in so doing enabled it to play an important role in politics. It seemed to occur to neither Democrats nor Republicans that they countenanced dual loyalties." As the war progressed, ethnic leaders and the foreign language press pleaded for active American partici- pation on behalf of the nationalist aspirations of the subjugated peoples of Austria-Hungary, Russia, and Germany. Democrats and Republicans seized upon these outcries for American involvement to appeal to foreign-born Americans and their children. This competition by the major parties, according to Gerson, "further accentuated the hyphen and persuaded the ethnic leaders in America, as well as in the native lands, of their power to influence American decisions." Wilson, a persistent Anglophile, antagonized both the Irish and the Germans but turned for support in 1916 to eastern and southern European immi- grants. After his nomination in 1916, he encouraged the groups in their liberation aspirations. He publicly opposed literacy tests for immigrants. He requested that the Central Powers provide or permit provision of relief for the starving populations of ravaged eastern Europe. In the 1916 election, Wilson won sizable majorities from ethnic groups from Eastern Europe, particularly Polish-Americans. By the time of the Versailles peace conference, he had committed himself to extending his policy of self-determination to the Poles, Czechs, Slovaks, Serbs, Croats, and Slovenes and to supporting the establishment of a Jewish national state in Palestine. The suffering of eastern and Central European Jews during the war and the threat to Jewish settlements in Palestine by the Turks profoundly stirred American Jews to aid and protect their coreligionists. At the out- break of the war, American Zionist membership was roughly 20,000 out of an estimated Jewish population of 3 million. By 1918 this membership had grown to about 145,000. Wilson's first public state- ment in support of Palestine as a national home for the Jewish people, as embodied in the Balfour Declaration delivered in August 1918, came on the eve of the congressional elections. Increasingly aware of the growing ethnic consciousness of his constituency and preparing for a November campaign in Massachusetts, Republican Senator Henry Cabot Lodge, in the spring of 1922, introduced and backed a resolution in the Senate supporting the Balfour Declaration. With passage of the joint Senate resolution, Zionism had bipartisan support. Every subsequent president has reaffirmed that stand. In 1948 Presi- dent Truman backed the partition of Palestine and the creation of a

Jewish state. The Jewish foreign policy issue in 1971 is still the guarantee of a Jewish homeland. To that end 78 United States Senators in October 1971 voted in favor of a resolution calling for the shipment of supersonic jets to Israel, "without further delay," plus any supporting equipment and assistance "as are essential to maintain Israel's deterrent capacity."

Wilson's policy of self-determination stimulated self-awareness among America's ethnic groups and raised their nationalistic expectations, but the realities of the peace conference and partisan American politics brought disappointment and conflict to American ethnic groups and electoral retaliation against President Wilson. Ethnic Americans felt that Wilson and his party had neglected, gone back on, or compromised at the conference the promises and wartime pledges made to them. In 1920 the Republican Party encouraged Americans of German, Irish, and Italian ancestry, as well as other ethnic groups, to avenge Wilson's war policies and the peace treaty of Versailles by defeating the incumbent president's party at the polls. German-Americans sought revenge against the man who had led America against their homeland and believed the Republican Party offered them a better opportunity to rebuild their prewar influence. Irish-Americans blamed Wilson for not applying his policy of self-determination to a free and united Ireland. Italian-Americans were embittered with Wilson's decision to support Yugoslavia in its claim to the port of Fiume. Greek-Americans believed their homeland should have gained more territory at the peace conference. Thus ethnic Americans contributed substantially to the election of President Harding in 1920. It is ironic that Wilson's stimulation of their ethnic expectations and their subsequent disappointments caused them to turn to the nativist, Republican Party which was to return America to an isolationist posture and end the waves of open immigration by passage of the highly selective Immigration Acts of 1921 and 1924.

By the mid- and late 1930s, Nazis and Fascists had infiltrated hundreds of American ethnic organizations. A report prepared by the Institute for Propaganda Analysis found that by late 1938, 800 organizations existed in the United States which "could be called pro-fascist or pro-Nazi," and many of them were ethnic organizations. The aim of the Nazis and Fascists was to promote American disunity, to stir the ethnic consciousness of Americans of German and Italian extraction, and encourage them to sympathize with Hitler and Mussolini. Such propaganda was more successful than most Americans realized. The Nazi plan called for the unity of all German communities and the communication of the Nazi ideology to people of German origin. Italian-Americans were stimulated by the activities of Fascists and pro-Fascists. During this time appeals by both political parties to Italian-Americans and other nationality groups served to heighten

their ethnocentrism. The president of the Federation of Italian American Democratic Organizations of New York went so far as to write
President Roosevelt in August 1936 explaining the necessity for the
United States to recognize Italy's annexation of Ethiopia in order to
capture the entire Italian-American vote for the Democratic Party.
The remark of the pre-World War II period which was to stir the
greatest ethnic emotions was Roosevelt's statement that the Italian
attack on France was a "stab in the back." Italian-Americans were
offended and pro-Fascist Italian-American spokesmen and press,
as well as Republican politicians, exploited the president's remark
to the fullest possible extent. In the 1940 presidential election the
Republican Party sought the support of Italian- and German-Americans,
while the Democrats concentrated on winning other nationality groups.
During the party conventions in 1940, Nazis and Fascists tried to
influence the parties and their platforms, their primary goal being to
keep the United States out of the war. The opportunities for foreign
governments and the major American parties to make political capital
out of foreign policy propaganda, rhetoric, and promises were ended
on the morning of December 7, 1941, by the Japanese at Pearl Harbor.
Americans were united in a common determination to defeat the Nazi,
Fascist, and imperial Japanese alliance.

In his book The Hyphenates in Recent American Politics and
Diplomacy, Louis L. Gerson concludes his chapter on the World War
II period as follows:

> Thus, throughout the war, while the Government of the
> United States attempted to unite ethnic Americans behind
> the war effort, the American parties in their appeals for
> the ethnic vote encouraged a large segment of the elec-
> torate to divide itself into competing units, each con-
> cerned with the future of its native land—concerns which
> may or may not have been in the true interests of the
> United States.

Following World War II, American foreign policy shifted
permanently from isolationism to involvement in world affairs because of Russian territorial aggression, the challenge of Communism,
and the American commitment to collective security through the
United Nations. This shift inevitably created more opportunities for
American politicians, ethnic leaders, and foreign governments to
excite, stimulate, and provoke ethnic Americans, and often to estrange
them from each other and their fellow Americans. The legitimacy of
the concern of ethnic Americans for the destinies of their former
homelands has never been the issue. Rather, the important questions
were whether the efforts of particular ethnic groups to influence

American foreign policy in favor of their former homelands were compatible with the best interests of the United States, and whether American politicians, ethnic leaders, and foreign governments were acting in good faith by appealing to and stimulating ethnic consciousness and thus promoting dual loyalties. The record of both parties before the cold war and since show that exploitation and tokenism have been the rule, not the exception. Not only was much promised and little delivered, but divisive forms of ethnocentrism have been encouraged. To win the ethnic vote in presidential and congressional campaigns from 1952 through 1964, the Republican Party relied heavily upon its support for the liberation of captive nations and its anti-Communist activities, but with the killing of more than 25,000 Hungarian civilians by Soviet troops during the 1956 uprising, while the United States made no meaningful intervention, the emptiness of the liberation rhetoric became clear. In the 1960 presidential campaign Richard Nixon courted what he believed to be the Polish interest by promising an audience in Buffalo's Polish Union Hall that, if elected, he would support Polish claims to formerly German lands by recognizing the Oder-Neisse line as Poland's western frontier. This appeal won Nixon few Polish votes in Buffalo, angered German-Americans and West Germany, and, in response to outcries from Bonn, the State Department was forced to issue a statement denying any change in America's attitude toward the Oder-Neisse line. Liberation of the captive nations and a strong anti-Communist posture have become increasingly difficult in the face of the realities of international politics. In 1959 President Eisenhower initiated an exchange of visits with the Soviet premier. Three years later the United States confronted the Russians over the installation of rockets in Cuba—an intrusion into the western hemisphere. But in 1968 when Czechoslovakia was invaded by Soviet troops, the Democratic administration simply offered its sympathies and verbal condemnation. The Republican Party was cautious in exploiting the inaction of the Johnson administration in the Czech invasion. In less than four years President Nixon has taken important steps in the interest of world peace and international cooperation, yet this activity is hardly compatible with the long-standing tough Republican stand on the cold war. Between 1968 and early 1972, Nixon has negotiated arms control, consular and trade agreements with Russia, and recognized Communist China by favoring its admission to the United Nations and visiting Peking. By the fall of 1971 the United States was selling large quantities of grain to Russia, and the United States Secretary of Commerce went to the Soviet Union in November 1971 to arrange for the sale of other American products. On his return, he spoke of new agreements to multiply American trade with Russia many times over. But Nixon, the politician, still backs financial support of the cold war through such means as Radio Liberty and Radio Free Europe. The latter beams its programs to Bulgaria, Czechoslovakia, Hungary, Poland, and Rumania; Radio Liberty directs its broadcasts to the Soviet Union.

The domestic political power of ethnic groups upon American foreign policy makers varies greatly. Ukrainian-Americans are more powerful than Russian-Americans, Slovaks more so than Czechs, the Irish more so than the English, the Greeks than the Turks, the Jews than the Arabs.

10

ETHNIC
AND RACIAL
BALANCING

Balanced tickets and ethnic and racial quotas for public jobs and appointments and for party councils are still very much an aspect of American political life. They have been forced upon and become a part of the federal government. Their desirability is infrequently questioned, and they are, for the most part, the result of political expediency. American politicians have always pretended that only the most competent receive important appointments. Training, ability, and performance, not political reward, have supposedly been the determinants for public employment. Obviously, this has frequently not been the case. Reformers have done much to make civil service and merit systems a permanent part of public employment in the last 70 years, but American politicians still have considerable freedom to reward individuals and groups. Groups are usually rewarded on the basis of the electoral support they provide, but rarely beyond what is absolutely necessary. Ethnic groups give their vote in exchange for jobs, petty favors, local appointments, and social welfare legislation. In the last two decades ethnic groups have sought and received significant political rewards from the national parties.

The balanced ticket and ethnic and racial quotas have usually meant that the group on top had to give up some of its power and status. WASP leaders were never keen on balanced tickets and quotas. The Irish made effective use of them to gain and then hold control of the urban machines in the North. The leaders of Jewish organizations by the late 1960s were opposed to quotas in educational institutions because their own educational achievement had enabled them to advance and provided them with a major vocational activity. Quotas for teachers in the New York school system often meant that blacks replaced Jews without regard to ability or seniority. When Ivy League universities and other colleges pledged themselves to take certain percentages of black students, it was often at the expense of the Jews.

The requirement that federally-financed construction projects hire certain percentages of racial minorities forced labor unions, to a significant extent, to recognize racial quotas.

The balanced ticket and quotas do not result from or reflect the numerical strength of a group at the polls. Rather they reflect the relative political strength and skills of particular groups within the parties. Minneapolis is probably the largest Swedish-American city in America, but it has had only a few mayors of Swedish descent. The Irish, numerically much less significant, have won the chief executive's office of that city time and again. They are politically more skillful and more predisposed to seek their fortunes in public life than are the Swedes. In his book The Irish and the Irish Politicians, Edward M. Levine concurs in this general observation. By militant assertion, heightened group consciousness, and organization, blacks have built their own political strength. Political strength in party councils is related to some extent to the percentage distribution of groups within the electorate. Some groups are too small numerically, or too poorly organized, to gain representation on a ticket. The dominant group never gives away more than it feels is absolutely necessary to maintain its power. To give away too many important offices is to relinquish one's power. To spread influential nominations and appointments too thinly is to threaten the maintenance of power, for if the leaders of too many groups are excluded, they will join one another to unseat the dominant group. Party boss Richard J. Daley and his predecessors in Chicago have held power by the shrewd manipulation of the balanced ticket and quotas. The balanced ticket, as exemplified in Chicago, represents a temporary equilibrium and compromise between proportional representation and the reluctance of established party leaders to relinquish their power. Needless to say, the balanced ticket strategy applies beyond ethnic, racial, and religious considerations. Organized labor, business, and reform groups are given recognition.

Group conflict is increasing. In front-page editorials in November 1969, the Polish American, a major Polish-American newspaper in Chicago, demanded a larger participation in major city jobs. "Why Irish Power?" was the title of one of these editorials. The editors claimed that of 50 top city jobs, 47 were held by people of Irish descent and 3 by Jews. In October 1971 the mayor of New York City ordered that the city's Commission on Human Rights conduct a racial and ethnic census of city employees. He had responded to group pressure and in so doing encountered group resistance. The American Jewish Congress criticized the census on the ground that it "could be misused to destroy the Civil Service merit system." The chairman of the Congress demanded a public hearing. The City Council president then requested the Council's Committee on Civil Service and Labor to investigate the mayor's order. Groups in the urban North have clashed before, but recent group competition and conflict have become more explicit and formalized.

11

THE DECLINE OF THE CITIES ENDS ETHNIC SUCCESSION AND PRODUCES RIGIDITY AND STRATIFICATION IN ETHNIC BALANCING

In the past, successive immigrant groups have moved upward through city government. The Irish and Germans won control from the Anglo-Protestants. The Irish and Germans have been succeeded by the Jews, Italians, and Slavs. In many large cities, blacks are pushing these latter groups and are themselves being pushed by the Latins. But the succession of groups appears to have markedly subsided. The flexibility which characterized the shifts of urban political power in the past hundred years appears to be greatly lessened. Political control of a large city traditionally carried with it jobs, financial opportunities, and prestige, but by 1970 urban political dominance offered fewer opportunities, less status, and much more hardship. Groups that had not escaped the central cities seemed trapped and destined to fight among themselves for the diminishing resources of the cities.

Balanced tickets and quotas have become more than temporary arrangements and now represent growing rigidity and stratification. In Chicago, for instance, blacks have gradually replaced the Irish and Germans in the local post office, but now face competition from the Latins for the diminishing number of jobs. They show little willingness to yield their gains for they have no place to go. As balanced tickets and quotas become institutionalized, they promote group conflict. From the 1850s to the late 1960s they functioned to open the political system to newcomers and were, for the most part, integrative. But as these mechanisms become more static, their harmful aspects outweigh their constructive ones. Ability, competence, and performance are subordinated to considerations of ethnic, racial, or religious background. Once a group wins office, it takes the attitude that it owns it. In Chicago, certain offices are traditionally held by representatives of a particular group, which is upset if it loses "its" office.

Large Northern cities have informally adopted ethnic and racial quotas
on a large scale, and New York City appears to be on the brink of
formalizing such arrangements.

At the national level, "balanced tickets" and ethnic and racial
quotas are growing in importance. Jews have felt entitled to the seat
on the Supreme Court granted in 1916 to the Court's first Jew, Louis
D. Brandeis. Brandeis was succeeded in 1939 by Felix Frankfurter,
who was succeeded in 1962 by Arthur J. Goldberg, who in turn was
succeeded in 1965 by Abe Fortas. The charges of judicial impropriety
that forced Fortas's resignation in 1969 gave President Nixon the
opportunity to break the succession of Jewish Supreme Court justices
and thus to deprive the Jews of their traditional representation on the
Court.

President Kennedy established the precedent of an ethnic seat
in the cabinet when he appointed Italian-American Anthony J. Celebrezze
as Secretary of Health, Education, and Welfare in 1962. President
Johnson's appointments of Robert C. Weaver as Secretary of Housing
and Urban Development in 1966 and of Thurgood Marshall as a Supreme
Court justice in 1967 were firsts for blacks in high positions, and
blacks accordingly expect no fewer of such high offices. President
Nixon was not persuaded by their demands for a cabinet post in his
administration, but did see fit to follow the Kennedy precedent of
appointing a white ethnic to his cabinet. Nixon's other cabinet members
have "low profiles."

They are gray men with bland personalities who represent no
identifiable region, class, nationality, race, or religion. But, as mentioned, Nixon has made hundreds of ethnic appointments. Both national
parties keep current records of all congressmen, federal appointees,
and federal judges with ethnic backgrounds. Nixon has appointed
United States delegates and alternates to the United Nations on the
basis of ethnic origin rather than prior experience or qualifications.

Many political observers have questioned the qualifications of
Anthony J. Celebrezze for his cabinet post in 1962. As mayor of
Cleveland he had been closely identified with urban ethnic America.
He had had little experience in federal government, and his three
years of service in the cabinet were not marked by distinction.
Supporters of ethnic balancing and quotas argue that the major ethnic
groups have adequate numbers of competent persons to fill any government position. While this may be true, the most competent ethnics
are not necessarily nominated or appointed. The leadership of the
national parties prefers highly visible ethnics, usually those associated
with national ethnic organizations. When an ethnic leader threatens
to defect from a party, nominations and appointments can be used to
coopt him and thus neutralize his adverse influence. Competency
aside, ethnic or racial appointees often do not truly "represent" their

group. Many ethnic "leaders" are self-appointed, self-serving opportunists. The majority of them, and sometimes the most able, prefer
to forget their old neighborhoods and enjoy their American middle-
class existence.

Opponents of the balanced ticket and ethnic and racial quotas
are frightened by the logical extension of these mechanisms. While
some of their fears may be primarily a defensive reaction to their
own loss of power, these opponents are nevertheless justified in their
concern that the primary qualification for a public job may shift even
more from ability to ethnic or racial origin. Explicit and formal
recognition of the ethnic vote in state and national politics, and the
acceptance of rewarding that vote with ethnic nominations and appointments, become self-perpetuating political practics. Indeed, the
practice becomes more elaborate and the competition among groups
more intense. The drive by a group for status and recognition gains
ever increasing impetus. Each grant of recognition stirs ethnic pride,
which subsequently requires more important appointments. It is this
logical extension that produces group conflict and is divisive in
American society. Group assertion and its recognition on the balanced
ticket and ethnic and racial quotas tend to separate the electorate
into specific blocs. Appeals are made to voters on the basis of prejudice and special interest without regard to the general welfare of
the nation. Political assimilation was always central to the melting
pot rationale. Balanced tickets and quotas as a political device do
not always produce negative consequences, for in their earlier forms
these practices were largely integrative. An ethnic group's access
to political office brought it into the mainstream of American life.

President Nixon's major appointments are not selected on the
basis of ability or performance. With one or two exceptions, his
cabinet members are loyal bureaucrats who came to office without
notable records and who have done little to distinguish themselves.
They are moderates and conservatives devoted to status quo positions
and the defense of established business and farm interests. Opponents
of the balanced ticket and quotas spend most of their energy attacking
the prerequisite of ethnic and racial origin as if such were inherently
bad, but they rarely examine the basis for nomination and appointment
of nonethnic Americans.

The ideal recruitment system remains a utopian one in which
equal opportunity is afforded everyone, competition is encouraged,
and ability and performance are the only prerequisites for advancement. The balanced ticket has already been carried to the point where
WASPs are treated as an ethnic group, and when the ticket is drawn
up for state and local elections, the party leadership sometimes
nominates only one WASP candidate, because "that's all the ticket
needs." Heightened group consciousness among Anglo-American

Protestants is not a development—given their overwhelming majority—that will help ethnic Americans in their political pursuits or encourage them to participate fully in American life. One can imagine a Balkanized American electorate in which it is meaningless simply to be an American. The difficulty with advancing one's self as an ethnic American is that it emphasizes the differences that set one apart from the mainstream. Thus, nomination or appointment as an ethnic representative denies one's identity as an American and underscores his outsider status, his second-class citizenship.

America is not the only country plagued with the problem of ethnic quotas. Marshal Tito of Yugoslavia recently scolded his lieutenants for favoring certain ethnic groups in job recruitment. The New York Times reported that Pravda "warned local officials against giving jobs to people on the basis of their ethnic origin," a warning, the report added, "apparently directed both at Russians who discriminate against Soviet minorities and at non-Russian local officials who favor members of their own nationality."

12

OTHER POLITICAL ACTIVITIES
PROVOKE ETHNIC AWARENESS

In addition to promoting ethnic consciousness through the use of the balanced ticket and ethnic and racial quotas, American politicians have encouraged it in other important ways. President Nixon has met with prominent Italian and Polish-American leaders, among others, at the White House and praised them for their activities which heighten ethnic consciousness. In 1968 Vice-President Humphrey, as the leading contender for the Democratic presidential nomination, attended Polish Constitution Day in Chicago and was photographed kissing a Polish-American girl at the headquarters of the Polish National Alliance. When Congress and President Nixon established Columbus' birthday as a national holiday, they aroused the pride of Italian-Americans to an unprecedented extent. Congress and the president have officially designated October 11 as General Pulaski Day. In 1971 the Senate passed an ethnic studies bill to do research on and teach the cultural heritages of all ethnic groups in America. The bill provided an appropriation of $30 million between the time of its becoming law and June 1973. Its Statement of Policy (Section 901) reads:

In recognition of the heterogeneous composition of the Nation and of the fact that in a multiethnic society a greater understanding of the contributions of one's own heritage and those of one's fellow citizens can contribute to a more harmonious, patriotic, and committed populace, and in recognition of the principle that all persons in the educational institutions of the Nation should have an opportunity to learn about the differing and unique contributions to the national heritage made by each ethnic group, it is the purpose of this title to provide assistance designed to afford to students

opportunities to learn about the nature of their own cultural heritage, and to study the contributions of the cultural heritages of the ethnic groups of the Nation.

President Nixon has expressed his support for an ethnic studies law.
Congressional hearings have investigated ethnic defamation in the
communications media. Requests for congressional and presidential
action on commemorative postage stamps honoring ethnic heroes and
groups are on the increase. Italian-Americans want a Fermi stamp,
Polish-Americans a Copernicus stamp, and the Greeks a stamp
commemorating their 150th anniversary of independence. In the 1960s
the Czechs were honored with a stamp commemorating the Sokols and
the Poles with a stamp in memory of Ignace Jan Paderewski. The
Congressional Record is filled with ethnic praise, promises, and
recognition. Congressional resolutions of an ethnic nature are frequently passed.

At the state and local level of government, resolutions and
proclamations are common. In May 1971 the Pennsylvania House of
Representatives adopted a resolution urging the United States Congress
to provide money for the restoration of General Thaddeus Kosciuszko's
last American home in Philadelphia, and for its maintenance as a national shrine. The action was initiated by State Representative John
Pezak of Philadelphia. Big city officials are more active than ever
in bestowing governmental recognition on ethnic groups. In September
1971 Mayor Daley urged that ethnic celebrations be part of the observ-
ance of the 100th anniversary of the Great Chicago Fire. "This can
and must be a parade which will show the world the real Chicago and
its people," he declared. Leaders of ethnic organizations were asked
to sponsor parade floats depicting the roles their nationalities had
played in the building of Chicago. They were also asked to mobilize
marchers in national dress. According to news reports, "myriads
of ethnic groups" marched down State Street past Mayor Daley. In
1960 the Daley administration initiated an annual Holiday Folk Fair
for Chicago's ethnic groups. In 1970 more than 100,000 people attended the two-day spectacle at Chicago's Navy Pier. A 1971 press
release reported: "No other city in the United States can stage a
program such as this which is possible only because of the many
ethnic groups of the city who have preserved the folklore of the countries from which they or their ancestors have come." The 12th
Annual Folk Fair in 1971 featured cultural exhibits, an international
bazaar, an international café, and entertainment by ethnic groups.
Forty-three nationality groups participated and major groups had as
many as 10 separate exhibits. Mayor Daley officially opened the
Fair by crowning the Queen of the Fair. When Miss Sweden was
chosen from among other ethnic representatives as queen in 1971,

she said: "The thing that comes to mind at this minute is that I'm very proud to represent Sweden." The city administrations of New York, Philadelphia, Detroit, and other large cities promote many similar activities. New York City recognized Puerto Rico Discovery Day in November 1971 by noting that 260,000 public school students are of Puerto Rican origin, and issued a proclamation calling for special activities to commemorate the 378th anniversary of the discovery of Puerto Rico by Christopher Columbus in 1493. District 7 in the south Bronx, which has the highest concentration of Puerto Rican students of any school district, held assemblies and evening programs for parents and the community. The New York Public Library exhibited books about Puerto Ricans in Spanish and English. At all levels of government, public officials send messages to and attend important ethnic affairs and never miss an opportunity to be photographed with ethnic leaders. The more public recognition given to America's ethnic diversity and to specific ethnic groups, the more likely it becomes that each group will assert itself and demand greater recognition. Each time an important politician singles out one group for mention in his public utterances, others feel slighted for his seemingly intentional omission of their group. It is the politicians and ethnic leaders who foster divisions in American group life.

13

POLITICIANS
INCREASINGLY STIR
ETHNIC CONSCIOUSNESS

Since 1960 politicians at the national level have contributed greatly to the increase of group consciousness among ethnic and religious minorities in America. The Catholicism of John F. Kennedy, the black assertion and recognition of the 1960s, and, more recently, the white ethnic movements are all inseparably related to the behavior of American politicians. Their speeches refer with decreasing frequency to "America—the great melting pot" and instead emphasize racial, religious, and ethnic differences. The issues of school busing, integration of the suburbs, and safe streets, in addition to the compelling economic issues, are the critical ones in the early 1970s. These social issues are largely racial. George Wallace's 13.53 percent of the presidential vote in 1968 was primarily a white versus black phenomenon. The religious factor in politics is shown by Kennedy's loss of 1.5 million votes because of his Roman Catholicism and by Nixon's hints of aid to parochial schools. The emergence of ethnic politics in the 1960s as an expanded and elaborated form of earlier nationality-group politics promotes ethnocentricity.

When Congress enacted legislation designating Columbus Day as a national holiday and the president signed the bill making it the law of the land, the federal government had acted to satisfy the demands of Italian-Americans and had thus exhibited to a significant extent an acceptance of cultural pluralism. One can expect new demands by Italian-Americans as their group consciousness becomes heightened through such official recognition. In November 1971 two New York congressmen introduced legislation in the House of Representatives calling for a postage stamp to commemorate nuclear physicist Enrico Fermi. Congressman Mario Biaggi, Democrat of the Bronx, complained that the only other Italian-American to be honored by a commemorative stamp was Christopher Columbus. Cleaning the local

statue of Christopher Columbus in time for the Columbus Day parade
is no longer a sufficient gesture, nor have bigger Columbus Day
parades—long the symbol of Italian-American pride—brought content-
ment. One Italian-American in the cabinet—why not more? Why not
an Italian-American Supreme Court justice, an Italian-American
president?

The inevitable question is that if regional and class differences
have been legitimate perspectives from which to view issues and
candidates, why are the racial, religious, and ethnic points of view
any less legitimate? The traditional explanation for rejecting these
grounds was that heightened ethnocentricity encouraged divisions within
society. Indeed, the genius of the American political process has been
its flexibility and assimilative influence. Resentment of nativist
Protestant prejudice fused diverse ethnic and religious minorities
into one cornerstone of the New Deal coalition. The balanced ticket
at the local level helped to assimilate diverse ethnic groups into the
political system, and to a great extent into American social and
cultural life. Rapid induction into public office fostered a sense of
respectability. Political participation by ethnic groups early in their
immigrant experience developed skills among many of their leaders
and engendered in them a concern for a community larger than their
own nationality group. Democratic ethnic adviser Andrew Valuchek
believes that succession to local political power by major ethnic groups
is not only a natural process but also one of the best safeguards to
American democracy since it prevents domination by any one group.
Americans are, according to him, a nation of minorities; when one
minority becomes too strong, the others "gang up on it" and prevent
it from becoming too confident, self-centered, and powerful. The
phenomenon of one ethnic group replacing another as the political
elite in the majority party results from the relatively open elections
in the North in the last one hundred years. The death of political
boss Edward J. Flynn of the Bronx in 1953 ended Irish political
leadership in New York City, and such leadership became open to
Jewish and Italian initiative. In 1972 Philadelphia was to have an
Italian mayor, Detroit a Polish one, Cleveland a second-generation
Czech Catholic, and Gary and Newark blacks.

Chicago has been the most striking exception to the rule of
ethnic political succession. Bohemian-born Mayor Cermak has been
followed by three Irish mayors, all born and raised in Chicago's
Back of the Yards area. The last of these—Richard J. Daley—has
shown extraordinary political skill in keeping the levers of local
political power in the hands of the Irish. Within the American political
process, group assertion and accommodation have tended to neutralize
group conflict and make national consensus a frequent reality. Ethnic
and religious groups serve to check and balance one another. No

national parties are deliberately and explicitly organized along ethnic, religious, or racial lines. The major parties make room for these groups; indeed, they actually court their support to build majority coalitions.

14

**PROSPECTS
FOR ETHNIC POLITICS
IN THE 1970s**

GROUPS NATIONALIZE TO PRESS THEIR DEMANDS

With the breakdown of traditional party loyalties, America
seems to have entered an era of interest-group politics, with ethnic
politics a legitimate subdivision of the new politics. Such legitimacy
has encouraged, and will continue to encourage, heightened ethnic group
consciousness. The Spanish-origin groups followed the lead of the
black caucus and black political leaders who held national conferences
in 1971 to discuss coalition-building black strategies for the 1972
presidential campaign. The Spanish-Americans met in Washington,
D.C., in October 1971 for a unity conference to nationalize their
movement. The conference, attended by more than 800 Latin leaders,
was organized by 4 Spanish-American congressmen and endorsed
two proposals—Puerto Rican independence and a separate Spanish-
speaking political party. White ethnic leaders have not yet formed a
national organization to represent white ethnic groups. It seems
doubtful that the Irish and German-Americans would become a part
of any such organization. Monsignor Baroni's Center for Urban
Ethnic Affairs, however, is headed in that direction. He has become
the major spokesman for ethnic America and legitimized his leadership by two national conferences and recognition by President Nixon,
congressional leaders, and the Ford Foundation. He has lobbied for
the National Ethnic Studies Bill and other programs which are of particular interest to white ethnic groups. His first lieutenant, an Alinsky-
trained community organizer, has used the "ethnic handle" when it
is expedient to his efforts to organize blue-collar white ethnics.
Whether Baroni can survive without foundation, church, and federal
funding is questionable. He does not appear to have sufficient financial
and leadership support from white ethnic communities to run a

self-sustaining national organization. It is doubtful whether the blacks could have realized their substantial gains without the support of white liberals and white institutions. Baroni is proceeding cautiously and avoiding high visibility.

Another national organization of white ethnics, the National Confederation of American Ethnic Groups, was formed in April 1956 in Washington, D.C. It grew out of the anguish and disappointment that followed the brutal suppression of the Hungarian uprising and the failure of the Republican administration to fulfill its campaign pledge to liberate the captive nations and repudiate the Yalta Agreement. The Confederation seeks to represent ethnic Americans and to exert direct influence on governmental decision-making bodies, thus bypassing both parties. Its avowed purpose is to unite nationality groups into one "giant confederation." In its prospectus, it appeals to nationality organizations to affiliate themselves with it because, in its words, "The Irish and Jewish groups—and now the Negroes—have learned the effectiveness and prestige that can be achieved through collective, unified action—and they are forging ahead. The many benefits these groups have derived from such action are self-evident. Have you ever stopped to think where this leaves the Nationality groups?"

Paul Deau, one of the organizers of the Confederation, became its salaried national executive vice-president and was still serving in that capacity in 1971. The Confederation had no staff in that year and operated out of Deau's private home. In Richard Lemon's book The Troubled American, Deau is quoted as saying:

> Right now, the ethnic vote is up for grabs. . . . New York liberals are dogs. The burning of cities, lawlessness, permissiveness in our colleges, is pushed as a weapon by progressive liberals to bring the nation to its knees so they can rule. . . . Nixon has said he would be the champion of the forgotten man. We're still waiting. . . . We're not going back to the liberal Democrats. They took our vote and shut us off from the benefits. Unless the GOP gives due consideration, they can't make any headway. We're not going to exchange one master for another. So Wallace may be the only answer.

The Confederation has survived for more than fifteen years but its impact on foreign policy and domestic political institutions and decision-making has been limited. The directors of the Nationalities Divisions of the two parties have given speeches to groups of Congressmen. Congressmen have remained on friendly terms with the Confederation, but the leadership of the two parties and their elective

officeholders know that the Confederation does not have a broad base
of support and therefore extend it only token recognition. As long as
the Confederation remains primarily tied to a capitve nations program,
its political influence will be minimal.

Both political parties have been largely successful in coopting
nationwide efforts to organize nationality groups. The leadership of
nationality groups has usually been given enough recognition and
enough token foreign policy concessions to keep them within the party
structure. The same pattern has prevailed at the local level. When
immigrant groups in Chicago began to assert themselves politically,
Mayor Anton Cermak assigned Chicago Congressman Adolph J.
Sabath, a Czech Jew, to organize them and bring them into the structure
of the local machine. While the Nationality Groups Organization
remained within the Chicago Democratic machine it was unable to
consolidate and exert influence as a separate entity because of the
local Party's desire to keep it weak and dependent and to minimize
internal conflict among the major nationality groups. Leaders of the
major nationality groups refused to let Sabath speak for them. In
1934 Joseph Rostenkowski, a Polish leader, openly defied Sabath at a
meeting at Democratic headquarters. Rostenkowski told Sabath:
"Don't you dare to say you represent the Poles. You're not a Pole,
and we will speak for ourselves. You don't control the Polish vote
and never will." Much the same has happened at the national level.
Louis L. Gerson writes in The Hyphenates in Recent American Politics
and Diplomacy:

> Nationality groups have been unable to unite internally in
> a common sustained and well-timed effort to compel the
> government of the United States to satisfy their demands.
> Political, social, or religious divisions, entanglements,
> and mutual distrusts present in the land of origin have
> often been transplanted onto American soil with each
> successive wave or ripple of immigrants, exile leaders,
> or refugees. This was true of the Irish-Americans in the
> late nineteenth and early twentieth centuries; this has been
> true of Slavic-Americans during both of the world wars and
> to some extent during the Cold War. At times a core of
> ethnic leaders has been able to gain control over all the
> members—active or inactive—of a given nationality,
> through the establishment of roof organizations or the
> "rigging" of a convention. Armed with the ostensible
> power to speak for the whole group, this small but
> articulate elite has been able to induce political leaders
> to attend its wants.

There has never been a significant effort in America to organize a third political party based on shared ethnic or religious backgrounds, or on foreign policy concerns. The record of political influence exercised by national nationality-group organizations such as the Confederation is very limited. The most competent ethnic leaders prefer to advance themselves within established American institutions. Of course, ethnic leaders who present themselves as representing their groups are no different from leaders of organized labor who claim to "control" the votes of their members. Recognition by the national parties also enhances the position of ethnic leaders. A conference with the president boosts the influence of an ethnic leader with his constituency. Ralph Perk is such an example, and he undoubtedly profited from his close association with the Republican National Committee and President Nixon. But the parties make enemies when they take under their official wing opportunists from ethnic communities who do not enjoy support within their nationality groups.

WALLACE RUNS AGAIN

By November 1971 it was reasonably clear that Alabama Governor George Wallace would seek the presidency in 1972. His chief political aides announced that he was "moving" and would again seek the electoral support of blue-collar workers in the urban North. The head of Wallace's various publications for the 1972 presidential campaign said in the fall of 1971 that Wallace had a labor coordinator and a constituency of workers among ethnic groups. He noted: "We are finding tremendous support among Americans of Cuban and Chinese extraction. . . . The main issue in 1972 will be busing . . . feelings about busing are running strong and deep." One of Wallace's six publications is entitled Labor Action, and 100,000 copies of this new monthly newspaper were distributed throughout the country to working-class readers. In 1968 the Wallace campaign forced organized labor to expend a substantial part of its energies and resources to neutralize the governor's appeal among union members. At one point in the 1968 campaign it was estimated that Wallace had 17 percent or more of the labor vote. A $50-a-plate dinner for Wallace in New York City attracted more than 1,000 adherents, and 900 people turned out for a similar dinner in Toledo. In the fall of 1971 polls showed Wallace winning roughly 12 percent of the vote as a third-party candidate.

Wallace slightly shifted his appeals in 1972 from racism to populism. By May 1972 he had won some Democratic primaries and made impressive showings in others. On the eve of the Maryland and

Michigan primaries, Wallace was severely wounded in an assassination attempt. Five bullets left Wallace confined, perhaps permanently, to a wheelchair. Most indications, as of the summer of 1972 were that he would not engage actively in presidential politics.

THE FUTURE OF REPUBLICAN ETHNIC STRATEGY

The Nixon ethnic strategy, outlined by Kevin Phillips and executed by Vice-President Agnew and the Republican National Committee, faces two serious obstacles. Conservative Republicans are no more committed to public spending and federal intervention to uplift ethnic minorities economically than they were to improve the lot of racial minorities. They simply are not prepared to share their wealth or risk serious social and economic change. Class issues, outside the deep South, remain stronger than racial ones. Ethnic Americans will not be fooled on the basic economic issues. The Republican Party retains its image as the party of big business and conservative economics. The results of the 1970 congressional elections showed that ethnic Americans were less persuaded by Agnew's rhetoric of resentment than by the issues of unemployment, inflation, and unfair taxes. On these basic issues, white ethnics still turn to the Democratic Party. The Republican strategy to weld together on social issues Southern whites and low- and middle-income whites of the industrial Northern states depends heavily on economic prosperity, for it pits economic allies against one another. This Republican strategy is synonymous with the politics of resentment. It keeps the white and black lower and middle classes fighting among themselves for self-respect, jobs, schools, housing, medical resources, recreational facilities, and welfare while affluent suburbanites and the rich retain their positions and assume a defensive posture. In additional, the Republican Party has a majority of the electorate from the large industrial areas of the Southwest and West. The Republican ethnic strategy is negative and makes no commitment to realize America's potential for greater growth and the more equitable distribution of its wealth. This is a "no-lose" rather than a "win" policy.

In an article in Commonweal (September 25, 1970), entitled "The Politics of Resentment," Michael Novak writes:

> Phillips is probably right that major ethnic groups, largely Catholic, are being driven from the intellectualist liberals and attracted by conservative rhetoric. . . .
> No doubt, ressentiment plays a great role in those primitive emotions which govern voting behavior—witness

the savage ressentiment on whose tide Hitler came to
power in Germany. But it is not at all certain . . . that
the Republicans will do anything concrete to meet the needs
of the lower-middle-class white. Those needs include more
self-determination and pride on the job, more prestige in
the nation, more dignity—as well as better housing, a sharp
control on inflation, full employment, more scholarships
and welfare (so that non-whites and whites don't have to
compete for the same small piece of pie), far more beauty
and peace and easy transport and security in the cities and
boroughs in which they live.

The other weakness of the Republican ethnic strategy is
revealed in Kevin Phillips' The Emerging Republican Majority.
Phillips' basic contention depends on Democratic inflexibility.
President Kennedy and then President Johnson shifted the emphasis
of the party from deprived whites to deprived blacks—or at least they
appeared to do so. But early indications in the 1972 presidential
campaign indicated that Democrat Edmund Muskie was modifying that
shift in priorities from blacks to whites in order to project a middle-
of-the-road image. It appeared that he wanted American voters to
believe that he would not be stampeded by black political activists.
His campaign revealed his commitment to the concerns of ethnic
Americans and included, in some instances, support of such law-and-
order candidates as Frank Rizzo. Much to the anguish of the liberal
left, Muskie telephoned his congratulations to Rizzo the day after his
November election and accepted an invitation to meet privately with
the Mayor-elect in Philadelphia in December. The title of Phillips'
book—The Emerging Republican Majority—postulates a permanent
shift in electoral support by ethnic Americans, but this does not
appear likely. In American politics, groups do not give their loyalty
to a party permanently.

The Republican Party, however, has recently achieved some
important white ethnic victories. In addition to statewide victories
such as that of Senator James Buckley in New York in 1970, there
have been urban successes. For example, Republican Ralph J. Perk
lost the Cleveland mayoralty to Carl Stokes in 1969 by the slim margin
of 3,473 votes out of the more than 238,944 cast. Stokes did not seek
reelection in November 1971 and backed a black Independent against
the white Democratic candidate and Republican Perk. Perk, a
second-generation Czech Catholic, surprised most forecasters by
winning by a plurality of more than 40 percent. He thus became the
first GOP mayor of Cleveland in 30 years. No American city larger
than Cleveland had a Republican chief executive in 1971. Perk was
founder of the American Nationalities Movement in Cleveland—a

campaign to encourage Cleveland residents to take pride in their
ethnic heritages and join together to influence local public decision-
making—and in 1971 vice-chairman of the National Republican Heritage
Groups Council, and thus closely associated with President Nixon.
Election returns revealed that Perk made substantial inroads into
traditionally Democratic blue-collar white communities and captured
the great majority of Cleveland's white ethnics. He stressed fiscal
responsibility, the failures of the Stokes administration, and law and
order in his campaign, and was frequently characterized by the media
as a conservative Republican. Former Mayor Stokes had stepped
down "to seek a more active role in national politics."

THE CASE OF EDMUND MUSKIE

Edmund Sixtus Muskie, a second-generation Polish Catholic,
might have finished the work begun by Alfred Smith and advanced
much further by John F. Kennedy, by making the presidency of the
United States accessible to all European stock, except, perhaps, those
of the Jewish faith. Had Muskie been nominated by the Democratic
Party and gone on to win the presidency, he would have affirmed one
of the promises of the American Dream. He represents a fusion of
Yankee background from the state of Maine, Polish ancestry, and
Roman Catholicism, and he presented himself to the American public
as a middle-of-the-road healer and unifier. He emphasized his
personal character and integrity, avoided charismatic appeals, and
stressed his trustworthiness and managerial expertise. He used none
of the ideological rhetoric of the European socialist and spoke only
as a pragmatic moderate. The news media used the words "centrist"
or "centralist" to designate the image he was trying to project.

At the turn of the century, Muskie's father, Stefan Marciszewski,
at age 17, emigrated to America from a Polish village in order to
escape conscription in the Russian army. He was a tailor and married
a Polish-American named Josephine Czarnecki. A cover article in
Life (November 5, 1971), entitled "Muskie—The Democrats' Front-
runner" notes that Muskie has been much influenced by his father's
self-reliance and his "Polish-Yankee legacy of right strivings." The
article quotes Muskie as saying: "His was a tough code, but a liberating one. He built his life in a company town, and you know what
company towns can be like. So many people subservient. But nobody
ever challenged my father." The elder Muskie, a Democrat, had
voted for Alfred E. Smith in 1928, and he died in 1953. Muskie's
mother still lives in the mill town of Rumford, in the ramshackle
neighborhood where Muskie was born and raised. The inhabitants of
Rumford were predominantly French-Canadians and largely Roman

Catholic. Muskie as a boy was subjected to heckling as a "Polack," but apparently was little affected by it. It was his father who changed the family name. Muskie attends Sunday Mass regularly, and his Roman Catholicism serves him as a source of inner strength. The article in Life quotes Muskie on the special significance that the family holds for him, and, as he believes, for most ethnic Americans: "A keen sense of family is what brought them here. For the sake of generations yet unborn. That's still true in my own life." He is close to his wife and five children. Muskie speaks little Polish and maintains no contact with his relatives in Poland, though he referred to them in general terms during his unofficial campaigning in 1971. "While Uncle Stefan was still alive," said a cousin in the old country, "we would hear about the family in America, but not any more."

While the Muskie family had none of the wealth and quasi-aristocratic background of the Joseph P. Kennedy clan, Muskie distinguished himself as a cum laude graduate of an Ivy League law school (Cornell) and worked himself up through Maine state politics by using a liberal WASP style. He married a WASP. He has lived by and espoused the Protestant ethic. Just as John Kennedy was perceived more as a WASP humanitarian and social liberal than as an Irish Catholic with conservative social views in the mold of Al Smith, Muskie remains cast in a largely Anglo-Protestant image. Muskie is different from Kennedy in that he married a salesgirl from a small town in Maine and has not been associated with international socialites and the Washington cocktail circuit. As Kennedy shattered the myth that no Roman Catholic could be elected president, Muskie might have shattered the myth that the American presidency is the exclusive province of those with WASP or wealthy Irish backgrounds.

Elections analyst Richard C. Scammon, co-author of the 1970 book The Real Majority, thought that Muskie appealed to the moderate middle and believed that the reason he showed a stronger rating in the opinion pools at that time than any other Democratic presidential prospect was because he did not project a "soft-on-crime" image. The thesis of his book, which Muskie did not challenge, is that it will be detrimental for Democrats to appear to be overly "permissive" in this area. For Scammon, the "social issue" (crime, busing, drugs, legalized abortion, pornography) will share the spotlight in the 1972 presidential campaigns with the economic issues. Muskie had joined other members of the Senate and House in proposing a special White House office on drug abuse and a federal program that would require nearly twice the present federal expenditure to establish local treatment centers for drug addicts. He was not in favor of liberalized abortion laws. Scammon had reasoned that Muskie, as a Polish-American and a Roman Catholic, would minimize defections in the Democratic big cities to George Wallace's conservative third-party

movement. Muskie would systematically court the white ethnic vote,
but with a low-key approach. Few Polish-Americans are unaware of
Muskie's ancestral roots, and the majority of them were intensely
proud of his imminent candidacy. While discussing the electoral
college system on August 25, 1970, Muskie had voiced his fears that
the social divisions in America would make it difficult for either of
the two major parties to form a majority coalition. He said that civil
unrest and bombings were "stirring up the right and moving the
moderate middle toward the right." He added that what is viewed in
the public mind as the "liberal approach" to dealing with violent
disorder has lost credibility with many Americans.

By November 1971 Muskie was making ethnic appeals to ethnic
groups in much the same manner as previous presidential candidates.
Before he attended Polish Constitution Day in Chicago in 1971, a
Chicago advance man prepared a memorandum for him about the
Polish-American community in Chicago. When Muskie was asked to
comment on the formation of the heavily ethnic Calumet Community
Conference, he said: "It is exactly what America must have if our
democracy is to become more responsive to the people's real needs."
On September 27, 1971, Muskie told a largely Jewish audience of 1,800
people in Chicago: "As long as I have any influence on the course of
this nation's history, I will do everything I can to assure that the
children of Israel have and hold their Promised Land." He criticized
the Nixon administration for not delivering fighter jets to Israel.
America, he said, must "provide Israel with tools to do the work of
survival." On Labor Day 1971 Muskie met with Catholic labor leaders
in Los Angeles, and two months later he and his wife attended mass
at the Our Lady of Guadelupe Church in predominantly Mexican East
Los Angeles. Muskie's national campaign coordinator, Anthony
Podesta, was a white ethnic, his Illinois campaign manager a Greek-
American.

It is ironic that though Muskie's election would have been the
most important breakthrough for ethnic America, it was Muskie himself who, in a moment of candor in September 1971, said that he did
not think he could win the presidency with a black vice-presidential
running mate "at this point in history." His assessment was probably
an accurate one, though an October 1971 Gallup Poll showed that
prejudice toward blacks in politics appears to have declined to its
lowest point. However, according to George Gallup, the nationwide
survey found that Muskie would have lost votes had he chosen a black
as a vice-presidential running mate. Nixon and many black politicians
wasted no time in making political hay of Muskie's remark. The
president said: "It is very important for those of us in positions of
leadership not to tell large numbers of people in America, whoever
they are, that because of the accident of birth, they don't have a chance

to go to the top." Muskie retreated slightly and said that he might later change his "judgment" but not his "mind."

Ethnic politics in America has taken new directions. They are less integrative and assimilative, and perhaps more divisive, as group identities become the poles toward which people gravitate and around which they are brought to rally to improve their status and power and to conserve whatever security or gains they believe they already possess. America has been relatively successful in surmounting group conflict. But the problem of how people of diverse racial, religious, and nationality backgrounds can live together peaceably and creatively within the same national society has become one of the most crucial issues facing America, second only to the overriding problem of international war. The best and most dedicated thinkers and social scientists in America must devote more consideration to this inadequately explored problem, particularly because of political efforts to stir and appeal to deeply felt racial, religious, and ethnic sentiments. And it is not only the politicians who are encouraging group identification. Newspapers, television, private foundations, intellectuals, and universities are promoting cultural pluralism. When the Ford Foundation grants $100 million for programs in black, Mexican-American, Puerto Rican, and Indian studies at the graduate level, and for financial support for black colleges, the ideological shift is obvious. The Ford Foundation granted nearly a million dollars for exploration of white ethnic alienation, but ethnic intellectual Michael Novak has reacted to this grant by calling it "guilt money."

Ethnic politics, as the term has been used so far, has included racial and religious groups but has focused primarily on the interplay of ethnic awareness and national politics. There is evidence that both politicians and ethnic leaders on the one hand and certain ethnic Americans on the other are influenced by ethnic considerations. Many observers are astonished at the persistence of the ethnic factor in American politics, but perhaps this results from their close identification of the ethnic with the immigrant. It has become apparent that attention should be given to the process by which immigrants and their children are acculturated, their continuing identification with their homeland, their resistance to assimilation, and the confused and tarnished symbols and goals presented to them by the American society. Second- and third-generation Americans may move away from the old neighborhood, sever most cultural ties, and blend into some vaguely defined national identity, but this identity is neither uniform nor standard. Ethnic groups have assumed an American form. Certain ethnic characteristics and attitudes brought to America are retained and take distinctive new shapes. While use of the foreign language is decreasing, the foreign language press and radio fading from the urban scene, and the ethnic social, religious, and fraternal organizations losing membership, the American hyphenate is emerging into public view more prominently as a hyphenated American than at any other time in American history. While the ranks of recent immigrants are being significantly replenished, immigration is a small fraction of what it was between 1850 and 1924. It is among the immigrants who settled before the Depression, as well as the post-World War II refugees, that the ethnic influence in politics has become important, and it has not diminished as was expected.

In their book, Beyond the Melting Pot, published in 1963, Nathan Glazer and Daniel P. Moynihan argued that it was religion and race that would define the next stages of the politics of the American people. They presented convincing evidence that the melting pot phenomenon had not really taken place, and that the group characteristics of ethnic social life had remained, especially with regard to religion and race. While they found that ethnicity was a factor in American politics, it was, they said, declining in importance and was likely to continue in that direction. Glazer and Moynihan originally underestimated the problems and political potential of the blacks and Puerto Ricans in New York, where they gathered their data. In a long introduction to the second edition of Beyond the Melting Pot, published in 1970, they revised their conclusions and explained their new one, namely, that "ethnicity and race dominate the city, more than ever seemed possible in 1963," but that "religion as a major line of division in the city is for the moment in eclipse."

New York City is not the only strategic area where ethnicity is a decisive political power. Directors of newly formed white ethnic organizations report that such presidential contenders as John Lindsay and Edmund Muskie had sought their counsel on how to appeal to white ethnics. They wanted to know the new symbols, rhetoric, and directions of the ethnic movements. Irving Levine, director of the National Project on Ethnic America, believes that the 1972 presidential campaign will "galvanize the white ethnic movement" and notes that

progressive Democrats are "covering their appeals to racial minorities with a white flank."

In an unpublished paper entitled "Ethnic Circumstance: Americans at the Polls," presented at the second national conference of the
Center for Urban Ethnic Affairs in June 1971, Richard M. Scammon
summarized his view of the new meaning of ethnic politics as follows:

> We all recognize a new kind of ethnicity in America today
> and we recognize it in politics as we do in so many other
> streams of American life. It is not only a pride in heri-
> tage and past achievement, it is a concern over present
> situations and values. That is why we can speak of a
> "Cosmo" vote in Cleveland, or of an "ethnic" vote in
> Chicago, because much of the voting of so-called white
> ethnic Americans concerns itself now not with voting for
> the " . . . ski," or the Irisher, or the Italian, but for some-
> thing else, for a value system which the ethnic may feel
> to be under attack as strongly, maybe even more strongly,
> than the N-N WASP (native-born or native-born parents,
> White, Anglo-Saxon Protestant).
>
> It is often in the defense of these values, in the de-
> fense of what some would call the white ethnic view of so-
> cial order, that a good deal of this new ethnic political
> vitality may be sensed. We do not know how far this new
> vitality will go, and indeed it is a vitality and a concern
> shared by many voters without a specific ethnic interest,
> by Blacks and Whites, by Jews and Gentiles, by Catholic
> and Protestant. In this "joined" sense this new vitality
> is non-ethnic and perhaps this, more than any other evi-
> dence, represents the paradox of the new importance of
> ethnic politics in a non-ethnic set of political and social
> values.

Speaking a year earlier at the Center's first national conference,
Scammon noted that the white ethnic voter would continue to play a
pivotal role in determining the outcome of future elections. He observed that while white ethnics support progressive "bread and
butter" legislation, they are against progressive social action, which
they deem disruptive. Their primary concern for "social order"
will not abate in the near future. Scammon warned that no ethnic
group has an absolute political or issue identity. For instance, the
Poles and Jews overwhelmingly favor the Democratic Party. The
high frequency of home ownership among Polish and Italian-American
voters relates significantly to their electoral attitudes and behavior
on issues of local taxation. The voting behavior of Irish-Americans

reveals a growing political conservatism which has increasingly put them at ideological odds with the Democratic Party.

In his book The Emerging Republican Majority, Kevin Phillips argues that as the Democrats shifted from the economic populist stand of the New Deal to what he terms "social engineering," the New Deal coalition collapsed. As a result, he writes: "In practically every state and region, ethnic and cultural animosities and divisions exceed all other factors in explaining party choice and identification." George Wallace's strong primary showing among the ethnic working class in Gary, Milwaukee, and other Northern cities in the 1960s and in 1972 was caused less by racism than by Wallace's appeal as an economic populist. Certainly the Democrats' "social engineering" most affected urban workingmen by pushing blacks into their neighborhoods, schools, and unions, but it was to their feeling of economic neglect and frustration that Wallace appealed with some success. The protests of urban white ethnics may be in terms of "get people off welfare," or "they are taxing us to death," or "we Poles brought ourselves up from nothing," but behind this rhetoric is their basic objection to paying the cost required to uplift society.

In the 1960s the emphasis of the Democrats shifted from poor whites to poor blacks. In The Hidden Crisis in American Politics, Samuel Lubell writes of America's dilemma as a "fierce Darwinian competition between a new militant economic individualism and an overloaded sense of responsibility." After a strenuous month of interviewing a cross-section of 27 New York City precincts, Lubell found that the new "conservatism," symbolized by the election in 1970 of New York's junior senator, James L. Buckley, has been mistakenly pictured as largely hard-hat and blue-collar. His interviews revealed that only about a third of Buckley's supporters were construction workers, truck drivers, factory hands, cargo handlers, etc. Outnumbering them two to one were white-collar employees, including four out of every five policemen. Nearly 70 percent of those who voted for Buckley also backed President Nixon on his Indochina policy; more than two-thirds favored Buckley's racial policies. Lubell concludes:

> It seemed evident that the contest was plainly stacked against the liberals. To get funds for their "programs" someone's taxes had to be raised or the money had to come from friendly governments in the state capital or Washington.
>
> The "conservatives" on the other hand, had the drive and means (as long as full employment continued) through which they could lift themselves by their own efforts, fighting to keep what they earned by opposing tax increases and new spending programs. . . .

> As a result, evidences of the breakdown of urban so-
> ciety are piling up like uncollected garbage. . . .
> What we are witnessing, I believe, is the rise of a
> new urban sectionalism, the equivalent for our time of the
> Populist revolt against 19th-Century laissez-faire indivi-
> dualism, whose squeeze was felt most harshly by farmers.

Lubell believes that American society has nearly lost the battle
for meaningful integration. The attraction of Wallace in the 1960s
foreshadowed the consequences of this failure—intensified territorial
racial conflict and the spread of racial voting. Job opportunities in
Cleveland, Gary, Newark, and other Northern cities are diminishing.
The Republican strategy to become the majority party is grounded
in the union of the South and white urban North into a conservatively
oriented coalition, and the cement for this union is opposition to school
busing and open housing.

Monsignor Baroni, director of the Center for Urban Ethnic
Affairs, is more optimistic. He looks to new and creative leadership
in 1972, emphasizing that the working whites of Gary voted for George
Wallace in 1964 and for Robert Kennedy in 1968. "Wallace catered
to their fears . . . Bobby catered to their hopes."

Theorists and practitioners of American public policy have done
very little to study the growing public commitment to cultural pluralism
and its consequences. With the exception of the stakes in American
foreign policy and American immigration laws at the federal level, and
positions of political power at all levels of government, the ethnic
politics practiced by most American politicians seem innocuous. But
it is too early and events are not yet in sufficient perspective to allow
judgment. Why ethnic leaders have permitted themselves to be exploited by politicians, why ethnic voters seem to be swayed by empty
rhetoric and promises made in bad faith, and why ethnic politicians
with ethnic constituencies have not been required to "deliver" more
for their electoral support are still sources of speculation. Increased
activity by the national parties may serve to improve communications
with ethnic Americans, but that is not their purpose. Gimmicks,
fakery, token recognition, and political expediency seem to be the
rule, not the exception. Messages to and appearances at ethnic
affairs, meetings with ethnic leaders, resolutions, proclamations,
stamps, holidays, parades, ethnic studies programs are far less costly
political "expenditures" than the relinquishing of positions of power.
Television and radio offer large national audiences and make it much
easier to engage in the practice of "instant" ancestry. Nixon is
suddenly Irish; Muskie, a Maine Yankee, struggles to learn enough
Polish to capitalize on his ancestry. Other foolish and dangerous
practices occur. The Republican National Committee overlooks the

fact that it has a former Nazi as its Slovakian adviser until it is highly publicized. Former Postmaster General John Gronouski speaks Polish so poorly that his voice must be dubbed on tapes, since his pronunciation would offend a Polish-speaking audience. The federal government provides a site in Washington, D.C., for an Ukrainian-American statue and both parties take credit for it. Politicians talk of "playing the game of ethnic politics." The growing sophistication of the American electorate, however, suggests that politicians may have to exercise more caution in their ethnic appeals. Ethnic Americans increasingly resent condescending political treatment.

While this bibliography is selective, it attempts to provide a survey of the literature on American ethnic groups. Emphasis has been placed on the immigrant experience, political and social development, and contemporary rediscovery and resurgence. The majority of the literature in this last category is popular and journalistic but does provide a means for understanding recent developments. Some effort has been made to include notable writings on individual ethnic groups. The author has not undertaken to divide these citations into categories. He has serious reservations about the benefits of categorizing, given the problem of overlapping. Important articles included in collections have not been repeated.

The growing popular and scholarly interest in ethnicity has already resulted in an increase in the literature on the subject. Much more is likely to follow. At least three series on American ethnic groups have so far appeared. The most valuable is Milton Gordon's Prentice-Hall series, to date covering Jewish, black, Japanese, Indian, and Puerto Rican Americans. Alexander De Conde of the University of California, Santa Barbara, is general editor of the "Minorities in American Life Series." This series has already provided books on Irish and Chinese-Americans, and books on Mexican, Polish, black, Japanese, Jewish, and Italian-Americans are forthcoming. A third "scholarly reprint" series published by R & E Research Associates, San Francisco, offers a wide variety of reference works. Its brochures state that they are "publishers and distributors of ethnic studies" and their listings indicate an emphasis on comprehensiveness without regard to selectivity.

Perhaps the most important research on American ethnicity under way at this time is being conducted at the Center for the Study of American Pluralism, headed by the Reverend Andrew M. Greeley. The Center maintains offices at the National Opinion Research Center and is associated with the University of Chicago.

I am grateful to the following for their assistance and suggestions in the preparation of this bibliography: the Reverend Paul J. Asciolla, C.S., the Reverend Andrew M. Greeley, Judith M. Herman, Louis H. Masotti, David G. Roth, and Robert W. Welsh, Jr.

Errors of commission and omission are the responsibility of the compiler-author.

Abell, Aaron I. American Catholicism and Social Action: A Search
     for Social Justice 1865-1950. Garden City, N.Y.: Hanover House,
     a Division of Doubleday, 1960.

_____. ed. American Catholic Thought on Social Questions.
     New York: Bobbs-Merrill, 1968.

Abramson, Harold J. "The Ethnic Factor in American Catholicism:
     An Analysis of Inter-Ethnic Marriage and Religious Involvement."
     Unpublished Ph.D. dissertation, University of Chicago, 1969.

_____. "Ethnic Pluralism in the Central City." Storrs: Institute
     for Urban Research of the University of Connecticut, 1970.

Allinsmith, Wesley, and Beverly Allinsmith. "Religious Affiliation
     and Politico-Economic Attitude: A Study of Eight Major U.S.
     Religious Groups." Public Opinion Quarterly (Fall 1948).

Allport, Gordon W. The Nature of Prejudice. Reading, Mass.:
     Addison-Wesley, 1954.

Allswang, John M. A House for All People. Lexington: University
     Press of Kentucky, 1971.

Almond, Gabriel A. The American People and Foreign Policy. New
     York: Frederick A. Praeger, 1960.

American Jewish Committee. "Pluralism Beyond the Frontier: Report
     of the San Francisco Consultation on Ethnicity." San Francisco:
     American Jewish Committee, 1972.

_____. The Reacting Americans: An Interim Look at the White
     Ethnic Lower Middle Class. New York: American Jewish
     Committee, 1968.

Anderson, Charles H. White Protestant Americans. Englewood Cliffs,
     N.J.: Prentice-Hall, 1970.

Anderson, Ellen. We Americans: A Study of Cleavage in an American
     City. Cambridge, Mass.: Harvard University Press, 1937.

Anderson, Theodore and Mildred Boyer. Bilingual Schooling in the
     United States (two volumes). Washington, D.C.: U.S. Government
     Printing Office, 1970.

Antin, Mary. Promised Land. New York: Houghton Mifflin, 1969.

Aya, Roderick and Norman Miller. The New American Revolution. New York: Free Press, 1971.

Bailey, Harry A. and Ellis Katz, eds. Ethnic Group Politics. Columbus, Ohio: Charles E. Merrill, 1969.

Bailey, Thomas A. The Man in the Street: The Impact of American Public Opinion on Foreign Policy. New York: Peter Smith, 1948.

Balch, Emily Greene. Our Slavic Fellow Citizens. New York: Arno Press and the New York Times, 1969.

Baltzell, E. Digby. The Protestant Establishment. New York: Random House, 1964.

Banfield, Edward and James Q. Wilson. City Politics. Cambridge Mass.: Harvard University Press, 1963.

Baroni, Geno C., ed. All Men Are Brothers. Washington, D.C.: United States Catholic Conference, 1970.

Barron, Milton L., ed. Minorities in a Changing World. New York: Alfred A. Knopf, 1967.

Bean, Louis H. "Research Project on the Influence of Nationality Groups on Election Returns." Unpublished report to Franklin D. Roosevelt, February 12, 1941, in the Roosevelt Papers.

Bell, Daniel. The End of Ideology, rev. ed. New York: Free Press, 1962.

Bennett, Levone, Jr. Confrontation: Black and White. Baltimore: Penguin Books, 1965.

Berelson, Bernard R., Paul F. Lazarsfeld, and William N. McPhee. Voting. Chicago: University of Chicago Press, 1954.

Berger, Bennet M. Working-Class Suburb. Berkeley: University of California Press, 1968.

Bernard, William S., ed., American Immigration Policy—a Reappraisal. ✓ New York: Harper and Row, 1950.

_____, ed. Immigrants and Ethnicity: Ten Years of Changing Thought. New York: American Immigration and Citizenship Conference and National Project on Ethnic America, 1972.

Berry, Brewton. Race and Ethnic Relations. Boston: Houghton Mifflin, 1965.

Berson, Lenora A. The Negroes and the Jews. New York: Random House, 1971.

Bettelheim, Bruno and Morris Janowitz. Social Change and Prejudice. New York: Free Press, 1964.

Binzen, Peter. Whitetown, U.S.A. New York: Random House, 1970.

Blumberg, Rae L., Scott Greer, and Robert F. Winch. "Ethnicity and Extended Familism in an Upper-Middle Class Suburb." American Sociological Review (April 1967), pp. 265-72.

Bogue, Donald J. The Population of the United States. Glencoe, Ill.: Free Press, 1959.

Bower, Robert T. "Voting Behavior of American Ethnic Groups, 1936-1944." Unpublished essay. Bureau of Applied Social Research, Columbia University, New York, 1944.

Bowers, David F., ed. Foreign Influences in American Life. Princeton: Princeton University Press, 1944.

Bradburn, Norman M., Seymour Sudman, and Galen L. Gockel. Racial Integration in American Neighborhoods. Chicago: Quadrangle Books, 1970.

Brenner, Saul. "Patterns of Jewish-Catholic Democratic Voting and the 1960 Presidential Vote." Jewish Social Studies (July 1964).

Brink, William and Louis Harris. Black and White. New York: Simon and Schuster, 1967.

Burger, Peter. "The Blueing of America." New Republic (April 3, 1971), pp. 20-23.

Campbell, Angus, Philip E. Converse, Warren E. Miller, and Donald E. Stokes, eds. Elections and the Political Order. New York: John Wiley, 1967.

Capek, Thomas. The Czechs in America. New York: Arno Press
and the New York Times, 1969.

Clark, Dennis. "Toward Assimilation or Ethnic Identity?" Urban
and Social Change Review (Fall 1970), p. 19.

Clark, Kenneth B. Dark Ghetto. New York: Harper and Row, 1965.

Clayton, Edward T. The Negro Politician: His Success and Failure.
Chicago: Johnson, 1964.

Cohen, Wegner. "The Politics of American Jews," in Sklare, Marshall,
ed., The Jews. Glencoe, Ill.: Free Press, 1958.

Coles, Robert and Jan Erikson. The Middle Americans. Boston:
Little, Brown, 1971.

Converse, Philip. "Religion and Politics: the 1960 Election." Unpublished essay, The Survey Research Center, University of
Michigan, 1962.

Covello, Leonard. The Social Background of the Italo-American
School Child. Leiden, the Netherlands: E. J. Brill, 1967.

Cox, D. N. How Does a Minority Group Achieve Power. New York:
John Wiley, 1969.

Cross, Robert D. The Emergence of Liberal Catholicism in America.
Cambridge, Mass.: Harvard University Press, 1958.

Cutsumbris, Michael N. A Bibliographical Guide to Materials on
Greeks in the United States, 1890-1968. New York: Center for
Migration Studies, 1970.

Dahl, Robert A. After the Revolution? New Haven: Yale University
Press, 1970.

_____. Polyarchy. New Haven: Yale University Press, 1971.

_____. Who Governs? New Haven: Yale University Press, 1961.

Danzig, David. "The Social Framework of Ethnic Conflict in America."
Paper delivered at National Consultation on Ethnic America,
Fordham University, June 20, 1968, sponsored by the American
Jewish Committee.

Dawidowicz, Lucy S. and Leon J. Goldstein. Politics in a Pluralistic Society. New York: Institute of Human Relations Press of the American Jewish Committee, 1963.

Dean, John P. and Alex Rosen. Manual of Intergroup Relations. Chicago: University of Chicago Press, 1955.

Deloria, Vine. We Talk, You Listen. New York: Macmillan, 1970.

Devine, Robert. American Immigration Policy, 1924-1952. New Haven: Yale University Press, 1957.

Dinnerstein, Leonard and Frederick Cople Jaher, eds. The Aliens. New York: Appleton-Century-Crofts, 1970.

Drake, St. Clair and Horace R. Cayton. Black Metropolis. New York: Harcourt, 1945.

Drummond, Andrew L. Story of American Protestantism. Boston: Beacon Press, 1950.

Duncan, Otis Dudley and Beverly Duncan. The Negro Population of Chicago: A Study of Residential Succession. Chicago: University of Chicago Press, 1957.

Duncan, Otis Dudley and Lieberson, Stanley. "Ethnic Segregation and Assimilation." American Journal of Sociology (January 1959).

Dunfee, Maxine. Ethnic Modification of the Curriculum. Washington, D.C.: Association of Supervision and Curriculum Development, 1969.

Edwards, David L. Religion and Change. New York: Harper and Row, 1970.

Eisenstadt, S. N. The Absoprtion of Immigrants. Glencoe, Ill.: Free Press, 1955.

_____. Essays on Comparative Social Change. New York: John Wiley, 1965.

Elinson, Jack, Paul W. Haberman, and Cyrille Gell. Ethnic and Educational Data on Adults in New York City 1963-1964. New York: School of Public Health and Administration, Columbia University, 1967.

Ellis, John T. American Catholicism. Chicago: Univeristy of Chicago Press, 1955.

Endleman, Shalom. Violence in the Streets. Chicago: Quadrangle Books, 1968.

Epstein, Benjamin R. and Arnold Forster. "Some of My Best Friends . . ." New York: Farrar, Strauss and Cudahy, 1962.

Essien-Udom, E. U. Black Nationalism. Chicago: University of Chicago Press, 1962.

"Ethnic Groups in American Life." Special Issue. Daedulus (Spring 1961).

Faderman, Lillian and Barbara Bradshaw. Speaking for Ourselves. Glenview, Ill.: Scott Foresman and Co., 1969.

Featherman, David L. "The Socio-Economic Achievement of White Religio-Ethnic Subgroups." American Sociological Review (April 1971), p. 211.

Feinstein, Otto. Ethnic Groups in the City. Lexington, Mass.: Heath Lexington Books, 1971.

Fellows, Donald K. A Mosaic of America's Ethnic Minorities. New York: John Wiley, 1972.

Fenton, John. The Catholic Vote. New Orleans: Hauser Press, 1960.

Finkelstein, Louis. The Jews. Philadelphia: Jewish Publication Society, 1949.

Fishman, Joshua A., ed. Language Loyalty in the United States. London and The Hague: Mouton, 1966.

Fitzpatrick, Joseph. Puerto Rican Americans. Englewood Cliffs, N.J.: Prentice-Hall, 1971.

Foner, Philip S. American Labor and the Indo-China War. New York: International Publishers, 1971.

Forbes, Jack D. The Education of the Culturally Different. Washington, D.C.: U.S. Government Printing Office, 1969.

Francis, E. K. "The Nature of the Ethnic Group." American Journal
   of Sociology, Vol. 52 (1945), p. 393.

Franklin, John Hope. Color and Race. Boston: Beacon Press, 1969.

_____. From Slavery to Freedom. A History of American Negroes.
   New York: Alfred A. Knopf, 1956.

Franklin, John Hope, Thomas F. Pettigrew, and Raymond W. Mack.
   Ethnicity in American Life. New York: Anti-Defamation League
   of B'nai B'rith, 1971.

Frazier, E. Franklin. The Negro Family in the United States. Chicago:
   University of Chicago Press, 1939.

_____. The Negro in the United States. New York: Macmillan,
   1957.

Friedman, Murray, ed. Overcoming Middle Class Rage. Philadelphia:
   Westminster Press, 1971.

Fuchs, Lawrence H., ed. American Ethnic Politics. New York:
   Harper and Row, Harper Torchbooks, 1968.

_____. John F. Kennedy and American Catholicism. New York:
   Meredity Press, 1967.

_____. The Political Behavior of American Jews. Glencoe, Ill.:
   Free Press, 1956.

Gans, Herbert. The Urban Villagers. Glencoe, Ill.: Free Press, 1962.

Garis, Roy L. Immigration Restriction: A Study of the Opposition to
   and Regulation of Immigration into the United States. New York:
   Macmillan, 1927.

Geertz. Clifford. Islam Observed. New Haven: Yale University
   Press, 1969.

Gerson, Louis L. The Hyphenates in Recent American Politics and
   Diplomacy. Lawrence: University of Kansas Press, 1964.

Gittler, Joseph B. Understanding Minority Groups. New York:
   John Wiley, 1956.

Glaser, Daniel. "Dynamics of Ethnic Identification." American Socio-logical Review, Vol. 23, No. 1 (1958), pp. 31-40.

Glazer, Nathan. American Judaism. Chicago: University of Chicago Press, 1957.

_____. "Black and White Ethnics: The Difference, and the Political Difference It Makes." Social Problems (Spring 1971).

_____. "Ethnic Groups in America." In Monroe Berger, Theodore Abel, and Charles H. Page, Freedom and Control in Modern Society. New York: Van Nostrand, 1954.

_____, and Daniel P. Moynihan. Beyond the Melting Pot. 2nd. ed. Cambridge, Mass.: MIT University Press, 1970.

Gleason, Phillip. "The Melting-Pot: Symbol of Fusion or Confusion?" American Quarterly (Spring 1964).

Glock, Charles Y., and Ellen Siegelman. Prejudice U.S.A. New York: Frederick A. Praeger, 1969.

Goering, John M. "The Emergence of Ethnic Interests." Social Forces (March 1971), pp. 379-84.

Goldsen, Rose. The Puerto Rican Journey. New York: Harper, 1950.

Goldstein, Sydney and Calvin Goldscheider. Jewish Americans. Englewood Cliffs, N.J.: Prentice-Hall, 1968.

Gordon, Milton M. Assimilation in American Life. New York: Oxford University Press, 1964.

Gorenstein, Arthur. "A Portrait of Ethnic Politics." American Jewish Historical Quarterly. March, 1961.

Gosnell, Harold. Negro Politicians: The Rise of Negro Politics in Chicago. Chicago: University of Chicago Press, 1935.

_____. Machine Politics: Chicago Model. Chicago: University of Chicago Press, 1937.

Gottfried, Alex. Boss Germak of Chicago: A Study of Political Leadership. Seattle: University of Washington Press, 1962.

Graham, Hugh Davis and Ted Robert Gurr. Violence in America: Historical and Comparative Perspectives. A Report to the National Commission on the Causes and Prevention of Violence. Washington, D.C.: U.S. Government Printing Office, June 1969, and New York: Bantam Books, 1969.

Grebler, Leo, Joan W. Moore, and Ralph Guzman. The Mexican-American People. New York: Free Press, 1970.

Greeley, Andrew M. and Paul B. Sheatsley. "Attitudes Toward Desegregation." Scientific American (December 1971).

_____. The Catholic Experience: A Sociologists' Interpretation of the History of American Catholicism. New York: Doubleday, 1967.

_____. The Denominational Society. New York: Schocken Books, 1972.

_____, and Peter H. Rossi. The Education of Catholic Americans. Chicago: Aldine, 1966.

_____. That Most Distressful Nation: The American Irish. New York: Quadrangle Books, 1972.

_____. "Political Attitudes Among American White Ethnics." Public Opinion Quarterly (Summer 1972).

_____. "The Positive Contributions of Ethnic Groups in American Society." Paper presented at a meeting sponsored by the American Jewish Committee, May 1970.

_____, and Joe L. Spaeth. "Stratification, Poverty, and Social Conflict in American White Ethnic Groups." In Lipset, Seymour Martin and Michael Miller, eds., Stratification and Poverty, forthcoming.

_____. Why Can't They Be Like Us? New York: E. P. Dutton, 1971.

Greene, Victor R. The Slavic Community on Strike. Notre Dame, Ind.: University of Notre Dame Press, 1968.

Greer, Scott. "Catholic Voters in the Democratic Party." Public Opinion Quarterly, Vol. XXV (1961).

Hadden, Jeffrey K. and Louis H. Masotti. "Suburbs, Suburbia and
    Suburbanization: A Bibliography." Evanston, Ill.: Northwestern
    University, Center for Urban Affairs.

Hagan, William T. American Indians. Chicago: University of Chicago
    Press, 1961.

Halpern, Ben. Jews and Blacks: The Classic American Minorities.
    New York: Herder & Herder, 1971.

Handlin, Oscar. The American People in the Twentieth Century.
    Boston: Beacon Press, 1963.

_____. The Americans. Boston: Little, Brown, 1963.

_____. Boston's Immigrants. 1790-1865: A Study in Acculturation.
    Cambridge: Harvard University Press, 1959.

_____. Race and Nationality in American Life. Boston: Little,
    Brown, 1957. Doubleday Anchor paperback, 1957.

_____. The Uprooted. Boston: Little, Brown, 1951.

_____, ed. Immigration as a Factor in American History. Engle-
    wood Cliffs, N.J.: Prentice-Hall, 1959.

Handman, J. B. S., ed. American Labor Dynamics. New York: Arno
    Press and the New York Times, 1969.

Hansen, Marcus L. The Atlantic Migration, 1607-1860. Cambridge:
    Harvard University Press, 1940. Harper Torchbooks paperback,
    1961.

_____. The Immigrant in American History. New York: Harper
    and Row, Harper Torchbooks, 1964.

Hapgood, David. The Purge That Failed: Tammany v. Powell. New
    York: Eagleton Institute of Politics, 1959.

Hartmann, Edward George. The Movement to Americanize the
    Immigrant. New York: University of Columbia Press, 1948.

Hartz, Louis. The Liberal Tradition in America. New York: Harcourt,
    Brace and World, 1955.

Haugen, Einar. The Norwegian Language in America: A Study of Bilingual Behavior. Bloomington, Ind.: Indiana University Press, 1969.

Hawgood, John Arkas. The Tragedy of German-America. New York: Arno Press, 1970.

Hawkins, Brett W. and Robert A. Lorinskas, eds. The Ethnic Factor in American Politics. Columbus, Ohio: Merrill, 1970.

Hearings before the General Subcommittee on Education on H.R. 14910. The Ethnic Heritage Studies Centers Bill. Washington, D.C.: 1970.

Hentoff, Nat. "Counterpolitics: The Decade Ahead." Evergreen Review (February 1969), p. 25.

Herberg, Will. Protestant-Catholic-Jew. New York: Doubleday, 1955. Anchor paperback.

Herskovits, Melville J. Acculturation: The Study of Culture Contact. Gloucester, Mass.: Peter Smith.

_____. The Myth of the Negro Past. Boston: Beacon Press, 1958.

Higham, John. Strangers in the Land: Patterns of American Nativism 1860-1925. New York: Atheneum, 1968.

Hofstadter, Richard. Anti-Intellectualism in American Life. New York: Random House, Vintage Books, 1966.

_____, and Michael Wallace, eds. American Violence. New York: Alfred A. Knopf, 1970. Random House, Vintage paperback, 1971.

Hoskins, Harold B. "American Unity and Our Foreign-Born Citizens." The Annals of the American Academy of Political and Social Science (March 1942).

Howe, Louise Kapp, ed. The White Majority. New York: Random House, 1970.

Hsu, Francis L. Americans and Chinese: Purpose and Fulfillment in Great Civilizations. New York: Natural History Press, 1970.

Hudson, Winthrop S. Nationalism and Religion in America. New York: Harper and Row, 1970.

Huebener, Theodore. The Germans in America. Philadelphia: Chilton, 1962.

Hughes, Emmet John. The Church and the Liberal Society. Notre Dame, Ind.: University of Notre Dame Press, 1961.

Hutchinson, E. P. Immigrants and Their Children. 1850-1950. New York: John Wiley, 1956.

"The Imperatives of Ethnic Education." Phi Delta Kappa. Special Issue (January 1972).

Institute of Public Affairs. Four unpublished papers prepared for the Leadership Conference, sponsored by the Institute. New York, 1970. The authors of these papers were Laplois Ashford, Russell Barta, Andrew Greeley, and Arthur Mann: their subject was group relations in the Chicago area.

Iorizzo, Luciano J., ed. An Inquiry into Organized Crime. Staten Island, New York: The American Italian Historical Association, 1972.

Isaacs, Harold. "Group Identity and Political Change: The House of Muumbi." Paper presented to the American Political Science Association in Chicago, September 1971.

"The Italian Experience in Emigration." International Migration Review. Special Issue (Summer 1967).

Itzkoff, Seymour. Cultural Pluralism and American Education. Scranton, Pa.: International Textbook, 1969.

Jaffe, Louis. "The Philosophy of Our Immigration Laws." Law and Contemporary Problems, Vol. 21 (1956), pp. 358.

James, Sidney V. A People Among Peoples. Cambridge: Harvard University Press, 1963.

Janeway, William R. Bibliography of Immigration in the U.S. 1900-1930. San Francisco: R & E Research Associates, 1972.

Jones, Maldwin. American Immigration. Chicago: University of Chicago Press, 1960.

Kallen, Horace M. Cultural Pluralism and the American Idea. Philadelphia: University of Pennsylvania Press, 1956.

Kane, Michael B. Minorities in Textbooks. Chicago: Quadrangle Books, 1970.

Kantrowitz, Nathan. "Ethnic and Racial Segregation in the New York Metropolis, 1960." American Journal of Sociology (May 1969), pp. 685-95.

Kazan, Elia. America! America! New York: Popular Library, 1961.

Kazin, Alfred. Starting Out in the Thirties. Boston: Little, Brown, 1965.

Kennedy, John F. A Nation of Immigrants, rev. and enlarged. New York: Harper and Row, 1964.

Kennedy, Ruby Jo Reeves. "Single or Triple Melting Pot? Inter-marriage Trends in New Haven, 1870-1940." American Journal of Sociology, January 1944, pp. 331-39.

Killian, Lewis and Charles Grigg. Racial Crisis in America: Leader-ship in Conflict. Englewood Cliffs, N.J.: Prentice-Hall, 1964.

Kitano, Harry. Japanese Americans. Englewood Cliffs, N.J.: Prentice-Hall, 1969.

Kobler, John. Capone. New York: G. P. Putnam's Sons, 1971.

Kolodny, Ralph L. "Ethnic Cleavages in the United States." Social Work (January 1969), p. 20.

La Gumina, Salvatoria J. Vito Marcantonio, The People's Politician. Dubuque, Iowa: Kendall-Hunt, 1969.

Lally, Francis J. The Catholic Church in a Changing America. Boston: Little, Brown, 1962.

Lasson, Kenneth. The Workers. New York: Grossman, 1971.

Leggett, John C. Class, Race and Labor: Working-Class Conscious-ness in Detroit. New York: Oxford University Press, 1968.

Leinwand, Gerald. Minorities All. New York: Washington Square Press, 1971.

Lemon, Richard. The Troubled American. New York: Simon and
    Schuster, 1971.

Lenski, Gerhard. The Religious Factor: A Social Inquiry. New York:
    Doubleday, 1961.

Lerner, Michael. "Respectable Bigotry." American Scholar (August
    1969).

Lesser, Gerald and Susan S. Stodolsky. "Learning Patterns in the
    Disadvantaged." Harvard Educational Review (Fall 1967), pp.
    546-93.

Levine, Edward M. The Irish and Irish Politicians. Notre Dame,
    Ind.: University of Notre Dame Press, 1966.

Levine, Irving M. "A Strategy for White Ethnic America." Paper
    delivered at Conference on the Problems of White Ethnic America,
    University of Pennsylvania, June 25, 1968, sponsored by the
    American Jewish Committee.

_____, and Judith M. Herman. "The Ethnic Factor in Blue Collar
    Life." An unpublished paper. American Jewish Committee,
    1971.

Levitan, Sar A., ed. Blue-Collar Workers. New York: McGraw-Hill,
    1971.

Levy, Mark R, and Michael S. Kramer. The Ethnic Factor: How
    America's Minorities Decide Elections. New York: Simon and
    Schuster, 1972.

Lewis, Oscar. La Vida. New York: Random House, 1965.

Leyburn, James. The Scotch-Irish: A Social History. Chapel Hill:
    University of North Carolina Press, 1962.

Lieberman, Jethro K. Are Americans Extinct? New York: Walker,
    1968.

Lieberson, Stanley. Ethnic Patterns in American Cities. Glencoe,
    Ill.: Free Press, 1963.

_____. "Suburbs and Ethnic Residential Patterns." American
    Journal of Sociology (May 1962), pp. 673-81.

Liebow, Elliot. Tally's Corner. Boston: Little, Brown, 1967.

Light, Ivan H. Ethnic Enterprise in America. New York: World, 1972.

Lincoln, C. Eric. The Black Muslims in America. Boston: Beacon Press, 1961.

Lipset, Seymour M. "Religion and Politics in the American Past and Present" in Lee, Robert and Martin Murray, eds., Religion and Social Conflict. New York: 1964.

Litt, Edgar. Ethnic Politics in America. Glenview, Ill.: Scott, Foresman and Co., 1970.

Lopreato, Joseph. Italian Americans. New York: Random House, 1970.

Lubell, Samuel. The Future of American Politics, 3rd. ed. New York: Harper and Row, 1965.

_____. The Hidden Crisis in American Politics. New York: W. W. Norton, 1970.

Macdonald, Dwight. Against the American Grain. New York: Random House, Vintage Books, 1962.

Mack, Raymond W. Race, Class and Power. New York: American Book Co., 1963.

Maisel, Albert Q. They All Chose America. New York: Thomas Nelson and Sons, 1957.

Malcolm X. The Autobiography of Malcolm X. New York: Grove Press, 1965.

Mann, Arthur. "A Historical Overview: Education, the Lumpenproletariat, and Compensatory Action." The Quality of Inequality: Urban and Suburban Public Schools. Chicago: University of Chicago Center for Policy Study, 1968.

_____. La Guardia Comes to Power 1933. Chicago: University of Chicago Press, 1965.

Marden, Charles F. and Gladys Meyer. Minorities in American Society. New York: Van Nostrand Reinhold, 1968.

Marrow, Alfred J. Changing Patterns of Prejudice. Philadelphia:
      Chilton, 1962.

McDonagh, Edward C. and Eugene S. Richards. Ethnic Relations in
      the United States. New York: Negro Universities Press, 1953.

Merriam, Charles. Chicago, A More Intimate View of Urban Politics.
      Chicago: University of Chicago Press, 1929.

Minority Cultures. Rochester: Catholic Curriculum Committee, 1970.

Mizwa, Stephen P., ed. Great Men and Women of Poland. New York:
      Kosciuszko Foundation, 1967.

Moore, Edmund. A Catholic Runs for President: the 1928 Campaign.
      Gloucester, Mass.: Peter Smith.

Morris, Terry. Better Than You: Social Discrimination Against
      Minorities. New York: Institute of Human Relations Press,
      American Jewish Committee, 1971.

Myrdal, Gunnar. An American Dilemma. New York: Harper, 1942.

National Association of Secondary School Principals. Minority
      Cultures in the Curriculum. 1970.

National Education Association. Index to Multi-Ethnic Teaching
      Materials and Teacher Resources. 1967.

Nelli, Humbert S. The Italians in Chicago 1880-1930. New York:
      Oxford University Press, 1970.

"The New Immigration." The Annals of the American Academy of
      Political and Social Science (September 1966).

Novak, Michael. The Rise of the Unmeltable Ethnics. New York:
      Macmillan, 1972.

O'Connor, Edwin. The Last Hurrah. New York: Bantam, 1956.

Parenti, Michael. "Ethnic Politics and the Persistence of Ethnic
      Identification." American Political Science Review (September
      1967).

Park, Robert E. The Immigrant Press and Its Control. Westport,
      Conn.: Greenwood, 1922.

_____. Race and Culture. Glencoe, Ill.: Free Press, 1950.

_____, and Herbert A. Miller. Old World Traits Transplanted. New York: Arno Press and the New York Times, 1969.

"Persons of Spanish Origin in the United States: November, 1969." Series P-20, No. 213. Washington, D.C.: U.S. Government Printing Office, 1971.

Peterson, William. Japanese Americans. New York: Random House.

Phillips, Kevin P. The Emerging Republican Majority. New Rochelle, N.Y.: Arlington House, 1969.

Pinkney, Alphonso. Black Americans. Englewood Cliffs, N.J.: Prentice-Hall, 1969.

Pisani, Lawrence Frank. The Italian in America: A Social Study and History. New York: Exposition Press, 1957.

Portal, Roger. The Slavs. New York: Harper and Row, 1969.

Pye, Lucian W. and Sidney Verba, eds. Political Culture and Political Development. Princeton, N.J.: Princeton University Press, 1965.

"The Rediscovery of Diversity." Special Issue. Antioch Review (November 1971).

Religion Reported by the U.S. Population, By Color, Sex and Residence: March, 1957. Current Population Reports, Series P-20 No. 79. Washington, D.C.: U.S. Government Printing Office, 1958.

Report of the National Advisory Commission on Civil Disorders. Washington, D.C.: U.S. Government Printing Office, 1968.

Reports of the Immigration Commission: Abstracts of the Reports of the Immigration Commission. Vol. 1. Washington, D.C.: U.S. Government Printing Office, 1911.

Reports of the Immigration Commission: The Children of Immigrants in Schools. Vol. 1. Washington, D.C.: U.S. Government Printing Office, 1911.

A Report on World Population Migrations as Related to the United
States of America. Washington, D.C.: George Washington
University, 1956.

Richter, Edward and Berton Dulce. Religion and the Presidency.
New York, 1962.

Riordan, William L. Plunkitt of Tammany Hall. New York: E. P.
Dutton, 1963.

Rischin, Moses. An Inventory of American Jewish History. Cambridge,
Mass.: Harvard University Press, 1954.

_____. Our Own Kind. Santa Barbara, Calif.: Center for the Study
of Democratic Institutions, 1960.

Rolle, Andrew F. The Immigrant Upraised. Norman: University of
Oklahoma Press, 1968.

Rose, Peter, ed. Nation of Nations: The Ethnic Experience and the
Racial Crisis. New York: Random House, 1972.

_____. They and We: Racial and Ethnic Relations in the United
States. New York: Random House, 1964.

Rosenthal, Eric. "Acculturation Without Assimilation." American
Journal of Sociology. November 1960.

Royko, Mike. Boss: Richard J. Daley of Chicago. New York: E.P.
Dutton, 1971.

Scammon, Richard M. and Ben J. Wattenberg. The Real Majority.
New York: Coward-McCann, 1970.

Schermerhorn, R. A. Comparative Ethnic Relations: A Framework
for Theory and Research. New York: Random House, 1969.

_____. These Our People. Boston: Heath, 1949.

Schrag, Peter. The Decline of the Wasp. New York: Simon and
Schuster, 1971.

Schulz, David A. Coming Up Black. Englewood Cliffs, N.J.: Prentice-
Hall, 1969.

Scully, Thomas. "Is the Door Open Again? - A Survey of Our New Immigration Law." 13 U.C.L.A. Law Review 227 (1966).

Segal, Bernard E., ed. Racial and Ethnic Relations. New York: Thomas Y. Crowell, 1966.

Segal, Ronald. The Americans: A Conflict of Creed and Reality. New York: Viking, 1969.

Senior, Clarence. Strangers Their Neighbors. New York: Anti-Defamation League of B'nai B'rith, 1961.

Sennett, Richard, ed. Classic Essays on the Culture of Cities. New York: Appleton-Century-Crofts, 1969.

_____. Families Against the City. Cambridge, Mass.: Harvard University Press, 1970.

_____. The Uses of Disorder. New York: Alfred A. Knopf, 1970.

Sexton, Patricia Cayo and Brendan Sexton. Blue Collars and Hard Hats. New York: Random House, 1971.

Shannon, Vincent J. The American Irish. New York: Macmillan, 1966.

Shibutani, Tamotsu and Kian M. Kwan. Ethnic Stratification. New York: Macmillan, 1965.

Shils, Edward. The Torment of Secrecy. Glencoe, Ill.: Free Press, 1956.

_____. "Primordial, Personal, Sacred and Civil Ties." British Journal of Sociology (June 1957).

Shostak, Arthur B. Blue-Collar Life. New York: Random House, 1969.

Silberman, Charles E. Crisis in Black and White. New York: Random House, 1964.

Simpson, George Eaton and J. Milton Yinger. Racial and Cultural Minorities. New York: Harper and Row, 1965.

Sinclair, Upton. The Jungle. New York: New American Library, Signet Classic, 1960.

Sklare, Marshall, ed. The Jews: Social Patterns of an American Group. New York: Free Press, 1958.

_____ and Greenblum, Joseph. Jewish Identity of the Suburban Frontiers: A Study of Group Survival in the Open Society. New York: Basic Books, 1968.

Skolnick, Jerome. The Politics of Protest. Washington, D.C.: U.S. Government Printing Office, 1969.

Smith, James W. and A. Leland Jamison. The Shaping of American Religion. Princeton, N.J.: Princeton University Press, 1961.

Smith, Timothy L. "Immigrant Social Aspirations and American Education." American Quarterly (Fall 1969) pp. 523-43.

Solomon, Barbara. Ancestors and Immigrants. Cambridge, Mass.: Harvard University Press, 1956.

Steele, C. Hay and Norman R. Yetman. Majority and Minority: The Dynamics of Racial and Ethnic Relations. Boston: Allyn and Bacon, 1971.

Steinfield, Melvin. Cracks in the Melting Pot. Beverly Hills: Glencoe Press, 1970.

Stone, Chuck. Black Political Power in America. New York: Dell, 1968.

Streiker, Lowell D. and Gerald S. Strober. Religion and the New Majority: Billy Graham, Middle America, and the Politics of the 1970's. New York: Association Press, 1972.

Suttles, Gerald D. The Social Order of the Slum: Ethnicity and Territory in the Inner City. Chicago: University of Chicago Press, 1968.

Szczepanski, Jan. Polish Society. New York: Random House, 1970.

Taeuber, Karl E. and Alma F. Taeuber. Negroes in Cities, Residential Segregation and Neighborhood Change. Chicago: Aldine, 1965.

Tax, Sol, ed. Acculturation in the Americas. Chicago: University of Chicago Press, 1951.

Thomas, William I. and Florjan Znaniecki. The Polish Peasant in Europe and America. 2 vols. Chicago: University of Chicago Press, 1918 and New York: Dover Publications, 1958.

Timm, D. W. G. The Urban Mosaic: Towards a Theory of Residential Differential. New York: Cambridge University Press, 1971.

Tobias, Henry and Charles Woodhouse, eds. Minorities and Politics. New Mexico: University of New Mexico Press, 1968.

Tomasi, Silvano M. and Madeline H. Engel, eds. The Italian Experience in the United States. Staten Island, N.Y.: Center for Migration Studies, 1970.

The Treatment of Minorities in American History Textbooks. Michigan Department of Education, 1968.

Tyler, Gus. Political Imperative: The Corporate Character of Unions. New York: Free Press, 1968.

U.S. Department of Commerce, Bureau of the Census. "Characteristics of the Population by Ethnic Origin: November 1969." Washington, D.C.: U.S. Government Printing Office, April 1971.

Vander Zanden, James W. American Minority Relations: The Sociology of Race and Ethnic Groups. New York: Ronald Press, 1966.

Walker, David B. Politics and Ethnocentrism: The Case of the Franco-Americans. Brunswick, Me: Bureau for Research in Municipal Government, 1961.

Warner, W. Lloyd and Leo Srole. The Social Systems of American Ethnic Groups. New Haven: Yale University Press, 1945.

Warren, Donald. "Anomia and Middle Americans." Paper presented to the Industrial Relations Research Association, 1971.

Wax, Murray. Indian Americans. Englewood Cliffs, N.J.: Prentice-Hall, 1970.

Weber, Max. "The Ethnic Group." In Parsons, Talcott, ed., Theories of Society, Vol. 1. Glencoe, Ill.: Free Press, 1961.

Weisberg, Bernard. The American People. New York: American Heritage, 1971.

Wheeler, Thomas C., ed. The Immigrant Experience: The Anguish of Becoming American. New York: Dial Press, 1972.

White, Lyman C. Three Hundred Thousand New Americans. New York: Harper and Row, 1957.

White, Theodore H. The Making of the President 1968. New York: Atheneum, 1969.

Whyte, William F. Street Corner Society: Social Structure of an Italian Slum. Chicago: University of Chicago Press, 1955.

Williams, Phyllis H. Southern Italian Folkways in Europe and America. New Haven: Yale University Press, 1938.

Williams, Robin M. Jr. Strangers Next Door: Ethnic Relations in American Communities. Englewood Cliffs, N.J.: Prentice-Hall, 1964.

Wilson, James Q. "Generational and Ethnic Differences Among Career Police Officers." American Journal of Sociology (March 1964), pp. 522-28.

Wilson, James Q. Negro Politics. Glencoe, Ill.: Free Press, 1960.

Wirth, Louis. The Ghetto. Chicago: University of Chicago Press, 1928.

Wittke, Carl. We Who Built America. New York: Prentice-Hall, 1939.

"The World of the Blue-Collar Worker." Special Issue. Dissent (Winter 1972).

Wright, Nathan, Jr. Black Power and Urban Unrest. New York: Hawthorn, 1967.

Wytrwal, Joseph A. America's Polish Heritage: A Social History of the Poles in America. Detroit: Endurance Press, 1961.

Yinger, J. Milton. A Minority Group in American Society. New York: McGraw-Hill, 1965.

Zorbaugh, Harvey W. Gold Coast and Slum. Chicago: University of Chicago Press, 1929.

ABOUT THE AUTHOR

PERRY L. WEED, a native of Philadelphia, is a postdoctoral fellow in political science at the Northwestern University Center for Urban Affairs. He has practiced law in Chicago since 1961, specializing in trial and appellate litigation.

He received a bachelor of arts degree from Hamilton College, Clinton, N.Y., and in 1961 a doctorate of jurisprudence from the University of Chicago Law School.

Besides the practice of law, he is currently engaged in a major study of the culture and politics of Chicago's ethnic groups. This work includes development of a television series on Chicago's ethnic groups for the City's educational television station. His articles on Chicago and Mayor Richard J. Daley have appeared in Saturday Review, the Progressive, other journals, and Chicago newspapers.